WAITING FOR
DIZZY

WAITING FOR

~~ DIZZY ~~

Gene Lees

New York   Oxford
OXFORD UNIVERSITY PRESS
1991

Oxford University Press

Oxford   New York   Toronto
Delhi   Bombay   Calcutta   Madras   Karachi
Petaling Jaya   Singapore   Hong Kong   Tokyo
Nairobi   Dar es Salaam   Cape Town
Melbourne   Auckland

and associated companies in
Berlin   Ibadan

Copyright © 1991 by Gene Lees

Published by Oxford University Press, Inc.,
200 Madison Avenue, New York, New York 10016

Oxford is a registered trademark of Oxford University Press

Library of Congress Cataloging-in-Publication Data
Lees, Gene.
Waiting for Dizzy / Gene Lees.
p.   cm.
Essays from Gene Lees Jazzletter.
ISBN 0–19-505670-1
1. Jazz—History and criticism.
I. Beiderbecke, Bix, 1903–1931.
II. Gene Lees, jazzletter.   III. Title.
ML3507.L47   1991
781.65—dc20   90-47883   CIP   MN

2 4 6 8 9 7 5 3 1

Printed in the United States of America
on acid-free paper

Foreword

by Terry Teachout

> The real war will never get in the books . . . Think how
> much, and of importance, will be, has already been,
> buried in the grave.
>
> WALT WHITMAN, on the Civil War

American newspapers first began covering jazz in 1917, the year
in which the Original Dixieland Jazz Band made the first jazz
recordings. Hundreds of books have been written about jazz since
then, and many of them have proved to be of permanent interest.
But the literature of jazz, for all its undeniable value, is still a partial portrait, a mosaic of isolated facts pieced together for the most
part by sympathetic outsiders. Not surprisingly, an important
piece has been left out of the mosaic: the inside story. Jazz, being
an improvised music, takes shape at the crossroads of the improviser's personality and the circumstances under which he is improvising. No outsider, however sympathetic, can possibly know what
it is like to stand at that crossroads. An outsider can tell you where
Duke Ellington was playing on the night of November 7, 1940,
and who was playing with him. He cannot tell you what it felt like
to play with Duke that night—or to ride the train with him the
next morning. Such inside knowledge is an indispensable part of
the history of jazz, and far too little of it has gotten into the history
books.

Waiting for Dizzy is a welcome exception to this rule, for it is the
work of an insider, a widely admired songwriter who has been a
part of the world of jazz for most of his life. As an insider, Gene

Lees knows that very few jazz musicians bear any resemblance to the pervasive stereotypes that continue to haunt jazz journalism, an ideology-ridden branch of literature in which all black jazzmen are customarily portrayed as alienated outcasts and all white jazzmen as soulless parasites.

"The jazz musicians I know," Lees points out, "are mostly gentle men and women, sensitive and cultivated, and very middle class. They don't consider themselves outcasts.

"They are witnesses to the history of jazz, and we are losing them very quickly. I want to ask them questions before they are gone. Indeed, I lived through a lot of jazz history myself, and I want to get my own memories on paper while there is still time."

Lees' sense of urgency is understandable. Until fairly recently, most jazz musicians learned their trade not at Berklee or North Texas State but through informal lessons cadged from old-timers in return for drinks and admiration; for them, "jazz history" consisted of the stories they heard at the bar or on the bus. Most of the legendary figures in jazz who didn't drink themselves to death or shoot up one time too many survived well into the '60s and beyond. If you knew how to play, the chances were better than even that you would sooner or later work with somebody who had worked with Benny Goodman or Duke Ellington or Charlie Parker and who had a tale or two to tell. Unfortunately, far too few of these revealing tales have made their way into the written record of jazz history. And every time a jazz musician dies without having told his story, an irreplaceable chapter in the annals of American music is lost forever.

In order to preserve some of the rich oral tradition of jazz and, in his words, "satisfy my own curiosity" about the lives and personalities of the great jazz musicians, Gene Lees started the *Jazzletter,* a monthly journal about jazz and American popular music, in 1981. Most of the *Jazzletter* is written by Lees himself, though he also publishes essays and memoirs by working musicians. *Waiting for Dizzy,* the third book quarried out of his *Jazzletter* essays, portrays in unprecedented and knowing detail the world of jazz as it really is. The musicians profiled in *Waiting for Dizzy* are not inarticulate sociopaths wandering from fix to fix. They are intelligent, well-spoken craftsmen who take a commercial commodity and turn it into an art form, the only wholly original one this country has produced. They live the shadowy lives of night people, working their mysterious musical alchemy in bars and country clubs and recording studios. Theirs is a world of friendship and mutual admiration, of unexpected kindness and extraordinary generosity, of hard times and empty pockets and four-in-the-morning courage.

It is impossible to understand jazz without understanding these remarkable men and women, and Gene Lees is as good a guide to their world as you are likely to find, not least because he is that rarest of birds: a historian who can write. As an insider he knows what questions to ask, but also knows how to shape the answers he gets into sensitively written essays that unerringly capture the essence of an artist at work. (What other jazz writer would have described the playing of guitarist Herb Ellis as having "the feeling of sun on warm dark loam"?) While jazz has spawned several solid historical studies and two or three first-rate biographies, it has produced precious little in the way of *belles-lettres*. Otis Ferguson wrote beautifully about jazz for *The New Republic* fifty years ago, and Whitney Balliett has been writing beautifully about it for *The New Yorker* since the 1950s. *Waiting for Dizzy*, like the rest of Gene Lees' work, is a part of that great tradition.

Composer Johnny Mandel—one of the many major jazz musicians who subscribe to the *Jazzletter* and eagerly await its arrival each month—has said of Lees' work: "Most writing about jazz seems like somebody looking through glass into a fish tank. Gene's sounds like he's in the tank, swimming with the rest of us."

Terry Teachout, formerly a jazz bassist, is a member of the editorial board of the New York *Daily News*. He writes about jazz for *The American Scholar* and classical music for *Musical America*. He is at work on a biography of H. L. Mencken.

Contents

WAITING FOR
DIZZY

There is properly no history; only biography.
RALPH WALDO EMERSON

Lost Innocence

Listening to jazz of the 1920s has been for many people more a matter of duty than pleasure, one of those labors you undertake with gritted teeth to try to understand your own epoch, such as reading French essays on the movies of Alfred Hitchcock. For myself, it was not just that I disliked the hissy surfaces and drainpipe sound of the records. When bass lines are inaudible or indistinct, I am harmonically disoriented. And I couldn't hear them on the old records. Composer Johnny Mandel remarked that listening to those records was like trying to see something through a dirty window.

In the late 1980s, this began to change as the record companies, taking advantage of the new market created by the popularity of the CD, the compact disc, withdrew from their vaults all sorts of important jazz long out of circulation and cleaned up the sound with new noise-reduction systems and computer technology.

The best recorded sound was achieved by an Australian collector and recording engineer named Robert Parker who turned jazz records of the 1920s and early '30s into albums with surprisingly—no, amazingly—good stereo sound. The results of his work were first heard in a series of radio programs on the Australian Broadcasting Corporation and then in England on the BBC. They were issued on disc on the BBC label, recordings by Louis Armstrong, Bix Beiderbecke, Duke Ellington, Red Nichols, Jelly Roll Morton, Bessie Smith, Joe Venuti, and Eddie Lang, as well as various less celebrated but nonetheless interesting figures.

One could not help wondering what the participants in some of these early record dates would think if they could hear them in the Parker restorations. I had the opportunity to find out.

The slightly out-of-focus quality of much overseas writing about America and particularly jazz turns up in Parker's otherwise informative annotations of these albums. He wrote of the Hoagy Carmichael recording, *Walkin' the Dog*, made in May 1928 in Richmond, Indiana: "[Carmichael's] early recordings did not necessarily employ the talents of . . . 'heavyweights.' Here, the band comprises an enthusiastic group of young friends from Indiana University." First of all, Indiana University has long had an excellent music school. The note suggests that the players were all inconsequential amateurs. The name Bud Dant, listed in the personnel, apparently didn't mean anything to Parker in Australia.

Charles Bud Dant and Carmichael had graduated from the same Indianapolis high school, though not at the same time. Trained on cornet by a bandmaster uncle, Dant went directly into a vaudeville band, playing jazz cornet. When he came home a year later after a long tour, Hoagy persuaded him to come to Bloomington, where Carmichael was completing his law degree at Indiana University, to play in and arrange for the new campus band to replace Carmichael's Collegians. This evolved into Bud Dant's Collegians. Dant took a bachelor's degree in music education, planning to teach, but Duke Ellington urged him and the band to turn pro, which they did. Dant became a successful arranger and conductor in network radio and later television, working with major stars of the period, including Bing Crosby, Jimmy Durante, Bob Hope, and Jo Stafford. Later he became a record producer, working with everyone from Pete Fountain to Ricky Nelson.

I sent tapes of the Parker restorations to Bud Dant, alive and well and living in Hawaii. At eighty-one, he was still an extremely busy musician, at that point engaged in re-arranging and re-orchestrating a suite composed by Carmichael in the early 1960s and performed then by the composer with the Indianapolis Symphony with Dant conducting. Of the 1928 date, and the Parker restoration of the track derived from it, he said:

"The session was recorded in Richmond, Indiana, at the Gennett Studio—on beeswax platters—of the Starr Piano Company, on an old railway siding. It was during spring vacation in 1928. I was at IU, running the band that Hoagy had organized. He called me and asked me to come over and bring Van Sickle, Wolfe, Habbe, Chauncey Goodwin, and Fred Murray. Fred was Hoagy's cousin, a good jazz cornet man who is not listed, I notice, in the liner information. Hoagy brought Drummond and Keating with him from Indianapolis. We also recorded Hoagy's tune *March of the Hoodlums*, *The Wedding Waltz*, and *Stardust*. *March* was released back of *Walkin'* but the other two were scrapped.

"I am the only living player from that session. I still play my old 1922 Benge cornet.

"I've studied the *Walkin' the Dog* track and also compared the Trumbauer-Bix *Singin' the Blues* with my Time-Life copy, and I cannot believe the remarkable quality this Australian engineer came up with."

The Parker albums are like a roomful of famous paintings that have been cleaned, revealing colors we did not know were there. They set a standard against which all other reissue programs had to be judged. Suddenly one could hear the music, all of it—including the bottom lines, whether tuba bass, Wellman Braud's string bass in the Ellington material, or Adrian Rollini's bass saxophone or Don Murray's baritone. I had always assumed the bass parts just weren't there in the grooves of the original recordings. They may have been weak, but they were there, and through Parker's electronic alchemy they were brought forward. You could hear not only the pulse but the pitch of the string bass, as played by Braud, Pops Foster, and others.

I had forgotten that the baritone and bass saxophones were used to play bass parts. The sound is odd; then you get used to it, and it is effective, producing a kind of chugging motion in the rhythm section. So the significance of Adrian Rollini strikes you immediately.

Much fun has been poked at Eddie Condon as a guitarist. He has been portrayed as a hard-drinking buffoon, author of witty aphorisms, who was able to put together good bands but contributed little if anything to the music. He never played solos, and his rhythm playing was quiet. There was even a joke that he didn't play guitar at all, just stroked his hand over the strings. Condon can be heard very well on some of the tracks in these collections, including *Nobody's Sweetheart*, made in 1927 with Jimmy McPartland, Frank Teschemacher, Bud Freeman, Jim Lannigan, and Gene Krupa—the Austin High Gang—and *Makin' Friends*, with his own Footwarmers group that included McPartland and Jack Teagarden. He plays banjo on the latter. He just sits there and makes a band cook.

The best of the tracks by Condon is a 1929 Fats Waller session for Victor. Condon was sent to see that Waller showed up sober and ready, which was pretty foolhardy on the part of somebody at Victor. They arrived hung over and unprepared, except for a couple of tunes Waller had written in the taxi on the way to the session. One of these is *Minor Drag*. (It was supposed to be called *Harlem Fuss* but somebody at Victor goofed on that too.) This is an astonishing track by Waller, Condon, and three horns, coherent, intelligent, humorous, and powerful. Both men knew how to swing, and they reinforced each other.

The Waller tracks are vivid reminders of his wonders: the total independence of his hands, his ability to cross over the time and never screw it up, the power of his left hand in stride passages. And he had the most delicate touch and tone. Like Armstrong, he achieved a success as an entertainer that overshadowed his gifts as a musician. Unlike Armstrong, he never descended to what has been interpreted as Tomming. Armstrong sang dross like *Blueberry Hill* with a big grin, as if he were enjoying it. And maybe he was. When record companies got Waller to sing and play drivel, he treated it with the contempt it deserved, and his sardonic performances are keenly funny. But, one feels on listening to the CD devoted to him, it is sad that more of his studio hours weren't expended on things such as *Minor Drag* and the solo-piano *Handful of Keys*.

It is probably impossible for anyone who grew up after Armstrong's arrival to perceive the impact he had—which is true, to be sure, of the new music of all periods. But these restorations of Armstrong recordings from the years of his greatest creative power give some hint of it. From the first notes, you feel the crackling authority of a soaring imagination.

Jelly Roll Morton's personality—his extravagant claim that he invented jazz—has clouded the issue of his ability. The CD on Morton lets you make up your own mind. His piano playing is weak, but his writing is his forte. The material is uneven, though the best of it is powerful, and his explorations of New Orleans polyphony are ingenious. *Black Bottom Stomp*, by his Red Hot Peppers, swings beautifully.

One CD is devoted to guitarist Eddie Lang and his violinist pal Joe Venuti, who shared an uncanny rapport. Lang, playing his chorded rhythms, is all over the instrument. His command of voicings is complete, his time a thing of beauty. And Venuti played exquisitely.

One of the tracks in the Venuti-Lang album is *Oh! Peter*, recorded with Red Nichols and his Five Pennies. There is no bass of any kind, just Nichols, Venuti, Jimmy Dorsey on clarinet, Fulton McGrath, piano, and Vic Berton, drums. But how that group swings. I have tended to accept the evaluation of Nichols as a pallid trumpet player. It is known that he wrote out his solos. But the various tracks by different editions of the Five Pennies caused me to re-evaluate his work. So too Jimmy Dorsey, who was a hot young alto player, a good clarinetist, a strong baritone player. He plays trumpet on one track, though only passably, and his brother Tommy is also heard on trumpet. Their father, a Pennsylvania music teacher, taught them all the instruments.

Jelly Roll Morton's *Milenburg Joys* is the vehicle that reveals just how brilliant the Detroit-based band called McKinney's Cotton Pickers, one of the orchestras in the Jean Goldkette stable, really was. Its music director was Don Redman, who is ubiquitous in these albums, turning up with several groups, including the 1925 Fletcher Henderson band, both as saxophonist and as arranger of *Sugar Foot Stomp*. Redman is, in common with his friend and fellow arranger Bill Challis, one of the most underestimated musicians in jazz history. He wrote for the Henderson band before Henderson himself did, and must be considered one of the major formulators of big-band jazz writing, more widely influential than Ellington, since more bands followed the pattern of the Henderson charts and format than those of Ellington. And the most under-recognized band is that of Jimmie Lunceford, heard here in a 1934 performance of *Stratosphere*, a clever but inconsequential piece that nonetheless shows what a polished, hard-swinging, fresh group it was, full of subtle mixings, dynamics, and inflections.

The Duke Ellington band between 1927 and 1934 is documented in a sixteen-track album. This was its Cotton Club period, and the band was evolving from Ellington's fascination with New Orleans players and polyphony into what would later be recognizable as the Ellington style. The rhythm section in *The Blues with a Feelin'* consists of Sonny Greer, who was always a strange drummer, and Wellman Braud. Braud plays arco bass here, and the effect is heavy, as if the band were slogging through mud.

The painted exoticism that Ellington devised for the audiences and management of the Cotton Club had nothing to do with the culture, or rather cultures, of Africa. The music caters to opulent ofays on shivery adventures into the "primitive" world of darkest Harlem, ogling feathered brown-skinned girls writhing around the stage, indulging fantasies of boffing these dark beauties in some steamy clearing. It is demeaning to everyone involved. I find nothing romantic about memories of the Cotton Club.

That this was another age, and that it is always dangerous to judge the behavior of a previous time by the standards of one's own, is obvious. Like Armstrong and Morton, Ellington must be viewed in context. Still, there was a time when it was acceptable public sport to feed people to lions, another when it was acceptable to keel-haul or even summarily hang sailors. These things are not acceptable to us now, even in retrospect. One might counter that at least the Cotton Club provided employment. But then so did the capture and care of lions.

The Mooche and *East St. Louis Toodle-oo* are examples of the affectations of the primal that Ellington contributed to the rites of the Cotton Club. That in them he does things original in popular music at the time is undisputed. But—to me—they bespeak distasteful things about the nature of man.

The album ends with the version of *Solitude* recorded January 10, 1934, *Stompy Jones*, recorded the previous day, and *Live and Love Tonight*, recorded four months later. The band has grown by now to four trumpets and two trombones, two altos, tenor, and baritone, plus the rhythm section. Braud plays pizzicato bass on *Stompy Jones* and the band swings hard. *Live and Love Tonight* is not an Ellington tune, but it shows how Ellington could convert pop material into something of his own. The band had advanced from the early Cotton Club time, it was heading toward the glory days of *Ko-Ko, Cotton Tail, Take the "A" Train, Harlem Air Shaft.*

The album is an invaluable historical record, and I have listened to it in deepest fascination—sometimes uneasy fascination, to be sure. And even in works such as *The Mooche*, Ellington was expanding the vocabulary of jazz. He is exploring shades of emotion not within the compass of the music before that. The music is leading toward the musings of Miles Davis, the palette of Gil Evans, and the lyrical broodings of Bill Evans.

If the affectations of exoticism of the Cotton Club days suggest the dark side of the Roaring Twenties, most of the popular music of that decade was in keeping with the giddy quality of the period, with its flagpole sitters and rolled stockings and bee's knees, raccoon coats and gin-flask irresponsibility. It was the era of the Volstead Act, rising hem lines, bobbed hair, cloche hats, marathon dancing, Teapot Dome, art deco, the Scopes trial, the Charleston, the St. Valentine's Day massacre, the John Held flapper, 23 skiddoo, I love my wife but oh you kid, Clara Bow, Chaplin, Valentino, Gatsby, Lucky Lindy, Dion O'Bannion, Al Capone, Shipwreck Kelley, and Erte.

The boys had come home (well, most of them; some were in Flanders Field, amid the poppies), America was prosperous, it looked like the party would go on forever. Few Americans even noticed it when as the decade dawned, the propaganda chief of the German Workers Party, one Adolf Hitler, publicly stated their program. He attacked Jews, capitalists, and large property owners. That was in February 1920. And no one much paid any attention when in Paris, the following January, the Allies announced the punishment they would impose on the Germans: payment of reparations of $56 billion over a period of forty-two years, and an additional payment of 12.5 percent tax on all her exports.

The thing that strikes you most forcefully in these albums is the ubiquity of the swinging. That, and the joy of the music. It is almost universally joyous. These records refute the later revisionist definition of jazz as the angered outcry of a down-trodden people. This music, played by black musicians and white alike, is enormous exuberant fun. Like all great art, it exists in and of itself, with no other purpose but to please the artist and his audience. It is frivolous and gay, like art deco. And the jazz of the 1920s has the additional charm of not being thought of as art at all by the men who were making it. It is devoid of pomp or pretense or claims for itself, which cannot be said of a lot of the jazz of recent decades.

And that isn't the only illusion dispelled by these albums, which give a fairly thorough representation of jazz in the twenties. So much fuss has been made over the hiring of Teddy Wilson by Benny Goodman that one is left with an impression that blacks and whites did not previously play together. Composer Milton Babbitt, who played jazz clarinet when he was a boy growing up in the south, said that mixed performances were quite common during that time, and that he played in funeral services himself. The Waller session with Eddie Condon, the Wingy Manone session with Dicky Wells and Jelly Roll Morton, were apparently not considered ground-breaking. Waller also recorded with Ted Lewis in a band that included Muggsy Spanier and Benny Goodman, and brought Mezz Mezzrow in on one of his own dates. Bubber Miley and Bix Beiderbecke are both on the Hoagy Carmichael recording of *Barnacle Bill the Sailor*. Certainly black and white musicians recorded together years before Goodman hired Wilson. In New Orleans, the light-skinned Creole clarinetist Sidney Arodin went casually back and forth between white and black bands, and he recorded with the New Orleans Rhythm Kings, with Manone and George Brunies, in 1934. Morton recorded with an earlier New Orleans Rhythm Kings, whose personnel included Ben Pollack and Don Murray, as far back as 1923. I had believed that mixed groups performed only on recordings, but Babbitt refutes even that.

Another thing I noticed, reading the personnel lists, is the scarcity, in proportion to population, of Anglo-Saxons in the ranks of white jazz musicians. The Irish were there—Eddie Condon, Dick McDonough, Jim Lannigan, Tommy and Jimmy Dorsey—and the Jews, including Artie Shaw and Benny Goodman, and the Germans: Paul Mertz, Frank Teschemacher, Jack and Charlie Teagarden, and Bix Beiderbecke. There is a Pole or two, Gene Krupa among them, though it must be remembered that Poland, like England, contributed comparatively little to European "classical" composition prior to the twentieth century. And Chopin was half French. Don Murray was almost certainly of Scottish descent. And when you consider how common it was for people with "funny" names to Anglicize them in that era, one wonders how many musicians bearing respectable WASP monikers were Italian or Jewish or middle European. These changes were still being made in later years, as in the cases of Joe Albany, Joe Farrell, Louis Bellson, Pete Jolly, and Jerry Gray, born Albani, Firrantello, Balassoni, Ceragioli, and Graziano respectively. Eddie Lang's name at birth was Massaro, and he was a member of that ethnic group with the largest contingent of white players, the Italians, among them Joe Venuti, Adrian Rollini, Frank Signorelli, Paul Graselli, Leon Roppolo, Pete Pumiglio, Wingy Manone, Sharky Bonano, Mike Trafficante, Tony Briglia, and Henry Biagnini, who was musical director of the Casa Loma orchestra when Glen Gray and Ray Eberle were its alto players. The Original Dixieland Jazz Band, the white group that came up from New Orleans in 1918 and started the national craze for jazz, contained Nick LaRocca and Tony Sbarbaro among its

players. Drummer Chauncey Morehouse, an authentic WASP, was
certainly a member of a minority in jazz.

Bix Beiderbecke has taken a place as a symbol of the Jazz Age
(music's equivalent of what F. Scott Fitzgerald was to literature):
the flawed and tragic poetic young men, somehow fated from
birth, who would be cut off prematurely by alcohol. It was Fitzgerald who named it the Jazz Age.

To get to the heart of the music Bix or anyone else made in the
1920s—or, more precisely, to let it get to yours—you have to
adapt yourself to a different concept of time and the rhythm section. There are more ways than one to swing, the cult of two and
four to the contrary notwithstanding. Samba swings on one and
three; or rather, on one, since in Brazil the bossa nova tunes that
became part of the North American jazz repertoire were notated
in two. It is also hard for us to know what the early jazz drummers
sounded like. Bill Crow, who has done some research on it, was
told by veterans of the era that drummers had to hold back
because of shortcomings in the recording equipment: on a King
Oliver track in this collection, despite the improved sound, you
can hardly hear Baby Dodds at all.

The bands with which Bix worked were *not* all inferior, as the
conventional wisdom holds. Bill Rank was a fine trombonist. Don
Murray was not only a very good clarinetist, he was an estimable
baritone player. One of the good groups Bix played with, despite
a myth created by Dorothy Baker's novel *Young Man with a Horn*,
was the Paul Whiteman organization, which is heard here in *Mississippi Mud*, a song with a lyric that is all the more unsettling in
that its cruelty is unconscious, its racism ingenuous: ". . . just as
happy as a cow chewin' on a cud, when the darkies beat their feet
on the Mississippi mud." How ghastly: an entire people characterized as being satisfied with, as aspiring to, nothing higher than the
pleasure of beating their feet in mud. Sometimes the smaller hor-
rors are the more revealing of a society and a time. Years later, in
a Red Skelton movie called *Whistling in Dixie*, a man awakens a
small black boy sleeping on the porch of a shanty and using his

little dog for a pillow. The man asks the boy for directions and leaves. The boy puts his head back on his dog and goes back to sleep. This scene is presented to us as comedy.

Thus too *Mississippi Mud*. It is admiring of its "darkies" and envious of their primitive pleasures. Finally, what is troubling about the song is its role in the perpetuation, perhaps even the creation, of a stereotype. Some people argue that "race relations" were progressing quite nicely until David Wark Griffith, in *The Birth of a Nation*, put into place a vision of the black American that set a pattern for later movies. Marlon Brando has insisted that the movie industry created the howling-savage image of the Indians. *Mississippi Mud* epitomizes the function of popular entertainment in the shaping of social attitudes, a power the executives of television, movies, and the record industry insist it does not have, even as the salesmen of radio and TV time argue out of the other side of the face that it does.

And, like the movies of Leni Riefenstahl, Hitler's favorite film-maker, *Mississippi Mud*—sung by Irene Taylor in one of those little-girl voices popular in that era, and by Bing Crosby and the Rhythm Boys—is the more disturbing for being well done. The playing on it, including that of Bix, is marvelous. A more satisfying track, because it lacks the described distraction, is *San*, played by the jazz group Whiteman carried within the band—Bill Rank on trombone, Jimmy Dorsey on clarinet, Frank Trumbauer on C-melody sax, Min Leibrook on bass saxophone, Matty Malneck, violin, and Harold McDonald on drums. And this is arranged chamber jazz, the chart by Bill Challis. It contains a soaring harmonized chorus by Bix and lead trumpeter Charlie Margulis.

I asked Paul Weston, who wrote for that band, if it were true that Whiteman couldn't read music. Paul chuckled and said that he certainly wasn't fluent at it. There were directions written on the music so that Whiteman could let it appear that he was conducting. "But I hope you're not going to put Pops down," Paul immediately said. "He made no pretensions about himself as a musician. It was all strictly among the boys. His attitude was: just don't let the advertising agency find out."

There is much for us to learn about America in the music on the Parker CDs. It is the gaiety, the joy, of it, its wonderful irreverence, that gets to you, now that you can really hear it.

In a sense, Bix does indeed live. When the word went around New York bars that he was dead, Hoagy Carmichael—who, let us remember, also played cornet and acquired Bix's mouthpiece and carried it in his pocket until his own death—said, "No he's not, I can hear him from here."

Bix becomes more an enigma than ever for the immediacy of his presence on the Parker CDs. If there was a dark lyricism in the playing of Bill Evans, it was there in the man. But if there was a darkness in Bix that made him drink himself to death, by the age of twenty-eight, it is not in the music.

Like Mozart's music, Beiderbecke's has a serenity in it, an almost angelic quality, as he makes perfect placement of those bell-sound notes. Nobody else ever got a sound like that out of a cornet, though some fine players have tried. Beiderbecke had a trick of laying back in soft passages and then suddenly cutting loose, strutting with an uncontainable exuberance. He had, as everyone knew, limited technique, and never played very high on the horn. But the selectivity and the perfection of the line seem to be the expression of an effortless musical eloquence.

Bix Beiderbecke was not long for this world, nor was the giddy age of which he was a somehow so perfect expression. In May 1927, Charles Lindbergh flew across the Atlantic, accelerating the diminution of the world begun by Columbus's caravels. In September Isadora Duncan strangled on her scarf. In July 1928, the first television set made in the United States went on sale (for $75). The next year the first color TV set was displayed by Bell Labs. On October 24, 1929, Wall Street, as *Variety* put it in a headline, laid an egg. After the Black Thursday crash, the gaiety was gone.

On May 21, 1930, seven months after the crash, Hoagy Carmichael recorded *Barnacle Bill the Sailor* with a personnel that included Bix, Bubber Miley, Tommy Dorsey, Benny Goodman, Arnold Brilhart, Bud Freeman, Irving Brodsky on piano, Lang and Venuti, Goodman's brother Harry on bass, and Gene Krupa on drums. This record is famous in jazz circles not for its musical merit—it hasn't any—but for the fact that at the end Venuti says in a basso voice, "Barnacle Bill the shithead." The enhanced recording reveals that he isn't the only one to use the phrase: Hoagy Carmichael and Carson Robison sing it through several choruses.

The joyous and often Rabelaisian irreverence of the 1920s, which makes so much of the jazz prior to this funny, has been replaced by a sophomoric and vaguely sullen scatology.

The Casa Loma band recorded *Casa Loma Stomp* in 1930. Bix died in 1931. By 1934, Ellington's style was defined in such pieces as *Stompy Jones*. His personnel, like that of other bands, had been enlarged after the manner of the Paul Whiteman band. Lunceford recorded *Stratosphere* that same year, on September 4, and eight days later, Earl Hines recorded *Maple Leaf Rag* with a rhythm section, three trumpets, three trombones, and four saxes. Five weeks later, in Cheraw, South Carolina, on October 21, a boy named John Birks Gillespie turned seventeen.

In Germany a young Hollander went to the guillotine for the Reichstag fire, which he didn't set. At the airport of Managua, Nicaragua, General Augusto Sandino, who was working to end peacefully the occupation of his country by the U.S. Marines, was executed by forces loyal to General Anastasio Somoza, who would soon take power with consequences we know. The Depression deepened and John Dillinger, who used a Thompson submachine gun in his bank robberies, was looked on as a hero by many people in the blighted midwest. Bonnie and Clyde died in a police ambush, then Dillinger was shot to death by FBI men in Chicago and Pretty Boy Floyd and Baby Face Nelson got theirs a few weeks later. The Gestapo was arresting and executing opponents of Adolf Hitler, who announced that he would no longer pay off Germany's foreign debts. Austrian Chancellor Engelbert Dolfuss was assassinated by Nazis, Mao Tse-Tung began the Long March, and Josef Stalin had one hundred of his rivals put to death.

The Jazz Age was over.

The tradition of New Orleans polyphony would be abandoned

by black musicians, its influence lingering on almost entirely in white players clinging to a style relevant to an era that was ended. When you have experienced the ebullience of 1920s jazz, you can understand why so many people were nostalgic for it. Something went out of the music. It was replaced by other things, valuable things, which would vastly expand its expressiveness, but something was lost. Still, you could not retain the Zeitgeist of 1920s jazz by imitating it. Music, like language, continually evolves, if only because its masters grow bored with what they are doing. Music that clings to a past inevitably becomes petrified. In time the New Orleans tradition with which jazz begins would deteriorate into an affected counterpoint, predictable from repetition, played by men in straw hats and shirtsleeves with arm garters.

Hines, Ellington, Armstrong, Goodman, Hawkins, Tommy Dorsey, continued to develop in the 1930s. Not everyone did. One of the records restored by Robert Parker somehow signals the end of the era perfectly. It is *Panama,* made September 12, 1934, by Wingy Manone, himself a native of New Orleans, George Brunies on trombone, clarinetist Sidney Arodin, Terry Shand on piano, Benny Pottle on bass, and Bob White, drums. The style is instantly recognizable. It is white Dixieland.

The best white jazz players—but not the black; they were silently excluded—had gone into the studios. They would sit around Jimmy Plunkett's and bitch about the music business.

Plunkett's, a forerunner of Jim and Andy's, Junior's, and Charlie's, was a speakeasy patronized by musicians, on 53rd Street under the old elevated railway, the El of legend, long since vanished. That was in the late '20s and early '30s. With the repeal of the Volstead Act at the end of 1933, a group of musicians, including Bunny Berigan, Tommy Dorsey, Dick McDonough, Manny Klein, Carl Kress, and Arthur Schutt among them, decided to open their own bar. It was the Onyx club, upstairs near the location now occupied by Twenty-one. There they could groan some more, hire musicians they admired, such as Joe Sullivan, Fats Waller, and Willie "The Lion" Smith, and let them play for an audience of pros who knew what they were hearing. They would do that and dream of playing a better kind of music.

In the summer of 1936 it became possible: Benny Goodman's band attained a sudden huge success, utilizing the homophonic kind of orchestral organization that had been taking form in the '20s, following patterns explored by the Casa Loma, Redman, Henderson, Challis, and others. A new fad was launched, and the verb, describing what the music was supposed to do, was turned into a noun to identify it: swing. The press agents jumped on it. The booking agents were looking for anyone who could put together a band that could "swing", and one after the other, these young musicians came out of the studio to do it, Benny Goodman and the Dorsey brothers among them.

At the same time, the admiration for soloists blowing in front of the rhythm section, brought about primarily by Armstrong but also by Coleman Hawkins and Bix Beiderbecke, grew among the jazz cognoscenti, although already stubborn loyalists, admirers of the old New Orleans style, said that this new music wasn't jazz.

On September 11, 1939, Lionel Hampton recorded Benny Carter's *When Lights Are Low*. Carter was in the ensemble. So was John Birks Gillespie, now twenty-two and sounding a lot like Roy Eldridge. Europe was mobilizing. The United States War Department placed a huge order for aircraft and engines. On September 30, Germany invaded Poland, and Britain and France declared war. Eleven days later, on October 11, Coleman Hawkins recorded *Body and Soul*, establishing irremovably the concept of the jazz soloist as culture hero, himself as one of its major figures, and the song as peculiarly his.

The Japanese bombed Pearl Harbor on December 7, 1941, a date Americans—older ones, anyway—know as well as they do the Fourth of July.

Remembering that day, Artie Shaw said: "I left the music business in 1954, but my career as a serious dedicated player of a musical instrument really came to an end before that. It ended in 1941, when World War II started. I was playing a theater in Providence,

Rhode Island. The manager of the theater asked me to make an announcement. I went out and asked all servicemen in the crowd to return immediately to their bases. It seems as if two thirds of the audience got up and left. We hadn't realized how many people had been going into service. With the whole world in flames, playing *Stardust* seemed pretty pointless. During the show I put the word out to the guys, two weeks notice. In the South Pacific I saw war face-to-face. Nothing was ever the same after that."

There is a photo of Shaw performing on an aircraft carrier, leaning back, bent around his clarinet. Young sailors are hanging off every protrusion of the carrier's island. Once he and his Navy band performed for marines under ponchos in the rain on some now-Godforsaken tropical paradise. Japanese snipers opened fire on them. During a concert on Guadalcanal they came under bombing attack. Shaw and his musicians and the boys they were sent to entertain plunged into slit trenches and tried to cling to the earth, which shook. In the darkness Dave Tough asked for a cigarette, got one, then asked for a lighter. Handing the lighter back, he said, "The cigarette is Joe's, the lighter is Jim's, and the shaky voice is mine," inducing much nervous laughter. Then a Japanese plane laid a stick of bombs, bracketing their foxhole. One of them blew in Shaw's left ear drum. His head rang for months, inducing shattering headaches. He would never again have full hearing in that ear. The band was eventually sent home, sick and exhausted. "Davey Tough was just a ghost," Shaw said.

Dave Tough went into the Woody Herman band, the one that would be known as the First Herd. In the early months of 1945, as German resistance was crumbling and it was obvious the war was nearing its end, he took part in a series of recordings which, in their dada-esque and sometimes even bitonal exuberance, were as characteristic of that time as *Singin' the Blues* and *West End Blues* were of theirs. This was the time of *Apple Honey, Caldonia, Goosey Gander, Northwest Passage, The Good Earth, Bijou.*

Dizzy Gillespie, Charlie Parker, Bud Powell, Thelonious Monk, Kenny Clarke, and a few more, were playing a new kind of jazz. Just as some of the New Orleans polyphony fans said that the

music of the big bands wasn't jazz, so some of the big-band fans—
and even musicians—denounced what the beboppers were doing.
Benny Goodman particularly disliked it.

Critic and cornetist Dick Sudhalter to this day says it is "nervous" music. For me, as a teenager listening to it, it was exhilarat-
ing. And if it was indeed nervous, it was the product of its age, as
the sunny and often frenetic jazz of the '20s was of its age. Time
has clarified that bebop was evolutionary, not revolutionary. A
number of CDs released on various labels since the Parker restorations remind us of the sheer, blazing genius of Parker and
Gillespie.

In July, 1988, Dizzy said to New York *Post* columnist Pete Ham-
ill that Louis Armstrong "is just as bright and shining today as he
was twenty, thirty, fifty years ago. Even today, all these years later,
we haven't gone too far from what he did first.

"It wasn't just trumpet he influenced. He left his print on everything: piano, trombone, saxophone, vocals. Listen to Billie Holiday, you'll hear Pops in there. Even me, I was a Roy Eldridge man.
But Roy came from Louis, so when I play a Roy Eldridge lick, I'm
also a part of the family of Louis Armstrong. Everybody is."

On June 13, 1953, Charlie Parker was interviewed by John
McLellan in Boston. McLellan asked, "Whom [*sic*] do you feel
were, beside yourself, the important persons who were dissatisfied
with music as it was and started to experiment?"

"Let me make a correction," Parker said. "It was *not* that we
were dissatisfied. It was just that another conception came along
and this was the way we thought it should go. Dizzy Gillespie, Thelonious Monk, Kenny Clarke, Charlie Christian, Bud Powell, Don
Byas, Ben Webster, myself."

MacLellan said, "Lots of musicians from the swing era are finding it difficult to work because the audiences are violently split
between Dixieland and Cool. There seems to be no room for these
middle-of-the-road musicians."

"I beg to differ," Parker said. "There is always room for musicians. There is no such thing as the middle of the road. It's either
one thing or the other—either good music or otherwise. It doesn't

matter which idiom it's in. Call it swing, bebop, or Dixieland. If it's good music, it will be heard."

"I notice," MacLellan said, "that you play *Anthropology* and *52nd Street Theme*, but they were written a long time ago. What is to take their place and be the basis for your future?"

"It's hard to say," Parker said. "A man's ideas change as he grows older. Most people don't realize that most of what they hear come out of a man's horn—they are just experiences. It may be the beauty of the weather. A nice look of a mountain. A nice breath of fresh air. You can never tell what you'll be thinking tomorrow. But I can definitely say that music won't stop. It will continue to go forward."

Parker himself had less than two years of future left. He died March 12, 1955. Louis Armstrong was still going strong, by now a world celebrity, used—cynically, some thought—by his country as its "Ambassador of Good Will."

Armstrong was even a movie star of sorts, appearing in 1956 in *High Society* with Grace Kelly, Frank Sinatra, and Bing Crosby, who'd been one of the voices on *Mississippi Mud*. Crosby and Armstrong had a duet in that picture. They sang *Now You Has Jazz*, Cole Porter's tacky tribute to the music, full of his idea of the argot of the idiom. Armstrong apparently is having fun and Crosby seems unembarrassed by this piece of trash. Art Farmer still could not sit with white customers in a Kansas City nightclub. J.J. Johnson and Kai Winding would feel a draft when they took their memorable group on the road even in the 1960s. It would take Autherine Lucy, heartbreak, bloodshed, and Martin Luther King to change all that.

In 1958, I was driving from Paris to Stockholm. By the side of a road in Germany I noticed a small arrow sign saying Belsen. Almost involuntarily, I turned in, making my way up a country lane amid fields of spring flowers until I reached the site of the camp. The buildings were gone, but there were huge long mounds of earth with signs in German saying "Here lie 1,000 dead . . . Here lie 3,000 dead." Anne Frank had died on a bunk on those cursed grounds in March of 1945, eleven days after Woody Herman recorded *A Kiss Goodnight.* There was no one there, only me, my emotions absolutely shattered, wandering bleakly in a terrible aloneness and in a chill wind in which, I swear, I seemed to hear moans and cries. No doubt it was just the sound it made passing through the pines. Long afterwards I described the experience to an English Jewish acquaintance, who—sign of our times—happens to be one of the world's leading authorities on terrorism. He too had been to Belsen.

He said, "Did you notice that the birds didn't sing there?" I was amazed. Because in memory, suddenly, I could hear, appallingly, their absolute absence from that scene.

After Guadalcanal and Saipan and the Coral Sea, Leningrad and Stalingrad, Gold Beach and Bastogne, Treblinka and Auschwitz and Belsen, Dresden and Hiroshima and Nagasaki, it was hard to realize that the giddy time called the Roaring Twenties, Fitzgerald's Jazz Age, the Lost Generation, had ever been. Now Pioneer Ten wayfares on into the endless night beyond the solar system. The players of that other jazz in that other time seem like a little group standing in an old-fashioned railway station, hands high in a forever arrested farewell, King Oliver, Nick LaRocca, the young Louis, Jimmy Noone, Johnny and Baby Dodds, Bix and Tram and Don Murray, Venuti and Lang, growing smaller in the distance as we look back from the platform of this train we wish we were not on.

But their music is traveling with us.

Fiddler Joe

Contrary to widespread impression, the violin is not an intruder into jazz. The instrument has been involved in the music since the beginning, as far back as the proto-jazz of Will Marion Cook's Southern Syncopators. References to the instrument crop up in early descriptions of jazz. The problem for the instrument, and its players, was that though it has great dynamic range, its volume is very light. In the days before amplification, one solo fiddle player wasn't going to be heard very well against a front line of saxophone or clarinet, trombone, and trumpet.

As for its use in sections, the bands of Artie Shaw, Tommy Dorsey, and Gene Krupa demonstrated that strings were not practical for exuberant up-tempo numbers. Sections of twelve or even eighteen men cannot outshout four trumpets and three trombones, much less five and four. A full-scale symphony orchestra employs up to sixty strings, and if you ever saw the Woody Herman band perform jointly with one, you know how easily a jazz brass section can drown them.

And string sections are incapable of jazz ensemble passages of their own: you could not round up sixty string players on this planet capable of phrasing jazz. They come from too different a tradition.

So those musicians who have played jazz on the violin have tended to be loners. They have not been many: Eddie South, Stuff Smith, Ray Nance, Joe Kennedy, Svend Asmussen, Jean-Luc Ponty, Stephane Grappelli, and the pioneering Joe Venuti. Four of those eight, one notes reflexively, were born in Europe. And Venuti was the first important jazz soloist on the violin.

Giuseppe Venuti always said he was born in Italy. He told me once he came from a family of sculptors and that he was trained entirely in classical music; jazz came later. But some researchers offer evidence that he was actually born in Philadelphia.

His birthdate is given as April 4, 1898, in John Chilton's *Who's Who in Jazz* and in Leonard Feather's *Encyclopedia of Jazz*. Robert Parker, in his annotation to the stereo album he engineered of the Lang-Venuti material, gives Joe's birthdate as September 16, 1903. On occasion Joe was known to say he was born on a boat to America around 1904. Dick Gibson says he once met one of Joe's uncles who told him that Venuti arrived in Philadelphia at the age of ten in 1906. And, he told Gibson, "Joe could play good when he got off the boat."

Joe said he was born in Lecco, which is near Milan. And his career, which began in the 1920s, was long and famous, despite his long and equally famous taste for the sauce.

Certainly Joe grew up in Philadelphia, specifically South Philadelphia, where he met Salvatore Massaro. Massaro, like Venuti, was a violin student. They played together in the string section of the James Campbell School Orchestra. Though they gave private performances of Italian folk music and material from opera, they were also experimenting with jazz by the early 1920s. Joe moved to New York. Massaro, who had changed his name to Eddie Lang and put aside his violin to devote the rest of his all-too-brief career to guitar and banjo, toured with Red McKenzie's Mound City Blue Blowers.

Venuti and Lang crossed trails in New York in 1926, which is when their true professional partnership began. Robert Parker

describes them as a "classic example of the attraction of oppo-
sites. Eddie was cool, logical, and a good businessman (also a
remarkably good billiards player, rumored to have made more
in the poolrooms than he did as a musician). Joe was a hot-
head, flamboyant and irresponsible (always spoiling for a fight
and much given to cracking violins over the heads of the
unwary)."

Venuti and Lang made some superb recordings together
between 1926 and 1933, in all sorts of contexts—sometimes as a
duo, sometimes with that other team, Bix Beiderbecke and Frank
Trumbauer, sometimes with groups of their own, sometimes as
part of Red Nichols and his Five Pennies. They had a marvelous
rapport.

Lang worked extensively in the New York studios, aside from
his jazz playing, which gives an indication of his musicianship. But
it is the collaboration with Venuti that endears him to history.
There is a captivating exuberance about their playing, and a kind
of nutty irreverence. They are fun to listen to, and more so than
ever in the Robert Parker restorations.

Lang was a great guitarist. In the praise of Django Reinhardt
and Charlie Christian, justified though it is, I am always mystified
that more credit isn't given to Lang and to Eddie Durham as the
pioneers they were. Because of Lang's influence on Reinhardt,
and Reinhardt's influence on the whole evolution of jazz guitar,
Lang is a true source in the French sense of that word, meaning a
spring—and in this case one that flowed on to become a river. The
Lang-Venuti duo records were the inspiration for the Quintet of
the Hot Club of France headed by Reinhardt and Stephane
Grappelli. Django is foreshadowed in Lang's linear solos. And
Lang could do things that Reinhardt, due to that damaged left
hand, could not. He could comp chords superbly. He was all
over the instrument when he played rhythm, with total command of the voicings, as far as the harmony in use at that period
went.

Possibly he doesn't get the credit he deserves because he didn't
live long enough. Jazz evolved enormously through the 1930s. But

Lang was not to take part in that development. He went into hospital in New York for a tonsillectomy and died of its complications, March 26, 1933. He was thirty.

Lang and Venuti recorded seventy sides together, in various contexts. In the early 1960s, Columbia Records issued their 1920s material in a three-album package.

"The first record Eddie and I made," Venuti told me in a conversation in Colorado Springs in 1974, "was a thing called *Doin' Things*. You'll hear *Musetta's Waltz* from *La Bohème*. But we did it in four-four, and I interpolated the melody in a different way. A tune we did called *Wild Cat* was just an exercise by Kreutzer." In another recording in that Columbia collection, Venuti uses the pentatonic melodic material of Debussy's *Maid with the Flaxen Hair*; he was one of the earliest to start assimilating the influence of the Impressionist composers into jazz.

Joe told me this story of how he came to join the Jean Goldkette band in 1924. He said he worked for short periods in both the Boston and Detroit symphonies. He said he was fed up with the forty bucks a week he was making in the latter orchestra and walked down to a club where some of Goldkette's musicians were playing and asked if he could sit in. They were playing a blues in C, he told me. He loosened his bow, looped the hair over the fiddle, and played his solo in four-note chords. All his life this was one of his most startling devices, and it was no trick: he could make real music that way.

Goldkette hired him, and he never again played "classical" music for a living, although backstage, when he warmed up, it was always on the old masters, with a particular partiality to Bach and Vivaldi. He was intimately familiar with the "classical" violin repertoire, and I remember that he had a great love for Palestrina. Jascha Heifetz, whom many violinists consider the ultimate master of their instrument, enormously admired Venuti's virtuosity.

Joe was as famous among musicians for his practical jokes as he was for his playing, and the stories about him are part of the folklore of jazz—in danger of fading now, I daresay, since there are no hangout clubs where the older musicians can pass them along to the younger.

One story concerns a tenor player he worked with whose foot-tapping so annoyed Joe that finally he came on stage with a hammer and nailed the man's shoe to the floor. I don't believe it. Unless he suddenly and psychopathically drove a nail through a man's foot, he would have to had to slip the nail through the edge of the sole. The image of someone sitting there and passively allowing this is not convincing.

One story that I know is true is this:

One Christmas Joe sent his friend Wingy Manone, the one-armed trumpet player, a single cufflink.

The next year he sent the other one.

Then there was the time he hit several balls into a golf course water hazard. In a fury he threw his club into the lake, then the rest of his clubs, then the bag, then the caddy, and finally himself.

This is one of the best-known Venuti stories, and I suspect it's true:

A certain famous singing-cowboy movie star, known for his flashy suits and self-admiration, succeeded in annoying Joe during some stage show they did together. The audience was full of mothers and their children. Joe slipped his bow under the belly of the cowboy's famous horse, just ahead of the legs, and began tickling. The cowboy brought the horse on stage. On signal it reared on its hind legs. It was immediately apparent that the animal was in the mood for love. The curtains promptly closed, and Joe left. "I wasn't going to stick around," he growled in that gravelly Italian voice.

Another time Joe telephoned thirty-six tuba players listed in the union directory and told them to meet him for a job on a certain corner. Joe told me it happened in Hollywood, not New York, as one version had it. He told them to meet him at Hollywood and Vine, and watched the chaotic scene from the twelfth floor of the Taft hotel with Jack Bregman of the publishing firm of Bregman, Vocco, and Conn.

"The joke was on me, though," Joe said. "They took me to the union and I had to pay ten bucks a man. Two weeks later, Jack

Bregman said, 'Call them again and I'll pay the fine.' But I said, 'No chance.'"

In the early days of television—and it was live television, remember—Joe was on a show sponsored by a hair cream company. In the middle of a commercial, he aimed his bald head at the camera and said, "This is what Wildroot Cream Oil did for me." The sponsor dropped the show.

The story of Whiteman, Joe, and the long pole is another of those with variant versions. This is the one Joe told me.

In 1936, Joe and his twelve-piece band were hired to work in Fort Worth opposite the Paul Whiteman band in a huge theater-restaurant called the Casa Mañana, as part of the Texas Frontier Centennial. The extravaganza was a Billy Rose production, with chorus girls, a revolving stage a block long, and a lagoon with a jet spray of water to separate the proscenium and the audience. Rose had suggested two bands be used; Whiteman had suggested Venuti as the other. At some points both bands played together. In his biography of Whiteman titled *Pops*, Thomas A. DeLong wrote, "The Whiteman bandstand was placed opposite the smaller platform holding Venuti and his players. As the open-air theater was generally dark, Paul decided to use a lighted baton so that both bands could see him directing them when they played together."

Joe thought this was a bit much. DeLong said he got a broomstick with a flashlight attached to the end; Joe said it was a fishing pole with a huge lightbulb on its end.

He came onstage in long underwear, carrying this "baton." "It lit up the wholllle arena," Joe said. "Billy Rose came back and said, 'What do you think I'm running here, a circus?'

"I said, 'That's exactly what you're running.'

"But they couldn't fire me, because I owed Paul five thousand dollars. I was with Paul on and off for nine years. When I quit the band . . . Well, I didn't quit, we all got fired. He couldn't hold the band. His payroll by then was something like $9,600 a week. And he said, 'Boys, I've given everybody notice with pay, and that's it.'

"I said, 'How are you gonna give me notice with pay? I owe you money.'"

"He said, 'That's all right, you'll make it.'"

"I said, 'I don't have a cent now. How're we gonna start our own band? Loan me five thousand.' And he loaned me five thousand dollars. So now I owed him ten, and I finally paid him back."

There's a bit of a problem with that story. Venuti's full-time period with Whiteman lasted from May 1929 to May 1930, with time off for Joe's recovery from an automobile accident in California. Joe was, let us keep in mind, recalling events forty years in the past. It is likely that the incident happened not in 1936 but in May 1930 at the Roxy, when Whiteman—faced by the Depression and shrinking audiences—lopped ten people off the payroll, including Joe, Eddie Lang, Lennie Hayton, Boyce Cullen, Bill Challis, Charlie Margulis, and Min Leibrook.

Like everyone else I ever met who worked for Whiteman or even knew him, Joe harbored an immense respect and affection for the man.

"Ooooh, to me," Joe said, with almost a reverence in his voice, "Paul was the greatest man in our business."

And, like all the musicians who knew Bix well, Joe categorically rejected the image of Bix so unhappy having to compromise art for the sake of commerce in the Whiteman band that he was driven to drink and death. That idea, perpetrated by the Dorothy Baker novel *Young Man with a Horn*, has done Whiteman's memory grave damage.

"Bix wasn't unhappy," Joe said. "He played all he wanted to in the Whiteman band. The only thing was, when we played a concert, Paul would never let us go out and play a solo. He'd play the [Gershwin] *Concerto in F* and *Rhapsody in Blue*, he'd play the [Grofé] *Mississippi Suite*. And on those concerts, we'd never get a chance to play any jazz.

"You know, I played in a symphony orchestra, and then I went to a dance hall, and then I cracked out of that and wound up in a cellar, the Silver Slipper. In the old days, in the early 1920s, jazz was always played in a cellar.

"Well, Paul Whiteman got a bunch of guys together and he took us out of the cellar. Actually.

"George Gershwin helped a lot with his compositions, and we

had a wonderful arranger in the Whiteman band named Ferde Grofé. He wrote . . . well, it was semi-jazz and semi-classical. But that helped us a whole lot. The band played Aeolian Hall, 1924, and did the *Rhapsody in Blue*. From there jazz went to Carnegie Hall, and Town Hall, and that brought the level up, and the college boys latched onto jazz."

Whiteman was known to be an inept conductor. As far back as his youth in Denver, his father, Wilberforce Whiteman—superintendent of music in the Denver Public Schools, and Jimmie Lunceford's teacher—had said of him, "He doesn't know how to conduct."

Venuti somewhat hesitantly confirmed that Whiteman used to instruct new players in the orchestra to watch not him but the lead trumpeter, and was quite capable of giving five beats where four should be. Still, it may be time for a re-evaluation of Whiteman's role in American music, which is a little analogous to that of Diaghilev's in ballet and twentieth century European music. He was a man who made things happen. Certainly Whiteman must have been blessed with immense tolerance, not to say a sense of humor, to put up with the antics of Venuti.

Another story that can be believed because members of the Whiteman band, including Bix, witnessed it, is this:

It occurred when the band was in Hollywood, waiting to film *King of Jazz* at Universal. There were endless delays as writers labored to produce a plausible script about the life of Whiteman. The band was at leisure, on full salary, and its members grew increasingly bored, particularly since it had to report for duty at the studio every afternoon. One day Venuti arrived at Universal leading on a leash a fox he had captured the previous day in Laurel Canyon. In the bright sunshine he called the band to silence and announced:

"Gentleman! Meet Mr. Reynard Vomit. Reynard would like it known that he can outrace any dog in the house." Somebody found a dog, and one of the musicians shouted, "Go!" Joe released the fox, which raced frantically into the nearby hills and disappeared.

While Whiteman was filming (or, more precisely, not filming) *King of Jazz* in Hollywood, he was also doing a weekly radio show for Old Gold cigarettes. Charles King, then starring in *Broadway Melody*, was a guest on one show. As he stepped up to the microphone to sing, Joe drew an old shotgun out of his violin case and aimed it at him. The musicians roared, of course. Whiteman was furious, and lost control of the band. The laughter went out "live" on the radio network, coast-to-coast as they used to say.

"Undoubtedly," Bing Crosby, a bandmate of Joe's at the time, wrote later, "Venuti helped age Whiteman."

At first I doubted the following story, which Joe told me, but I've concluded since then that it may well have happened—when *King of Jazz* was playing at the Roxy in New York. It opened May 2, 1930. Whiteman's band was combined with the Roxy Symphony to form an orchestra of 130 musicians. As always, *Rhapsody in Blue* was to be featured, with Gershwin playing the piano part. Concertmaster Kurt Dieterle was to lead the orchestra as it came up out of the pit, and then Whiteman would appear. What Joe said he did may have been at the opening night dress rehearsal. That was the impression he gave me. In any case, by now you should know that Joe had a conspicuous intolerance for anything that smacked of bombast.

Joe said, "We had no fanfare or tympani roll to open the curtain. There was a big tuba note.

"George Gershwin was a good friend of mine, and I thought I ought to come up with something special for the occasion.

"So I put five pounds of flour in the tuba.

"We had blue full-dress suits, and all of a sudden as the curtain went up, the tuba player blew that note and they became white full-dress suits. We looked like snowmen. Paul came out and said, 'Pardon me, where are we?' We had to close the scrim, and get ourselves dusted off, and then we played."

In 1944, Venuti settled in California to work as a studio musician at MGM. He led a West Coast band in the late 1940s. But in time he began to be forgotten. He seemed to have dropped off the planet and a good many people assumed he was dead. The stories about him began to take on the tone of legend.

The reason for this disappearance was liquor. He told me that at that period he drank two quarts a day, which very nearly destroyed his liver. It also, he said, destroyed a happy marriage.

And then he quit drinking. That must have been around 1960. He began turning up in nightclubs. Dick Gibson presented him at his Colorado jazz party in Vail in 1968. Gibson has written that Zoot Sims stood at the apron of the bandstand and listened to Venuti transfixed. Gibson said Zoot told him later, "I never saw him before. I've heard stories about him all my life. Wild stories. I wasn't sure he was real, you know, maybe he was invented, like that Paul Bunyan guy with the ox. Man, he's real though. Gee, he can really swing."

I saw Venuti in person for the first time in my life in Toronto, sometime in the early 1970s. I was as flabbergasted as Zoot. (Joe and Zoot were later to do some excellent recorded work together.)

It was later that year—in September—that I talked to Joe at Gibson's jazz party, held in the Broadmoor hotel in Colorado Springs. Joe played with various groups during that party. In one of them, the pianist was Roger Kellaway. Roger was then thirty-five, Venuti was seventy-six, if Chilton and Feather are right, seventy-eight if Joe's uncle was right. Roger said afterwards, "That old man will run you ragged. You constantly feel as if you're being goosed."

Joe and I talked on a terrace by a lakeside behind the hotel. It was a soft sunny afternoon, just prior to fall. Beyond the lake the Rockies rose steep against the sky. He told me that he had relatives—including twenty-three grandchildren—scattered from Seattle, where he was living with his second wife, to Milan, which he visited at least once a year to hang out with cousins. Other Italians told me Joe had no American accent in Italian; he had no Italian accent in English. Photos taken in the early days of his career show him as a handsome young man. But by that September afternoon, he had grown thick-waisted. He was bald and he wore dark-rimmed glasses.

"Looking at his waddling walk and potbellied figure," Leonard Feather wrote in the Los Angeles *Times* shortly thereafter, "you would never guess that this man is one of the few certified geniuses of jazz . . . along with Armstrong, Tatum, and Bix."

Seeing us sitting there talking at a table on that terrace, other musicians began to pull up chairs and enter the conversation. They talked to him about Gershwin, about Ravel, whom he said he'd met during the composer's period in America. He talked to them of Ravel's orchestration with broad and detailed knowledge. He talked to them about Milhaud.

Though they weren't, you had the feeling that they were sitting at his feet.

"The amazing thing about you, Joe," I said, "is that above and beyond the music, and the jokes, and all the rest of it, you are one of those rare people who has reached an age, and can look back and know that you've lived."

"Well," he said, "you reach a peak, and you go on, and you reach another peak, and that's the way I like to do it in music."

Someone came to tell him a car had arrived for him. He was leaving for a gig somewhere, and then a European tour.

And I never saw him again.

Cincinnatus Afternoon:
Spiegle Willcox

He wore a woodsman's shirt. His hair was full, thick, and silver-white. He stood in front of a huge picture window, which framed an idyllic tableau: a perfect round lake, frozen over now, and surrounded by forest: the gray-brown of deciduous trunks and branches relieved by tall green cones of the conifers. A heavy wet snow fell steadily into this picture.

"Do you want to hear me play?" he said.

"Sure."

He burred his lips a few times, then put the trombone to his mouth and ran up some arpeggios, and then scales, topping it all off with a strong accurate note. "That was a high D," he said with a grin, and put the horn aside.

It was a marvelous room in a marvelous house, with a big stove throwing the penetrating kind of dry heat that only wood seems to produce. My mother used to say nothing matched a wood stove for baking pies. The room was a strange combination of lazy living-room and kitchen, and the big beams in the ceiling were hand-hewn, the marks of the adze on them. They'd come from some old barn somewhere; the house itself was not all that old.

He sat down by the table.

"High D, was it?" I said.

33

"Yeah," he said. "You'll notice I didn't hold it very long!"

"Spiegle," I said, "you're lucky you've still got all your teeth."

"Well," he said, baring them and tapping them with a forefinger, "I just spent seven thousand bucks on them."

It's more than luck, of course. Longevity runs in his family. These are hardy people from old New England stock, and they have been in these hills for generations. Nonetheless, it is quite remarkable that at eighty-seven Spiegle Willcox can not only play his trombone but is again very active in music. For years a great many people assumed that he was dead, as they had assumed it of Joe Venuti, his buddy of more than six decades.

Spiegle Willcox was born May 2, 1903, not far from where he lives now. And where he lives now is a few miles outside Cincinnatus, New York. They pronounce it Sinsin-ay-tus in these parts, and they'll correct you if you try to pronounce it like Cincinnati. It is a small town east south-east of Cortland, New York, the seat of Cortland County, and home of an excellent branch of the State University of New York, on Interstate 81, between Binghamton and Syracuse. The house, which he built, is huge. It lies at the end of a winding single-lane road through the woods, which is marked by signs, one of which says Elephant Crossing. Another says Graystone Ballroom. That was the dancehall in Detroit where he played in the Jean Goldkette band, seated between Bix and Tram.

"My dad lived to be ninety-two, my mother was eighty-four," Spiegle said.

The country around here is unbelievably beautiful, comprising rolling wooded hills and long ridges, flat alluvial valleys, and small pretty lakes. On the backroads, it is like a land time forgot, its wise old barns and silos at peace in the earth. Only the cars tell you that we're nearing the end of a century that Spiegle almost began. His name is really Newell Willcox; Newell was his mother's maiden name. A member of the Newell family was a principal in launching the famous Cardiff Giant Hoax in the mid-nineteenth century twenty-five or so miles from here, just south of Syracuse.

This house is huge. It has all sorts of bedrooms, and, upstairs, an enormous living room with another big window overlooking the lake. It contains a grand piano and posters from his Goldkette days. His wife died a few years ago.

This isn't the way the mythology holds that jazz musicians end up, in a paid-for rustic mansion in seclusion by a lake, still in demand and still playing music.

"You didn't end up dead at thirty-five of dope," I said, laughing at the incongruity. He is such a vital man, his voice so strong that it almost shouts. He's also a funny man, with a sly sense of humor.

"I don't remember any dope," he said. "Booze was the thing. Oh they used to smoke, what did they call them, reefers. There was very little of that. It was booze."

What caused him to come back to the business?

"Joe Venuti's the guy who pulled me out from under the rug," Spiegle said. "In 1975, in Carnegie Hall, George Wein promoted it. What we did was we re-created the Goldkette stuff. They did two concerts. The first one was with Paul Mertz, who played sometimes with Goldkette. He played piano that night. He's alive. Bill Challis is alive. He lives about a hundred miles from here. He was up here a few weeks ago. The bass player on the first gig was Milt Hinton. Bobby Rosengarten on drums, Bucky Pizzarelli on guitar. Johnny Mince, Kenny Davern, Bob Wilber, Pee Wee Irwin, Bernie Privin, and somebody else on cornet. And there was Bill Rank and myself again on trombones.

"It wasn't recorded. Three months later we opened the Newport Jazz Festival with the Goldkette stuff. We had a little different personnel. Marian McPartland was on piano. We had Dave Hudson from Detroit. He's the guy who kind of copied the Goldkette stuff. Bill Challis is not a pusher. He's very quiet, just a gentleman. He's not the New York City type. Panama Francis played drums.

"At the end of that first concert, Joe Venuti said, 'Hey, Spiegle, why don't you get your trombone to where I'm playing these nightclubs and things, we can have a lot of laughs, a lot of fun, it won't cost you anything.' And I was seventy-two."

"Well," I said, "that's not as old as it once was. A lot of guys are playing well at that age. Look at Dizzy."

"I know, but they played all their lives, they were on the scene. I lived up in Cortland. Mind you, I didn't put the horn away.

"When I first came home from Goldkette, that was in 1927. I broke away and I went home to the family business, the coal business. I had my firstborn, Newell Jr."

"Where did the nick-name come from?"

"I don't know. I got the name Spiegle up in Manlius Military School, up near Syracuse. That was a mini-West Point. That was about 1918. I never graduated. I said, 'This isn't for me. I want to play.' My mother was broken-hearted.

"I'd give so much to know how I got Spiegle. Let me tell you something, people forget Willcox, they forget Newell. Lots of times they just say, 'Spiegle's playing.' Dizzy is another name like that. There's a pure example. There are not too many of those, not too many people called Dizzy. Or Spiegle."

"How did you get to play trombone in a little town like Cortland?"

"My dad. He played valve trombone. He was born in a little town called Smyrna, that's about four miles from Sherbourne, 'way up on the top of a hill. He and his brother, and his father, my grandfather. He must have died early, I never did see him. My dad and his brother; he played clarinet.

"The only times they'd play were Sunday afternoons in a parlor or sitting room. They'd have a few people come in, and we'd play orchestrations or play out of a hymn book. And we'd pull taffy. You ever heard o' that? That's the kind o' sport we did."

I said, "I was browsing in the Cortland library last night, and I found out they had quite a music school in Cortland before the turn out of the century."

"Yeah, they had the Cortland Conservatory. Prof Bentley was the head of it."

"I read that they had a chorale amounting to three hundred voices. In a little town like that. They even had an opera house."

"Oh, the Cortland Opera House! Sure! The Dillon Brothers ran it."

"So your father started you on trombone."

"That was a valve. When I went to Manlius, I played baritone, see. And of course there's the three valves. All you've got to do is figure out which ones to press at the right time. If your ear is bad, then you don't know and you'd better quit. We were all kids. And what a brass band! It was a super military school. Wealthy people sent their kids up there to keep them out of their hair. And the band, we were the inspiration with those drills and marches and parades.

"One of the trombone players showed me the slide positions, and I'm still trying to figure the damn things out. Seven positions. And I hear some guys play and I think they've got a hundred. Jesus, how some guys can play.

"Jack Teagarden was something else. He was super. Anybody who didn't like him . . . So many trombone players, even today, do little things that he did, or try to. There were some awful good players."

"Bill Crow, the bassist, told me that some of the older players had told him that rhythm sections didn't sound the same on records as they did in person because drummers had to hold back in order not to jump the cutter out of the track."

"I don't remember that we *had* drums on those 78s with Gold-kette. I think all Chauncey Morehouse did was hold a cymbal and come in on the end. At the Graystone, he had a great mass of props. He was a great guy to have chimes, tympanis. He was a great showman. He was from Chambersburg, Pennsylvania."

"How did you jump from Cortland to Detroit?" Like most people of our time, I understimate how much people traveled in those days. Because we live with the automobile, we forget how efficiently the country was served by the railways.

"That's a story," Spiegle said. "In 1922–23, I played in New York. It started out as a Cornell band, a jazz band. Most of them went to Cornell University. Bob Causer's Cornellians. He was the only son of the man and wife who owned the Ithaca hotel, which was the heart of Cornell in downtown Ithaca. All the college functions! It was a gold mine.

"Bob Causer was a half-assed drummer, but he was a good promoter. He got into the Whiteman office, and we worked through them. We were booked as Paul Whiteman's Collegians.

"That was right at the time, 1923, when Paul Whiteman was playing at the Palais Royale in New York. He only had one trombone, Sammy Lewis played trombone. Henry Busse played trumpet. I don't remember who played the other trumpet. Ross Gorman was in the saxophone section. Busse would come over to the Rendezvous, where I played with the Collegians. Our main attraction there was Gilda Grey, a shimmy queen out of the *Ziegfeld Follies*. Busse's girlfriend was in the little floor-show with Gilda.

"Busse would rehearse us a little bit. He was hot-lips Busse. Beiderbecke hadn't got in there in the Whiteman band yet to knock him down.

"What happened was that our piano player stole Busse's girl. I remember she was a cute little thing. After the *Ziegfeld Follies*, Gilda would bring about five or six girls in grass skirts, and that was the floor show. I remember Will Rogers coming in. William S. Hart, who was in silent movies, a two-gun man, he used to come sit beside me.

"That band made in the Victor recording studio, we made three records under the name The Collegians. One of the tunes was *Papa, Better Watch Your Step*, a real corny tune typical of the time. Another tune was *That Redhead Gal*. A good tune, too. Another tune that I still play once in a while was *I Cried for You*. I had a whole chorus on the damn thing.

"In 1924, I went with the Collegians down to the Chase hotel in New York for six months. I dropped out after six months. I came home in January or so to Cortland. I stayed around Cortland, because in that summer of 1925, I took a job over at Auburn, where Auburn Prison is. There is a lake there called Owasco Lake. And there was a big dance pavilion—I'm sure it's still there.

"We had jitney dancing, with turnstiles. Dime a dance. Put in your dime. Just like in the New York subway. Same damn thing. Everybody comes in and we'd play ten or twelve minutes, stop, everybody gets off the floor. Put their dime in, start right up again.

"Well, it came Labor Day of 1925, and Fuzzy Farrar, the first trumpet player in the Goldkette band, from Freeland, Pennsylvania, came by. The Dorsey brothers and Itzy Riskin, they were all from the Scranton area. Fuzzy Farrar happened to be in Auburn. He was on a vacation from Detroit. He came up to Auburn Park to be with his buddies from around Freeland, Pennsylvania, in their National Guard band. They parked on the park, and they'd play concerts. He came over to the pavilion one day. We were on a break. We were outside the pavilion, right close to the band door, and we got talking.

"I said, 'Where you from?'

"He said, 'Detroit. I play in a band out there—Jean Goldkette.' I'd heard enough about Goldkette. I figured he must be pretty good.

"I said, 'Why don't you come over and sit in with us tonight?' So he did just that. You could tell. Right away.

"We hadn't played very long when he said to me, 'Hey, how would you like to join the Goldkette band?' He said, 'Tommy Dorsey's in the band and he's leaving.' Only musicians knew Tommy Dorsey then. Bill Rank was the other trombone player in the band.

"I said, 'I have a commitment. I've got to go down to New York for two weeks at least and play with the California Ramblers.' I went down there. All of a sudden I began to realize how I didn't like New York City. Too busy, even at that time. And I'm just too corny. I'm a home-town guy. In those two weeks I had three wires from the Goldkette band.

"I heard later that he had the authority to fill Tommy's chair. So, I said, 'I'm going.' I left the California Ramblers, and that's how I got with the Goldkette band.

"I went out to the Graystone ballroom and joined the band in October, 1925.

"Venuti had been in the band but he'd left by then. Goldkette had recorded a tune that caught my attention back in Cortland, called *It's the Blues*. And Joe was playing that four-string stuff.

"Every time we recorded in New York, Joe and Eddie Lang would be in the studio to visit.

"When I joined the band, the only guy I knew just a little was Fuzzy Farrar. And who was leading the band by stick? Russ Morgan. Bill Rank was my side-kick. I don't remember who was on piano. Maybe Paul Mertz, maybe Itzy Riskin. In the trumpets were Ray Lodwig and Fuzzy Farrar. Steve Brown on bass, Chauncey on drums, Howdy Quicksell on banjo. The immediate sax section was Don Murray, and Fud Livingston, and Doc Ryker. And in two weeks, Fud Livingston left the band and in came Jimmy Dorsey. Jimmy stayed six months.

"In December they gave me one day to come back to marry my wife, Helen, in Binghamton. Early in January, I think, with Jimmy Dorsey still in the band, we made some records. On *Lonesome and Sorry* I had a whole chorus.

"Somewhere around in March of 1926 Jimmy left, and in came Frank Trumbauer with—who?—Bix.

"Frank played different. But Beiderbecke! Oh we liked him. He played so good. I sat over on the end in the second row. Bill Rank next to me, Beiderbecke next, Ray Lodwig, Fuzzy. I just can't describe him. He had a marvelous tone, attack, ideas. He was a kind guy. The damn booze."

"He remains a bit of a mystery, kind of evasive."

"Kind of, yes. Kind of quiet. He was born March 10, 1903, and I was May 2. He was just a little bit older than I. He went to military school too. And his father was in the coal business, like mine.

"The summer of 1926, the Goldkette band left the Graystone and split. Once in a while during the time I was with Goldkette, I'd go down to a place not too far away called the Silver Slipper. There was a band called Henry Theiss. He must have had a trombone player. I know he had a trumpet and cornet and maybe three saxes. I played with him enough that he asked me to join him down at Castle Farms in Cincinnati. I worked seven days and I got a hundred and twenty-five bucks, and I worked my ass off. I was getting a hundred with Goldkette. Newell, my son, was born September 12, 1926. We came back from Cincinnati to have the baby in Binghamton. I hung around three weeks or so. I got maybe two wires about joining the Goldkette band again. I said I'd come back for a hundred and quarter.

"Charlie Horvath, the band manager, said Okay. I joined the band on a famous two-week tour from Detroit up to the Boston area. Bix was still in the band. I stayed through till about June 1, and I said, 'I'm going to quit. I'm going home and join my daddy in the coal business.' By September they were running out of steam, no bookings. They were appearing down at Atlantic City. Helen and I went down just to see them. They were kind of close to us. We drove down. That's when the band split up, though.

"I think Jimmy Dorsey must have told Whiteman. Whiteman went down. He didn't want to steal Goldkette men, but if the band was splitting up, he'd take some of them.

"Immediately after they broke up, Adrian Rollini had a band for six, eight weeks at the most in a place called the New York. The piano player was Frank Signorelli. Drums, Chauncey. Bill Rank. Beiderbecke.

"For a while I was kind of a big shot. They'd invite me as a guest at Cornell, or Syracuse. About two years after I got home, I said, 'I'm gonna start a little Friday-Saturday night band of my own. For years and years I played in my own band.

"As I got older, rock-and-roll came in. I got to be fifty-five, sixty. It was that re-creation of the Goldkette band that got me back into it. Joe got me back in the music game, big.

"Joe finally broke away from booze. And I lived with him there on and off for three years, as he went around to these clubs. I didn't make 'em all, but I made a lot of 'em. It was cute the way he'd use me. I never got any money. That was something else. He was a loner. To tolerate me, I must have been doing something right.

"Spiegle the Beagle, he used to call me. He'd say, 'Here's Spiegle the Beagle, from ten miles from nowhere.' I played his last job with him, in Rochester."

In all those years when he was forgotten, Spiegle ran the family coal business and played weekends with his group for local organizations and dances. He still does that. The Finger Lakes region is close by, and for many of those years he played engagements in or near them. He raised a family, two sons and a daughter. He never really missed the music business. Friends from the bands knew perfectly well where he was, and they'd drop by on their way from Binghamton to Syracuse, or Syracuse to Binghamton. His office at the coal company was decorated with the same posters he now has in his living room.

I was surprised by Spiegle's ebullience. I have resented the incursions of time all my life, and have never understood how people face its inexorable arithmetic. Often, you'll find, such people find their consolation in religious.

"Are you religious, Spiegle?" I asked.

"Nope," he said cheerfully.

So much for that thought.

It came time to go. Spiegle was getting ready to go out on a jazz cruise aboard the S.S. Norway, and he had to pack. I had not brought my car to the house: there was ice on his road. He'd met me there with his four-wheel drive vehicle. Now he drove me back to my car.

We shook hands. He waited solicitously until my car was back on the wet pavement, then headed back to his house in the woods.

Weekend at Dante Park: Benny Carter

A small table stands by the window, which faces north. Lying on a sheet of score paper is a Scripto pencil, and near it a slim little blue carton of IBM Electrographic leads. Some composer or arranger in Los Angeles long ago discovered the smooth fluid quality of those leads, designed to be used on the early computer cards. They're magnetic. It was also discovered that these leads would fit not only IBM mechanical pencils but Scriptos as well. Scriptos are cheaper than IBMs and easier to find. This unknown explorer further found that Scriptos with IBM leads are near-perfect implements for writing music. Some of his friends tried out his pencils, and became instantly addicted to them, and the use of them spread like a benign epidemic on the coast. Eventually it seemed every composer and arranger in Southern California used them, while in New York they were still getting along with Black-wings and electric pencil sharpeners. The only place I ever found those IBM leads is Joe Valle's music shop in the San Fernando Valley, where composers take their work for photocopying. When I was living in New York, I had a friend send me a box of them because I couldn't get them in Manhattan.

The evidence then is in that still life by the window: a golden alto saxophone lying with its neck on the arm of a sofa, some score paper, a Scripto, and a box of IBM leads. You can deduce that the occupant of this room is a working saxophonist, since he has the horn out to practice, and an arranger and probably composer, and he lives in California. He is no neophyte, either: IBM quit making those leads a few years ago as computer technology advanced beyond the need for them. He has pulled the table to the window because it gives him a north light, which will not cast a shadow of his hand and pencil on the paper. He has efficiently rearranged the room to suit his needs, which suggests that he is habituated to writing on the road. He is in the middle of writing an arrangement, and somewhere a copyist is standing by awaiting it. But what is he writing? What is the assignment?

Look out the window. It faces north over that X-shape intersection of Columbus Avenue and Broadway, which at the south end forms a small equilateral triangle on which stand eight or nine large bare plane trees and a statue. It bears the grand name Dante Park, since the statue is of Dante. He stands tall, wearing a cap around which is a laurel wreath, and in his right hand, held high and close to his shoulder, is a copy of his latest best-seller, on the cover of which is engraved *Divine Comedy*. He looks as if he's displaying it on a television show. Over to the left, that is to say to the west, in the gathering evening, is Lincoln Center, its travertine surfaces and broad steps off-white in the lights.

So the arrangement that is being written in this hotel sitting room probably has something to do with a concert at Avery Fisher Hall, whose floors are visible through its tall windows. And you might have noticed on your way here the name of Ella Fitzgerald on one of those small billboards in front of the place. There is to be a concert for the American Heart Foundation in tribute to her, and Mayor Dinkins has declared the date of it, February 12, 1990, Ella Fitzgerald Day in New York.

Think of a composer from the west coast who travels constantly, plays alto saxophone, and is in some way associated with Ella Fitzgerald.

Bennett L. Carter of Beverly Hills. Elementary, my dear Watson.

"Is that mine?" Benny Carter said of the music we were hearing. "I probably haven't heard it since it was made." He referred to the Fletcher Henderson recording of *Wang Wang Blues*, waxed, as they used to say, May 6, 1929. The music was coming from one of the Robert Parker restorations, this one devoted to the late years of the Henderson band. I could reply only that Parker's annotation said it was Benny's arrangement. Benny didn't recognize it. He listened to it through, but it remained unknown to him. Next I played him, from the same CD album, the Henderson band's performance of his chart on *Happy as the Day Is Long*, a Harold Arlen tune the band recorded in September 1934.

"But *that* one I remember," he said when he heard the opening phrase. The tune is taken at a fast tempo. The guitar-player, Lawrence Lucie, is in four, but the bassist, Elmer James, remains in two. The trombone solo came up. "Claude Jones," Benny said instantly, with a smile.

Then came the Ben Webster tenor solo. "Now where does he come from?" Benny said. "What's the source of that?" It was a terse allusion to the tendency in writings about jazz to make it all seem little more than a Mendelian exercise in bean genetics: so-and-so begat so-and-so who begat so-and-so. It is a vision of jazz that precludes individuality, the very thing (or one of the things) the music is about. Influences there are, to be sure. "Jazz is a synthesis," Benny said, although he remarked at one point that he has trouble with the very term *jazz* because of the impossibility of defining it.

And he was right, of course. Ben Webster seemed to burst into the music fully original, with his big sound and slurs and push and bluff determination. The conventional theory is that he came out of Coleman Hawkins, but it's hard to see it. Coleman Hawkins was a man of considerable and complex intellect, very conscious of what he was doing. Ben Webster was another thing entirely. Great-hearted Ben with the big shoulders and big chest and sharp face and fierce concentrated mien, always going bluntly to the subject, musically and otherwise. God help you if you caught him when he was drunk and in a bad mood. And the rest of the time he was wonderful. But he was far more direct than Hawkins, and I don't think their sounds were really similar.

I was looking at the arranging credits on the Fletcher Henderson album. Some of the arrangements were by Bill Challis, who had gone from the Jean Goldkette band to that of Paul Whiteman and is considered one of the pioneering arrangers. Some others were by Russ Morgan, who also had written for Goldkette. I had, years ago, known Morgan only through the polite and somewhat corny society band he led. I had had no idea of his credits in jazz. "He was a good trombone player, too," Benny said. I noted that while I had been aware almost from my earliest interest in jazz of the black arrangers who wrote for white bands, as in the cases of Henderson with Goodman and Sy Oliver with Tommy Dorsey, I had not realized that white arrangers had written for black bands, including Challis and Morgan for Henderson. "Oh yes," Benny said. "Bill Challis was one of my heroes."

Then came a solo by Henry (Red) Allen, fierce and hot, the man's control of the horn absolute and authoritative. I ventured to suggest that he was one of the under-appreciated players in jazz history, and Benny nodded agreement. "I'll tell you another one who's under-appreciated," he said. "Paul Desmond. And do you know a trombone player named Willie Dennis?"

"I knew him very well."

"Is he dead?" Benny said.

"Back in the '60s. He was killed in a car crash in Central Park. I was thinking about Willie an hour or two ago, because I helped arrange his funeral with Father O'Connor and my room faces onto Columbus Avenue and I can see just to the south the church where we held the service. The Church of St. Paul. I remember that Joe Williams sang." Joe was scheduled on the concert for which Benny was writing the arrangement lying there on the table, this tribute to Ella Fitzgerald with an orchestra to be led by Benny.

"I heard a Phil Woods record and looked to see who the trombone player was," Benny said. "Willie Dennis. How did he get by me?"

"I can never pass that church without thinking of Willie and Joe

Williams and Morgana King. Willie was Morgana's husband. Both Italian, of course."

"He was some trombone player," Benny said.

I was a little over a year old when Fletcher Henderson made that record of Benny's chart on *Wang Wang Blues*, if indeed the annotation was correct. Since Benny has twenty years on me, that means he was twenty-one when he wrote that chart he doesn't remember. And when he wrote that 1934 arrangement, he still was only twenty-six. I don't approve of hero-worship, but I must confess that I idolized Benny Carter when I was a kid, he was one of my early heroes, and I still feel a trace of a sense of honor, which I hide from him, to be in his presence. I first heard him not on alto saxophone but on trumpet.

"Somebody told me you're playing trumpet again."

"A little. I don't have time to practice. If I could give equal time to both instruments . . . " He made a vague gesture of resignation at the impossibility. And he didn't even mention the time he spends over a hot Scripto.

Earlier that day, a Jamaican housekeeper who was taking care of both Benny's room and mine asked me who he was: with the clamp of gray hair that surrounds his bald head and his impeccable dress, he is obviously someone of great distinction. I told her his name, but she had never heard it, and I told her his was the longest continuous active career in the history of jazz, running all the way from the 1920s to the present, more than sixty years. She asked how old he was, and I told her: eighty-two.

"My goodness, darling!" she said in astonishment. "He looks in his fifties." And he does. And he moves as if he were no more than that. A couple of years ago he had a dizzy spell and went to a doctor, something he has never had much reason to do. The doctor asked his age. Benny told him. The doctor just shook his head, said there was nothing wrong with him, and sent him home.

But it is not just longevity that distinguishes Benny Carter. Oscar Peterson calls him "the true gentleman of jazz." His is an astonishing career. "My influences," Phil Woods once said pointedly, in comment on the comparisons of his playing to Bird's, "were Benny Carter, Johnny Hodges, and Charlie Parker, in that order." Benny is one of the major soloists on his instrument, spinning out airy, elegant, understated contours of sound. It is logical that he would like Desmond. We talked about Desmond for a while. I told him I'd made a discovery recently—what I suspect is the true headwater of Desmond's inspiration. Not Lester Young's saxophone playing, but his clarinet: Desmond's alto sounds a lot like Prez's clarinet. Prez in turn had said that his early idol was Frank Trumbauer.

How important was Trumbauer's influence?

"That's how *I* started," Benny said. "With Frank Trumbauer. Do you know a saxophone player I liked? Wayne King. Not jazz of course. But the sound and the way he played melody. He played beautifully." That one, I must admit, took me by total surprise. I thought about it. Wayne King played very well; not my kind of music, but . . .

Benny Carter's career has been nothing less than protean. He wasn't the first black film composer: by all evidence, Will Vodery was. Vodery was an arranger and orchestrator of Broadway musicals in the 1910s, and '20s, who then went to Hollywood and broke in. But Benny was almost certainly the first jazz musician to break in as a film composer. At that, there was discrimination. In his early film days, the discrimination ran so deep that he would be assigned to write arrangements for black singers making guest appearances in films. But in time he—along with another jazz musician, Shorty Rogers—orchestrated for Dmitri Tiomkin. He wrote a good deal of music for television series, including *M Squad*. Benny opened the way for J.J. Johnson, Oliver Nelson, Benny Golson, and others. For a long time, Benny Carter was absent from the jazz scene. And then he turned up again on the festival and concert circuit and recording a great deal for Pablo and other labels. He was playing as well as or better than ever.

After we'd listened to some more of the Fletcher Henderson album, we went out into the early night, Benny wearing an exquisite blue-gray suede overcoat. We ate at The Ginger Man. Benny ordered an excellent wine. I once asked him how he survives on the road. "Always go first class," he said. He is firm about it: he will not tolerate shabby lodgings.

Benny had been in the audience of the Apollo theater on that semi-legendary occasion when Ella Fitzgerald appeared on one of the theater's amateur contests as a dancer. It is part of the legend of jazz—but it's true—that she was immobilized by stage fright. The stage manager told her she had better do something, so she sang instead: *The Object of My Affection.* She was fifteen at the time; some accounts say thirteen. Benny went straight to Fletcher Henderson about her. Henderson had her audition, but wasn't interested. Neither, apparently, was John Hammond, to whom Benny also recommended her. Nor even Chick Webb. So she went on singing in amateur contests, winning one after another, until finally Webb tried her out at on a college date at Yale, and then hired her, and then adopted her as his daughter.

Benny mentioned in passing that he was a New Yorker. I'd never thought of him that way. He'd been born in the Bronx and grew up not three blocks from where we were sitting.

We somehow got onto the writing of William Styron. I said I enormously admired his book *Nat Turner.*

Benny frowned thoughtfully for a second. "*The Confessions of Nat Turner.* That's the name of it," he said.

I told him the reasons I liked it. "It's a chilling book," I said.

"I must re-read it," he said. "How is Styron? He used to be a neighbor of my wife's."

"As far as I know, fine," I said. "I saw him on a television show, discussing how depression had immobilized him. But he's over it."

Benny paused, and then said something startling, significant, indicative of his whole life. "I do not know the meaning of depression," he said.

How I envied him that.

We parted early that evening. Benny planned to write most of the night.

And he did, though you'd never have known it from the manner of the man as the orchestra gathered in a big room on the mezzanine of the hotel the next morning at eleven. It was a formidable orchestra, with a trumpet section that included Jon Faddis, Clark Terry, Red Rodney, and, substituting for Sweets Edison, who couldn't make it, one John Birks Gillespie. The saxophones were Phil Woods, David Sanborn, Stan Getz, Jimmy Heath, and Nick Brignola. The trombones were Al Grey, Urbie Green, Slide Hampton, and Jack Jeffers. The bass player was Ray Brown, the pianist Hank Jones. The drummer, Louis Bellson, hadn't arrived yet and so for a time Bobby Durham substituted.

Benny sat on a stool, conducting, relaxed and concentrated.

That night he sat up until six a.m., writing arrangements. When he appeared for rehearsal the next day, he was as relaxed as ever. The concert was that night. I spent most of it backstage, writing fragments of script for the performers, among them Lena Horne, who was mistress of ceremonies, Itzhak Perlman, and the mayor of New York who arrived with a coterie of tough-looking men and read the tribute to Ella I'd prepared for him. I'd come into New York for this. The show was being produced by Edith Kiggen, who'd asked me to help. It didn't take much writing: just bits of continuity here and there. I remembered that Oscar Peterson had written a poem to Ella. He sent it by fax from Toronto, and Lena Horne read it.

The unexpected guest arrived: Oscar himself. Itzhak Perlman had said it was the dream of his life to play with Oscar, and Oscar was delighted by the idea. I went with the two of them up to the so-called Green Room—why do they always call it the Green Room? it's never green—and they chose a couple of tunes, *Summertime* leading into *Stormy Weather*. The biggest problem was settling on keys, not because either of them had preferences but because both were utterly indifferent. They talked about Art Tatum. Perlman probably startled Oscar—he certainly startled me—by playing a couple of Tatum runs on his fiddle, a Guarnerius.

Sitting somewhat behind him during that rehearsal, I noticed Perlman's unorthodox left-hand position. One of the first rules of violin technique is that you do not let the neck of the instrument slip down into the crook between the thumb and index finger. You're supposed to hold it up out of the crook, usually with the neck supported between the knuckle of the thumb and the top joint of the index finger, where it meets the palm. This is supposed to give you flexibility. The same rule applies to classical guitar. If you let it slip down into the crook, the conventional wisdom holds, you lose flexibility and tone. You can't get over the instrument that way. Try telling that to Perlman, because that's exactly what he does. He uses the left-hand position of a country-and-western fiddler.

I commented on this to him, noting that Horowitz too did something forbidden: he curled the pinky of his right hand. It would strike out to hit a note at the top of a phrase or a chord, like a snake, and then retreat, curled tight into the palm. That's an absolute non-no.

Perlman said, "Rules in teaching are designed to cover the greatest number of people. You have to adapt them to your own needs."

I mentioned that when Eddie Harris long ago asked Lester Young a question about embouchure, Prez said, "I can only tell you about my mouthpiece in my mouth. I can't tell you about your mouthpiece in your mouth."

"Exactly," Perlman said.

The band played. Dizzy Gillespie performed, brilliantly, with his old sidekick James Moody. Manhattan Transfer sang. Joe Williams sang a song for Ella. Benny Carter directed the orchestra in an instrumental he'd written called *First Lady*. I suppose that's what he'd stayed up so late writing. I went over the lines she was to read with Lena Horne. I could not believe the condition of her skin. She remained an incredible beauty in her seventies, looking twenty-five years or more younger than she was. She was gentle and gracious and self-effacing.

Oscar Peterson walked onstage. He had not been billed; the audience levitated. Itzhak joined him, and they did their part, with Bobby Durham, Ray Brown, and Herb Ellis joining them in the second tune.

Ella sat through all this in a front-row seat. She wasn't supposed to perform at all, but she did: at the very end she got up and sang *Honeysuckle Rose*, and brought the house down, and then it was over.

Always I was conscious of Benny Carter, onstage without interruption, cuing the orchestra, holding it all together. The master. The absolute master. I listened to his charts, new and modern, of our time, and thought back to the *Wang Wang Blues* chart for Henderson.

They don't make movies about this kind of triumph over life. They don't make movies about happy musicians. The myth grows that all jazz musicians die young, like Bix and Bird, and in misery, and it overlooks Benny Carter, and for that matter Dizzy Gillespie. It overlooks Spiegle Willcox.

Benny out there with his alto case under his arm, making the festivals and concert circuit, Spiegle with his trombone, enjoying life.

What do these two men have?

Spiegle retired into the coal business, but never stopped playing. Benny faded into the anonymity of movie-studio orchestrating. Then both re-emerged.

Are you religious, Spiegle? Nope.

And Benny Carter doesn't know the meaning of depression.

Benny checked out of the hotel next morning. He said—no kidding!—he was tired. He was on his way to a gig.

One of the Jones Boys

The question of nature versus nurture is particularly vexed in music. There is a bit of suggestive evidence that abilities in athletics and music may be inherited. But if parents love music and the children take after them, how can you determine whether genetics or exposure played the more significant role?

Capable siblings, from the Dodds brothers to the Heath and Marsalis families, are by no means unusual in jazz history; and for that matter, recent years have seen the emergence of the gifted sons of accomplished fathers. Even when the parents were not professional, you will hear time after time some variant on this:

"Both my mother and father were musical. This is not to say that they played professionally in any sense. They didn't. My father played guitar a little and my mother a little piano. That was about the extent of it. At least they had a beginning influence. They influenced us to think in terms of music, whereas if they had not been musical, who knows where our energies would have gone? I think they impressed us, inspired us, to go as far as we could in music."

The speaker is Hank Jones, and the "us" in question comprises three of the finest musicians in jazz, in chronological order Henry, Thaddeus, and Elvin.

I had known Elvin well during his period with John Coltrane. And I knew Thad moderately well, particularly toward the end of his life when his writing had attained such levels of brilliance. He died in 1986 of a cancer about which he told almost no one. I had never really known Hank.

He lived quietly, and was never seen leaning on the bar of one of the New York musicians' taverns. And now he lives nearly two hundred miles out of New York City, on a hilly stretch of farmland. I ran into him backstage at the Ella Fitzgerald concert and he piqued my curiosity, this pianist of exquisite taste, with his open, gracious and unsuspicious manner. He struck me as a man at peace with himself.

And so I sought him out. I called to tell him I would be driving from Buffalo to New York City, and if it were convenient for him, I would like to drop by for an hour or so on the way.

On March 28, 1990, I got off the New York State Thruway at Herkimer and headed south, then drove five or six miles out the road that runs west from Cooperstown, best-known as the home of the Baseball Hall of Fame. Cooperstown is about sixty miles almost due west of Albany. The country there is a matter of creeks and small lakes and round eroded hills, some of it farmland and some of it woodlot, at that time all browns and grays under a lowering sky, though some of the branches were faintly colored by the first hesitant buds of spring.

As evening deepened, I turned into a dirt road off the highway, found the right mailbox, then ascended a long blacktop driveway to a white clapboard house into which was built a two-car garage. A second garage, also white, had doors for four cars. Between the two buildings, a basketball practice backboard on a thick metal pole leaned away from the driveway about thirty degrees from the vertical.

Hank greeted me at the front door and led me into a large paneled living room, where he introduced me to his wife, Teddy. Hank is dark. Teddy is very light, and in a rational society she would be called white as a matter of simple description. This is pertinent to something Hank said. After we had spoken briefly and I noted her accent, I said, "You're certainly a southerner."

"South Carolina," she said, adding that when she goes home to visit, her friends think she sounds like a northerner.

Hank urged me to join them at dinner. I said that first I had to reserve a motel room somewhere. Hank and Teddy said that had been taken care of: they had set up their guest room for me. I protested only feebly; almost immediately I felt as if I had known them a long time.

I asked what had happened to the basketball backboard in the driveway.

"No comment," Hank said with mock gravity, and Teddy giggled.

"No comment," he repeated.

"Don't tell me the wind did it," I said.

"No comment." As Teddy's laughter grew more helpless I realized I had stumbled onto a family tale.

Teddy said, "The funny thing is that when I hit it, it didn't even bother the car!"

"No comment."

"I backed the car into it," Teddy confessed, still laughing. "I must say, the ground was very wet."

"No comment," Hank said yet again, and at last burst into laughter himself.

"Who plays?"

"My daughter Cecelia," Hank said. "In high school, her coach thought her ability at basketball would get her an athletic scholarship to college."

Teddy said, "I played basketball until I was in my thirties."

"Where's your daughter now?"

"She finished four years of college, and now she's thinking about going to law school," Hank said.

Most jazz encyclopedias give his birthplace as Pontiac, Michigan. Hank was born August 31, 1918, in Vicksburg, Mississippi. His parents moved to Pontiac when he was a few months old. He was the third of ten children, eldest of the boys. The brothers and sisters after him were born in Pontiac, an automotive city. Thaddeus was born on March 28, 1923, Elvin on September 9, 1927. A brother, Paul, who lives in Detroit, plays piano, though not professionally.

"Elvin is one of twins," Hank said over dinner. "He had a twin brother who died as an infant of an infection. He was two or three months old. I had an older sister, Olive, who was a tremendous pianist, playing concerts at the age of twelve. She was skating on a lake and went through the soft ice and got caught in the current underneath the ice and drowned. She was, I think, the most talented of our family. It was something my mother never got over.

"As brothers, there was a certain familial closeness. We weren't that close on a playing level. Thad, Elvin and I did only two recording dates that I can recall. That's all. There was a six-year difference between Thad and me. Between Elvin and me there is a nine-year difference."

Their father had narrow ideas about music, Hank said. "He thought all my energies should be directed toward playing in the church. He thought playing jazz was the work of the devil.

"Most of the people that I grew up knowing were church people. They were very deeply religious. They frowned on anything that wasn't connected with the church. Rock music wouldn't have had a chance in those days. I think rock, blues, and that kind of thing, have always been around. But it certainly wasn't played in church services. One of my uncles was a minister in what they called at that time the Sanctified church. And the music they played in the Sanctified church was kind of finger-popping music. It was totally alien to the kind of music that was played in the Baptist church where I grew up. And I really grew up in the church. One of the earliest memories I have was reciting a poem in church. It was my first exposure to an audience. It was long before I ever tried to play a note on the piano. That was it. The church was a part of our lives. It was a seven-day part of my father's life. Every single day. He was very sincere about it, deeply deeply religious.

"This kind of staid, conformist approach to music began to change a little later on. We used to get quartets of singers from Detroit, which was twenty-five miles away, who gave concerts at our church, the Trinity Baptist Church in Pontiac. They brought a new style of singing, which later you heard in Aretha Franklin. It was a little bit left of center. This kind of Gospel singing was more of the hand-clapping revival, jubilee kind of singing. This, I think, started a new trend. It had a great influence on the musical thinking in Pontiac. It may or may not have started in Detroit, but certainly Detroit was one of the focal points of that new trend of singing in the church. It became less Gospel, more—not secular but jubilee. It became more rhythmic. It still retained the religious flavor."

What secular music was he listening to as he grew into music in the 1920s?

"I could hear Louis Armstrong on records. I heard a lot of blues singers on records, a lot of guitar players who played blues very well. One of the first bands I heard was Duke Ellington, the Mills Blue Rhythm Band. And I think Don Redman. Don Redman played with McKinney's Cotton Pickers out of Detroit, one of the best little-known bands ever organized. I think Don had a lot to do with it. Also the Jimmie Lunceford band, one of the major bands of the day.

"I had the sheet music of Bix Beiderbecke piano compositions like *In a Mist*. Bix left a lasting impression, partly through Bill Challis, who transcribed his piano pieces. I remember when I first played *In a Mist*, I was very much impressed by the harmonic changes, which I thought were a complete departure from anything I'd heard up to that time. He had this immense talent for harmonic organization and melodic integration. He put everything together so well. I think he created a style, and it had a tremendous influence on the thinking of the arrangers of the day, via Bill Challis and via his solo work."

He paused a moment, then said, "I wonder who Bix liked?"

"According to people who know more about him than I do, it was Nick LaRocca of the Original Dixieland Jazz Band."

Hank said, "It just proves that nothing and no one exists in a vacuum. Somebody is always influenced by someone else.

"I had a very good teacher, Pauline McCaughan. When I was taking lessons from her, she was still going to high school. There again was another great, great talent. She had a marvelous singing voice. She later came to New York and was then in *Carmen Jones*, which was an adaptation of *Carmen*. She was a tremendous singer, in addition to being a wonderful pianist and teacher. Later on I had several other teachers.

"I played a few nightclubs in Detroit, but nothing significant. I played actually more in Flint than Detroit, in various nightclubs and dancehalls and with local bands. I worked with a singing group called the Melody Lads, a very good group. We sang at a number of places in and around Detroit. We did a two-week engagement at the Fox Theater. The group was that good. We did an engagement in a church outside of Detroit. The church was composed of a congregation none of whom was as dark as my wife. This is a fact. When we came in, it must have been like they were slumming. Very strange. Why would they all be so light? So that tells you a story right there. There's really nothing new.

"When you have a race—in the U.S. the white race—that has a majority of numbers, it is bound to occur. When a country grows to the point where this is no longer an important or influential factor, then that country probably has arrived as a nation, a really integrated nation, without reference to color or difference of race.

"I would venture to suggest that discrimination, segregation, have occurred throughout history in all countries. What we're going through now in this country is, I believe, a repetition of what has gone on throughout history. Hopefully it will resolve into the kind of world that we know can exist, but which takes time to mature. When that happens, the nation as a whole will begin to make real progress. Because all those things, which are now standing in the way of progress, will be behind. They occupy too much of a person's thinking, to the exclusion of the things that really matter: scientific progress, educational progress, artistic progress.

"But that's what that church was like. It tells you something.

"After Detroit I moved to Cleveland, where I worked in a small band in Cedar Gardens, with the line of chorus girls and the comedians and the fights on Sundays. It was a very strange period. Then I went to Buffalo, playing in a small bar called the Anchor Bar. I understand it's still there. A wonderful Italian restaurant. That's when I first heard Art Tatum.

"Art Tatum played in a bar across town called McVan's. Our club closed before his club closed. So we used to go over and catch his last show. After his last show, Art would go to a restaurant downtown and hang out, play till eleven o'clock the next day. I went with him every morning that I could. I guess that was his method of practicing. And the owner would set a case of Pabst Blue Ribbon beer beside him.

"In 1944 I moved to New York, and I studied with Jascha Zayde."

His training was extensive, disciplined, and classical. You can hear it in his technique. I posed a question, one I had asked Oscar Peterson, who studied with Paul DeMarkey, who had studied in Hungary with Istvan Thoman, who had studied with Liszt. Given Oscar's discipline in the Baroque and Romantic keyboard literature, would he, had the doors been open to him, have become a concert pianist? Oscar replied that, no, he wouldn't; the creativity of jazz was too appealing to him. I asked Hank, "Since you had similar training, do you think you might have gone in a different direction if you'd been white?"

He said, "If I'd had *enough* of the formal concert training, I might have thought about it. In fact, that's what my mother wanted me to do. André Watts came two generations later. As you correctly stated, the door was not open. In fact it was slammed *tight* in those days. Witness what happened to Marian Anderson in Washington, D.C. I might have given it some thought, even so, because there might have been opportunities in Europe that may not have existed in this country."

Sometimes, at record dates, I have heard Hank warming up on Chopin.

The traces of a religious upbringing are still apparent. He always says grace at table, he never smoked or drank, and he doesn't seem to use profanity. His manner is always that of a gentleman, in both senses of the word, and he has a whimsical sense of humor that breaks into his conversation in slow chuckles and sly asides followed by "Only kidding, only kidding." He is highly articulate, a characteristic he shares with most jazz musicians, speaking easily and unhesitatingly. He talks as he plays, another characteristic common in jazz musicians. His enunciation is lovely, like his articulation on the piano, and he speaks in musical rises and falls of pitch, pauses as he thinks something through alternating with long clear phrases. If these are his ideals on the piano, and they obviously are, inevitably they would inform his talk.

He is slim and moderately tall and quite handsome, with a wide mouth and lively eyes. The only sign that he was approaching seventy-two was the gray that tinged his mustache and hair. He does not move like a man that age; there is no touch of that arthritic caution that inhibits, even if only slightly, the movements of most men in their eighth decade.

There is nothing wrong with his memory, either. I couldn't remember where we first had met. He reminded me that it was at a Johnny Hartman record date, produced by Bob Thiele at Rudy Van Gelder's studio in New Jersey. Hank had been the pianist on that session, which took place in the mid-1960s.

Hank said, "Johnny never seemed to get anywhere. He had the greatest voice. You could compare him with Dick Haymes, even Perry Como. So relaxed. He used to do some pretty tough things. I worked an engagement with him at Michael's Pub. He was doing some difficult things. He was good looking, and pleasant. Easy to work with. But it never happened."

After Teddy cleared away the dishes, she brought out a plate of fruit-cake, saying, "This cake is five years old." I assumed from this that it was soaked in booze, which Hank confirmed with a chuckle and:

"If I eat this fruit-cake, my observations might become a bit garbled."

By now I could see that if I let him, he would talk about others, not himself. I asked what happened after he started studying with Jascha Zayde.

"I went to work with Hot Lips Page on the recommendation of

Lucky Thompson, who had joined that band six months or a year earlier. All during the preparation—Cleveland, Buffalo—I had been promised that job. Hot Lips was working the Onyx Club. It was almost the end of the war, and just about the end of Fifty-second Street. When I got there, there was about eight months or a year of it left. I got to play on Fifty-second Street. I worked with Lips for about three months at the Onyx, and then I went on the road with him in a big band, a three-month tour of the south, one-nighters, the roughest way you can do it.

"Lips was a blues player. He liked Louis Armstrong. There were several trumpet players who came along about that same time, King Kolax, Frank Humphreys, Hot Lips Page, one or two others, who all played more or less like Louis Armstrong.

"That tour wasn't easy. It was a trying time.

"I remember very clearly that whenever we would go to a town, inevitably we would go to the section where most of the black people lived. You would see signs saying 'Boarders accepted' or 'Roomers accepted'. We would stay in private homes or small hotels that catered to musicians.

"During the war, things began to change almost imperceptibly for the better. It wasn't that noticeable at the time. I remember those cheap hotels—the Milner hotels, a dollar a day and all the cockroaches you could eat. The better hotels were not available to us. Segregation was rife. It was the order of the day. You could not break that line. You had to eat in segregated dining rooms, you traveled on segregated buses, you traveled on segregated trains, you drank from segregated water fountains. Even if you had your own bus, and you wanted to stop for a sandwich, you had to send somebody in the back door of the restaurant and get the sandwiches to take out. Most musicians, especially the younger musicians today, really can't conceive of this, but believe me, it happened.

"There was one instance where it didn't happen, and we were the most surprised people in the world. We were on a train going from Fort Worth to San Antonio in Texas. We were sitting in a segregated coach. Three or four of us decided that we would like to go back and have something to eat. Whether it was segregated or not, we wanted to have something to eat. So we went to the dining car, about three cars back. The waiters were standing around in nicely starched white coats, and I guess we had questions on our faces. They said, 'Please have a seat. Anywhere you want.' This was strange. It happened in the middle of Texas in the middle of that period when there was intense segregation all over the South and even parts of the North as well.

"We were standing in a railroad station waiting to take a train. In Mississippi, I think. Our luggage was at the end of the platform at ground level. And a guy with a truck came along and ran over it. He could see perfectly well that there was luggage there.

"After Hot Lips Page I worked with Andy Kirk. Shirley Green— it sounds like a girl's name but it wasn't—was a very fine tenor saxophone player, an excellent player. I often wondered what happened to him. Ben Thigpen, Ed's father, played drums. He had been with the earlier group, Andy Kirk and his Clouds of Joy band with Mary Lou Williams. We did the Apollo theater, we did the State theater in Hartford, the Royal theater in Baltimore. We did a couple of dances. Then I went with John Kirby in the time Charlie Shavers and Buster Bailey were in the band. It was a great little band. I first heard the band when I was in Michigan. They used to broadcast every Sunday afternoon, so it was kind of a thrill for me to work with them.

"When I first heard bebop, I was partially confused, because it was different. I'd never heard anything like it. It seemed to be the way to go. I wasn't going to be a seer and predict that this would be the wave of the future, but I did see it as a departure and a step forward, interesting harmonically. It required prodigious technique to do it properly. The players who were playing it all had that—Charlie Parker, Dizzy Gillespie, Bud Powell.

"It seemed to be a logical development. It employed the same chords that had always been used, but in different progressions. When I first came to New York, I listened to them. Monk, a little bit. Not as much Monk as Bud Powell. And a few others. There weren't too many around. I thought it was definitely forward-looking. I guess my assessment was correct, because it is still with us.

"There was a line, a division. There are many turning points in the history of jazz in this country, if jazz is the right term to use. I don't know about it."

"You and Benny Carter and Duke Ellington and quite a few other people."

"As a matter of fact, *Down Beat* ran a contest to find another name for it. Remember that? They came up with 'crew cut.'"

"As opposed to 'long hair'. That was before the rockers grew long hair."

"I suppose it had some logic to it. But 'crew cut'? To describe jazz? One of the reasons I have some reservations about the word 'jazz' is that, according to most historians, it was a derogatory term to describe the kind of music played in so-called bawdy houses of the day. It has a sort of negative connotation. I wish there was another term. And it's limited. Jazz is a much bigger field than any particular style. It encompasses a multitude of styles, all embodied within the term . . . we won't say it!

"It comes down to personal taste. Jazz is many things to many people. There are a lot of people who like what we call off-the-wall jazz. It doesn't seem to have a lot to say to people like myself, but hey, I'm not the final authority. I can only speak from my personal preferences. I have my personal preferences, my wife has her personal preferences. I don't tell her what to think, although if she doesn't think the way I think, well then, things could go very badly for her." And he and Teddy laughed.

"I think the bottom line is personal preference. I think, however, that people who review music, critics, have an obligation to report things more objectively regardless of personal preferences. I think a reviewer has an obligation to report things of a technical nature. This affects everybody, no matter what style. The technical proficiency, or lack of it, perhaps determines the degree of enjoyment.

"That's an obligation. We all have obligations. I have an obligation to try to perform at peak level at all times. I don't always do this. Maybe when I'm not doing this, a critic sitting in the audience might say, 'Well this didn't happen the way it was supposed to happen.'"

I suggested that you can be wrong about your own work, and not only when you thought more highly of it than the critics. You could underestimate it.

"Yes," he said. "One reason is that maybe at the time of the performance you are very close to it and have in mind what you wanted to do. Maybe you almost did it, but you knew what you wanted to do and in your own mind you didn't accomplish that objective. So it's a sub-criticism of something you tried to do and didn't think you did. On the other hand, it also could happen that the listener felt that whatever you did satisfied a certain standard that he or she had in mind. It's a hard question. There are two sides of it, maybe more than two."

I said, "Maybe you don't achieve what you tried to, and do achieve something else you didn't notice you'd achieved."

"That's true. Things are happening so fast. Your mind is racing ahead of your body. Whatever you play at a given time, you're already thinking beyond that, you're into the next four bars or maybe thinking of the end. Maybe you forget what you just did, it's already happened, it's already in the past.

"But getting back to bebop, if we can use that term, which I'm not too crazy about either, there weren't an awful lot of people around playing it. One reason is that technically it was very difficult to play and play well, and coherently. This may be the key to the whole thing. If you're going to play a style, it has to be believable, and in order for it to be believable, it's got to be understandable. In order for it to be understandable, it's got to be coherent. *Somebody*'s got to know what you're trying to do. That's what separates the men from the boys. Those guys who were playing it were so capable that there was no question about what they were trying to do. Either you understood it or you didn't. And if you understood it, then that was the way to go. If you didn't understand it, nobody was going to convince you that it was right.

"*I* thought it was right. I could see the correlation of the harmony to melody, I could hear the harmony they were playing, even though my knowledge of harmony was extremely limited at the time—then as now!" (Before taking this disclaimer seriously, one might look at the lead sheets of the tunes Hank writes.) "But at least I could figure out the direction they were going. It made sense to me. And still does. I listen to some of those old records and I'm still amazed by what those guys do.

"And the tunes Charlie Parker wrote . . . Nothing could be compared to them in originality. *Confirmation* . . . The melody and the harmony were perfectly integrated. It had movement. It had excitement. It had originality—it was different from anything ever heard before. I guess that's why it became such a bebop standard."

He suggested that the rhythm sections, excepting some of the drummers, particularly Kenny Clarke and Max Roach, weren't up to what Parker and Gillespie were doing. I told him of Bobby Scott's remark that the rhythm sections were ten years behind Charlie Parker.

"If not more," Hank said. "Some of the bassists, and I don't want to name them, I could never understand it. We have all agreed that this kind of playing and harmonic thinking were at least a generation ahead of anything that had been done previously. I think we're really talking about bass players of that time."

He soon found himself surrounded by the boppers. In 1945, he joined the—for its time—revolutionary band of Billy Eckstine.

"We had Fats Navarro in the band," he said. "I remember once we had occasion to sit down and talk on 110th Street, Central Park North. We sat there on a bench by the low stone wall. We started talking about guys who were hooked on narcotics, and we agreed that this was a terrible thing to do and musicians should know better than to get into that sort of thing. All the time I didn't realize that Fats was hooked. And that was what took him away. A *great* trumpet player.

"I also worked with Coleman Hawkins at the Spotlight on Fifty-second Street. In that band were Miles Davis and Max Roach. Not a bad band! We did a lot of dance dates around the Northeast."

"Dance dates?" I said, a little incredulous.

"That's right," Hank said, and laughed

"Miles playing dance music?"

"That's right. Coleman Hawkins had a lot of these dates. And he paid very well."

"But the idea of Miles playing dance dates . . . ."

"Incredible, isn't it?" he said, laughing again. "He probably wouldn't even admit it today. All the engagements with Coleman Hawkins were very educational.

"I also worked with Billy Daniels. He'd done *Black Magic* by then.

"In 1947, I joined Jazz at the Philharmonic. We used to do two tours a year, in the spring and in the fall. During the four and a half years I worked for them, I must have done just about every major city in the country. While I was with JATP, I joined Ella Fitzgerald." (He was to be her accompanist for several years.)

Hank was present at Carnegie Hall on the 1949 night when Norman Granz introduced Oscar Peterson as a visitor from Montreal and sent him onstage with Ray Brown. Oscar astounded the audience and the press, and his international career was launched. So was a friendship between Hank and Oscar, who always cites Hank among his favorite pianists.

"Oscar and I and Norman Granz planned to make a two-piano LP together, pretty much as I did with George Shearing for Concord a year ago," Hank said. "For some reason we couldn't get it off the ground. Probably the fault was as much mine as anyone else's. I'll take the blame for that one. There were certain things I wanted in the contract that I couldn't get in there. Oscar and I will probably still do that album. That's one of my ambitions, one of my priorities, and I hope Oscar feels that way too. It came up at Oscar's home in Toronto, when I was visiting.

"After Jazz at the Philharmonic, I worked with Tyree Glenn at

the Embers and at the Roundtable. I worked with Artie Shaw with
the New Gramercy Five, which included Artie, Tal Farlow, Irv
Kluger, Tommy Potter, Joe Roland. That was a very interesting
period. We did Las Vegas, East St. Louis, Cleveland. It didn't last
long, but it was very interesting. I must have worked with Tyree
twice. The second time Lester Young and my brother Elvin were
in the band. I remember once Lester was sick and didn't come to
work. It was the end of the week and I took his money over to him
at the Alvin hotel. He must have died the same year. That must
have been about the same time I went to work at CBS.

"Let's see. Oh. Yes. I also worked with, you should pardon the
expression, Benny Goodman." Again there was laughter; but
there was no malice in the remark. "I worked with Benny off and
on for almost twenty years. I would get calls from his office to do
single engagements. In 1957, I worked with the big band. I went
to the Far East with him for the State Department. Everybody got
along with Benny for shorter or longer periods. Not necessarily
longer periods. I always had great admiration for Benny for his
musical ability. The man could play the horn, there's no question
about that. Even during the CBS period, when I had a free day, I
would sometimes go with Benny.

"I did the Jackie Gleason and Garry Moore and Ed Sullivan
shows, and some others you've never heard of. I used to do a Dixieland jazz show on the radio, and a more modern jazz show too.
We had Hal McKusick and Trigger Alpert. The drummer was
either Specs Powell or Sonny Igoe. I was at CBS from 1959 to
1974. Close to fifteen years.

"I wasn't able to go on the road all that time. When CBS closed
down the music department, no more staff orchestras, everything
became open. I had the option of going out. I did a lot of recordings. They were coming out of my ears. Then I began to do tours,
festivals. I did the festival at Nice for about four years. I went on
a tour of Japan with Marian McPartland and John Lewis. It was
the first time I'd been there since 1957, when I was there with
Benny Goodman. I've been back nearly every year since then,

sometimes twice a year. There hasn't been any lack of work, I must say. I've had to turn down a lot. I did a lot of jingle dates.

"About five and a half years ago, I moved up to this part of the country. That canceled automatically all the jingle dates. You can't go four hundred miles round trip for a jingle date. When I go in to New York to do an album, I stay at a motel in New Jersey, because the parking's easier."

"And it's a little safer," I said. "You may come back and find you still have your hubcaps."

Again the laughter: "And also your wheels, your motor. I came out of Bradley's one night. I was parked on Tenth Street. Teddy and I walked back to the car between sets, and there's a guy sitting in the car. He'd gone through the glove compartment. He jumped out and ran. And he left his gloves behind. Lousy gloves. I still have them." And still more laughter.

"After CBS, I got a lot more calls. The recordings I've done lately are mostly my own dates, trio recordings, for Concord and for Japanese companies.

"J.J. Johnson worked for ten years or more in Hollywood, writing scores for TV and movies. They tell me those deadlines in Hollywood are murder. I think that had a lot to do with Oliver Nelson's death. I think it takes a deadly toll on some people. Oliver couldn't take that physical strain. It led to drinking, and he did a lot of it, and he was overweight.

"I think when you finally do come back to playing after years in the studios, you have such a wealth of musical ideas to express that it wants to come forth all at once. At CBS I was in a more or less restricted kind of environment, playing a lot of show music, oom-pah, oom-pah. It didn't stretch my musical mind; it was all there on paper. When I left CBS, it was almost like starting over again. You had to rebuild your muscles for playing again, mentally as well as physically."

I looked at my watch. I couldn't believe it; it was after midnight. I apologized for keeping Hank and Teddy up, they protested that I had done no such thing. They showed me to a room with a king-size bed. I could hear them, though faintly, still talking as I fell asleep.

There was a bright light on the drawn curtains when I awoke. The ground was covered with thick fresh snow. Great wet snowdrops were still falling, and the sky was lost to sight. I wondered if I would be able to leave.

Hank and Teddy were already awake, and I could smell breakfast, bacon and sausage and grilled liver. The conversation resumed as if it had never been interrupted. I wake up quickly, and so apparently does Hank. He made jokes about Teddy's coffee, insisting she had once made a pot of it that you could stand a spoon in. It was just my kind of coffee. Obviously Hank loves to tease her; obviously she loves him to do it, though occasionally she gets her own back.

While he was out of the room, I asked her if they farmed these 277 acres. "Oh no," she said. "He wanted to. But I said, 'You'd better make up your mind. Are you going to be a musician or a farmer? You can't be both.'" He told her he wasn't ready to give up music yet, and that was the end of his agricultural aspirations.

When he returned, I mentioned that on the car radio the previous day, I'd heard a Teddy Wilson solo performance of *Ain't Misbehavin'*. I said, "He was playing a moving bass line, rather intricate figures built out of the harmony."

Hank said, "I've never heard Teddy take that particular approach. But when you're playing solo you have poetic license. You can do just about anything you like, and make it come out. If you're lucky!

"Your conception of harmony changes over the years, as you gain experience. Your concept of melody changes too. You start to think more involved, complex melodies, sometimes not within the thirty-two-bar frame. You start thinking in terms of the overall melody—the story you're trying to tell—instead of confining yourself to thirty-two bars, or eight bars. Your harmonic conception changes greatly. I think that's what's happened to Oscar

Peterson, and I think it's what's happened to me, on a much lesser scale. I think the more technical ability you have, the more complex the harmony. I think it changes in direct correlation to that, because you can conceive many more complex patterns, more complex harmonic ideas. Sometimes it is even more than a thirty-two bar pattern. It could be a forty-two, forty-four, sixty-four-bar pattern. The number of bars doesn't seem to be as important as the ideas you're trying to express. That's the prime consideration.

"The first pianist that I really became aware of, I think, was Duke Ellington. Then Earl Hines, Fats Waller, then Teddy Wilson, then Art Tatum. Over the years other pianists, Tommy Flanagan, Barry Harris, Bill Evans, Dorothy Donegan. So many, some not so well known. Oscar Peterson. Oscar Peterson is head and shoulders above any pianist alive today. Oscar is at the apex. He is the crowning ruler of all the pianists in the jazz world. No question about it.

"There are some younger pianists around. I'm thinking of James Williams, Mulgrew Miller, Kenny Barron, and still younger ones. Roger Kellaway is an exceptional pianist. We both were judges in the Thelonious Monk contest in Washington, D.C., a couple of years ago. We each had to play a little bit of a solo in places. I got to hear him better, and much more intently, and I was very much impressed with his approach. He has delicacy but a definite firmness. Whatever he's trying to say comes through very clearly. He plays almost effortlessly.

"One of the characteristics of the best of them is that these pianists, beginning with Teddy Wilson, Art Tatum, then Oscar Peterson, play bass lines so highly developed that they provide perfect support and foundation for whatever is happening in the right hand. Without that bass line, the right hand would have no meaning. It would be floating in the air, by itself. The harmonic foundation, the harmonic justification for the right hand, is in the left hand. I have never understood how certain pianists can completely abandon the left hand, almost as if it were tied behind their backs. If you're building a house, you start with the foundation. This is an over-simplification, I realize, but it might illustrate the point. You've got to start somewhere. With music, you start with

the root of the chord. You build on that. If you don't, you've got
no foundation. Even if it's a slab house, without a basement, you
have to start with the foundation."

Let me suggest that you go back to the point where I mentioned
the bass line of Teddy Wilson's *Ain't Misbehavin'*. Notice how
Hank starts on the subject, explores several other ideas and dis-
cusses other pianists, and then returns to the point from which he
departed: bass lines. That is parallel to the way his musical thinking
flows across the eight-bar and even thirty-two-bar lines. He then
developed the point about solo playing into this:

"Nat Cole was one of my idols. One of Oscar's too. Nat was a
great influence on a lot of people. His tone and his attack were
quite different. That was a departure from his original style. The
way he plays when he's really relaxed, or maybe thinks nobody is
listening. I once went up to Andy Kirk's apartment, where Nat
used to stay. He was well-known by then. He was working a series
of theater engagements with Andy Kirk's band. I went by to see
Andy for some business reason, and I heard someone playing the
piano. I thought maybe it was a Tatum record. I peeked around
the corner and there was Nat, playing like Art Tatum. I was totally
amazed. I didn't think he played that way. It was a very relaxed
Tatum sound. He may have changed his style to accommodate the
vocal style he used, and also the trio style.

"Because as much as I loved Tatum, I loved him better playing
solo. When a pianist is playing a certain way alone, you have to
assume that the style that he uses with a group is something that
he does to accommodate the other musicians in the group.

"That simple style Basie used was the only thing that would cut
through the band sound, fit the holes. Basie was a very intelligent
musician."

"You mentioned Roger Kellaway," I said. "You know that
experimental band Thad had in Europe toward the end of his life.
Roger played piano in it at a festival. When he got back, I asked
him how he, as a composer, felt about Thad's writing. He thought
for a moment and said, 'I think Thad Jones may be a genius.' And
Roger doesn't use that word lightly."

"I think he was," Hank said. "I don't like to talk about him and Elvin because they're my brothers."

"Talk about them," I said.

At first with a touch of reluctance, Hank resumed, "Thad was an outstanding talent. Before Thad came on the scene, with his arrangements and with that big band he had with Mel Lewis, I didn't hear these things from anyone else. It was a completely new approach. I think Thad would be the first one to tell you that he was greatly inspired by Duke. But he didn't sound like Duke. The writing was innovative, it inspired the other musicians. I don't know of anybody who has had the influence that Thad had on the thinking of arrangers in maybe the last fifteen years. I think his influence will be felt for a long, long time. Perhaps as much as Duke and Billy Strayhorn. Completely original. Arrangers now are beginning to think that way. You hear little traces of Thad in a lot of things current today. That's one of the hallmarks of greatness, isn't it, that your influence can be felt long after you're gone.

"Elvin is an innovator of the first order. He has influenced a whole generation, or two, and even past generations of drummers. There's just no way to describe his playing. Elvin is the only one who could explain what he's doing. I get the impression that he's using a multiple, multiple series of triplets—triplets upon triplets, a whole pyramid of triplets. To me that's what his style is based on. As a drummer he could explain it a lot better than that. There's no question that he's an innovator, he's a stylist. A drummer I just worked with in California, Jim Plank, an excellent drummer himself, said he loved Elvin. I have not met a drummer yet who doesn't like him, even the drummers who don't play like Elvin. They say his style is completely original."

I said, "Thad once gave me an interesting description of the difference between the Ellington and Basie bands. He sort of waved his hands in parallel, and said that the Basie band came right straight at you, and the Ellington band had a broader sound, like Technicolor and CinemaScope or Cinerama. Another thing he said: he said Basie had an uncanny feel for tempos, he said Basie could walk on a bandstand at a dance and without even trying one number, get such a feeling for the audience that the first thing he played was exactly right for them.''

"Basie was like that,'' Hank said. "The ability to pick tempos is a rare, rare talent. For bandleaders or anybody else, but particularly bandleaders. If the tempo is not right, then everything sort of falls apart. Basie really had it. I was on a record date with Illinois Jacquet. We were recording a tune called *Black Velvet*, which later became *Don't You Go 'Way Mad*. We could not find the right tempo. It was Basie's date. They had me there because Basie couldn't be there at the time the date started. Jacquet could not find the right tempo for this tune. Basie came in about an hour and a half after the date started, and stomped off a tempo. That was the tempo. That was it. Fantastic.

"Basie was one of the two people I've worked with who had this great ability to pick right tempos. The other was Benny Goodman.''

Hank showed me a discography of his work that a Japanese researcher had compiled. It was well over three hundred pages. He has recorded with seemingly everyone. I noticed that he had recorded with Chet Baker. I said that Baker's work had evaded me in the early years. Only later did I become captivated by its spare, selective simplicity.

"He was a great player,'' Hank said. "Chet Baker's playing affected many people, from the standpoint of its simplicity. Probably this is the best testimonial to his over-all artistry. His playing was simple—perhaps! But he had complex chords in mind. He may have been dancing all around, but he was conforming exactly to the chord progressions of the tune, or of the tune as he had *arranged* the chords. It only appeared to be simple. This is probably the best expression of an artist—when the artist can make something appear to be simple. And yet underneath, it was complicated harmonically.''

I said I'd been told that Baker couldn't read. Hank said, "I find it hard to believe. He gave me a set of chord changes. He certainly knew what he was doing. I think he could read.'' (Some weeks after this conversation, Gerry Mulligan, with whose quartet Baker came to prominence, affirmed that Baker could read. The rumor that he couldn't, Mulligan said, "is all part of that mythology of jazz.")

Hank said, "The worst you could say is that Chet had a terrific ear. People say that Erroll Garner couldn't read, but Erroll played some of the most fantastic things. I would settle for not being able to read if I could play like that. Erroll had a wonderful way of playing that made you feel happiness. Fats Waller had that quality, although the style was not the same. But they had this quality of making you feel good. You got into the spirit of it.

"You know the joke about Louis Armstrong. Knowing Louis, I think he really said it. Somebody asked if he could read. He said, 'Not enough to hurt my playing.' Or was it 'Not enough to help my playing'?"

I mentioned Wes Montgomery, who swore to me that he couldn't read and had no idea what chord symbols meant. Buddy Rich couldn't read. And of course Bix Beiderbecke was never a proficient reader.

Hank said, "These people who couldn't read had exceptional ears, highly developed. They had an ingrained sense of harmony, and perhaps were writing the harmony as they played. It just proves that the ability to read is not absolutely necessary. It helps. You certainly couldn't hold a studio job or go to a recording date and play a sheaf of music sitting on your stand. On the other hand, the guys who can do that are not always the guys who can sit down and play the most interesting solos."

"Well," I said, "Clark Terry told me once that when he was in the *Tonight Show* band, he could read like a shark because he was doing it every day, but when he left and went out just to play jazz, his reading slipped."

"True. You have to read all the time to keep that skill. When I was on staff at CBS, my reading developed."

Breakfast was over. I drank some more of Teddy's powerful coffee. The snow had stopped. From the front window of the house, beyond a long sloping lawn, all white, and a large pond, black in the snow, you could see that the highway was clear. I quoted to

Hank something the Chicago pianist Fred Kaz had said to me long ago:

"My music has what my life does not: emotional freedom."

Hank said, "Music offers a means of emotional outlet. That is not practical in normal life. I don't want to sound dogmatic about this, I'm no psychiatrist. I feel that sports serve somewhat the same purpose: an activity that provides emotional outlet that is not practical in real life. I think there's something there."

I almost could hear the unfinished thought. I said, "Then it's crossed your mind too that there must be a strong correlation between emotional repression and high blood pressure in the male black population."

"Oh yes. Along with the realization that you're repressing something that should not have to be repressed, because there's a certain inequity involved, a certain denial of rights. More and more, though, I think you will see this manifestation of repression of feelings diminish, as the whole scene changes, as more and more people are given means to express them. When there's nothing to repress, I think you'll see high blood pressure gradually diminish in black men. They have been slighted. They traditionally have had to bear the brunt. Hopefully this will diminish in the future. You always have to have hope, even though the hope is not necessarily justified.

"I think it's possible to overcome it, if you have it within yourself to keep a cap on your emotions without repressing them, without allowing them to build to the point where they need to be repressed, and not having the freedom, the outlet for them to escape.

"Music does that in a sense. It allows you an avenue of expression. Emotions can be transposed into musical thought, musical feeling. There's a transfer that goes on between emotions and musical expression."

The snow in Hank's long driveway was turning to slush. I gathered my things from the guest room. It was now mid-afternoon.

I mentioned that there had been a controversy of late over the claim by European writers and critics that Europeans were the first to recognize and appreciate jazz and the growing body of evidence that this is not so.

Hank said, "I disagree with the notion that Europeans initially appreciated jazz more than Americans. I don't think there's ever been a problem of appreciation. The problem has been, and is, that jazz has not been adequately compensated. They forget that musicians who play jazz for a living have to play jazz *for a living*. Jazz has never been adequately compensated in this country. That is not to say that it has been adequately compensated in Europe either. That is the universal problem with jazz, with the possible exception of Japan."

I bade my farewells to Teddy. Hank walked me to the front door and we shook hands. "Drive carefully," he said.

I walked out past the tilted basketball pole and got into the car. The road wound south through the Catskills, magnificent under the fresh snow. Wide white ski trails descended through the pines on the mountains. A soft rain started and it seemed likely that the winter was over.

Bix and Bill

One afternoon in 1958 I sat in a Paris cafe with the French critic and composer André Hodeir, author of *Jazz: Its Evolution and Essence*. Americans are inclined to be flattered by European praise, and Hodeir's book caused a stir in the jazz intellectual community in the United States—not the musicians, to be sure, but editors and writers on the subject.

Alan Jay Lerner, who lived extensively in France and spoke the language, said that the French considered themselves the cultural Supreme Court of the world. If they did not discover something first, then it could be of little value. Hence the passion, shared with the English, in their claim that they discovered jazz before the benighted Americans appreciated its value. To like the music, they had to be its discoverers. Actually, the French are slow to accept the new in art to the point that Pierre Boulez went to live in Germany in protest against their conservatism.

Hodeir said to me that sunny afternoon, "No white man ever contributed anything to the development of jazz." I accepted this passively enough. It was the conventional wisdom, held by any number of writers not just in England and France but in the United States too. It was only much later, when I got into conversations—not interviews, but easy and off the record conversations—with the likes of Coleman Hawkins and Ben Webster that I began to have an uneasy feeling that the conventional wisdom was not the whole truth. Gradually I came to feel, on the testimony not of white critics but of black musicians, that a number of white musicians had exerted important influences in the development of jazz.

The huge preponderance of inventive exploration and influence has been by black musicians: Bechet, Morton, Armstrong, Ellington, Hines, Waller, Basie, Hodges, Redman, Carter, Fletcher Henderson, Lester Young, Coleman Hawkins, Parker, Gillespie, Monk, Bud Powell. They made the massive cultural achievement of jazz in less than thirty years.

However, a hypothesis of the total irrelevancy of white jazz musicians can be sustained only by the willful denial of historical record and the testimony of any number of black jazz musicians. Anthony Braxton lists Paul Desmond as one of his early influences. Herbie Hancock speaks of the influence of Bill Evans on subsequent jazz pianists, and only the deaf could fail to notice it. Art Tatum said that one of his influences was the Chicago radio pianist Lee Sims. Since many writers on the subject seem unfamiliar with Sims' work, which we know today chiefly from his compositions, they ignore what Tatum said. Edmond Hall said he was influenced by Benny Goodman. Buster Bailey said he was influenced by Larry Shields of the Original Dixieland Jazz Band, which indisputably was the first nationally popular jazz band and the group that established the widespread American fascination with this music.

Lester Young stated firmly that he was influenced by Frank Trumbauer (who, we should note for the sake of strict accuracy, was part Indian) and Jimmy Dorsey.

In his biography of Lester Young, *You Just Fight for Your Life*, the Danish writer Frank Buchman-Moller quotes an interview with trumpeter Lester Phillips, who played with Lester Young in the band run by the latter's father:

"Everybody in the band listened to the Casa Loma Orchestra and Jean Goldkette. We had plenty of records with them and Red

Nichols, Trumbauer and Bix. And Benny Goodman. We had *Davenport Blues* with Bix, and after Bix got with Whiteman we used to listen to him a lot . . . Jack Teagarden with Red Nichols changed the trombone around. Before he came around they played a slide horn, but he wouldn't slide, and everybody would copy him, like our trombone player . . . When a band came to Minneapolis, we'd all go to hear them—Ben Bernie, Goldkette, Coon-Sanders, Vincent Lopez and Paul Whiteman . . . . Lester was crazy about Bix, crazy about Trumbauer and Benny Goodman. We heard the Ben Pollack records with Goodman. Lester was playing *Singin' the Blues* around the house, and I said: 'Man, who is playing that trumpet?' And Lester said, 'His name is Bix.' We played Bix's record of *In a Mist* too. We picked up the lead on it, Lester played the lead and gave us the harmonies . . . Red Nichols was out there 'way before Bix and was more popular than Bix. Lester liked him too. He learned Goldkette's *Clementine* because Trumbauer had a solo on it. *Mississippi Mud* with Whiteman, too, with the Rhythm Boys."

Lester told an interviewer: "Trumbauer was my idol. When I first started to play, I used to buy all his records. He played a C-melody, and I tried to get the sound of a C-melody on a tenor . . . . Bix sounded just like a colored boy sometimes . . . I have great big eyes for Bix. I used to be confused between him and Red Nichols, but finally I had to put Bix on top."

The influence of Bix Beiderbecke on Miles Davis seems obvious during the *Kind of Blue* period of his career, in the spaced selective way of playing, and even in the curious sense of joy undercolored by darkness. When I asked Miles, famed for purported militancy, if he had listened a lot to Bix, he, far from being offended, answered, "No, but I listened a lot to Bobby Hackett. And *he* listened to Bix." Furthermore, in his autobiography, Miles confirms what Gil Evans—whom he describes as his best friend—said: that one of the influences on Miles was Harry James who, when he turned away from lugubrious ballads and broad vibrato, was a hot and hard and dazzling jazz player.

Rex Stewart, a writer as well as a cornet player, had much to say on the impact of Bix Beiderbecke. Saxophonist Billie Mitchell told me that his big early influence was Artie Shaw. Artie Shaw told me that he spent his early days trying to play like Bix on a saxophone.

Hodeir's statement, then, is simply silly. And given the scope of Lester Young's influence on jazz, including his influence on Charlie Parker, the statement of one English critic that Bix made history but did not influence it is in the same class.

One read too that white bands had to bring in black arrangers—Fletcher Henderson with Benny Goodman and Sy Oliver with Tommy Dorsey—to give them some soul and make them swing. I accepted that, too, not bothering to reflect that writing won't swing without players who swing. Basie, who knew a thing or two about swing, used a number of white writers, among them Neal Hefti, Sammy Nestico, and Chico O'Farrill. But three white writers—Will Hudson, Russ Morgan, and Bill Challis—wrote for Fletcher Henderson's band several years before Benny Goodman commissioned arrangements by Henderson, and incidentally Don Redman wrote for Paul Whiteman and Goldkette. Challis and Morgan were alumni—along with Tommy and Jimmy Dorsey, pianist Itzy Riskin, and lead trumpeter Fuzzy Farrar—of a Pennsylvania dance orchestra called the Scranton Sirens. They were from coal country, and they knew each other early.

Dance bands were burgeoning all over America to supply the music required by the dance craze catalyzed by Vernon and Irene Castle and their famous black music director, James Reese Europe, after World War I. Given the quality of the musicians who came out of it, the Scranton Sirens must have been a very good band. Not very far to the north, Spiegle Willcox was playing in local bands in pavilions and dance halls. He and Challis did not know each other then. They still live only an hour or so of driving time apart.

Challis began writing for the Jean Goldkette band in 1926. His arrangements were far ahead of their time, harmonically and rhythmically, and highly admired by musicians. A strange thing happened to those Challis charts for Goldkette.

The Goldkette arranging staff included Russ Morgan and a vio-

linist named Eddy Sheasby. Sheasby, who at one point shared conducting duties with Frank Trumbauer, was a volatile, temperamen-
tal drunk, and even the musicians, tolerant though they often are
of human vagary, didn't like him. Something set him off. Nobody
seems to know what. In a fit of rage he disappeared just before an
important engagement in St. Louis. The band's library, including
the Challis arrangements, went with him. Goldkette saw him several years later, but the band's book was never recovered. Its loss
contributed to the orchestra's eventual collapse.

When Paul Whiteman hired Challis, he asked the arranger to
reconstruct his Goldkette pieces. Challis adapted the charts to
Whiteman's larger instrumentation. All the Challis charts for
Whiteman are in the Williams College Library. In 1975, a Carnegie Hall concert resurrected some of the Goldkette music. Then a
young New York bassist named Vince Giordano, who had studied
arranging with Challis, urged his mentor to recreate some of his
Goldkette charts with their original instrumentation. Withdrawing
some of the Whiteman versions of the charts from Williams College, Challis went to work to scale them back down to the size of
the Goldkette band, thirteen men. Giordano put together a band
to record the material, made up of musicians sympathetic to the
music of that earlier era, including Bob Wilber and the late Dick
Wellstood. One of the trombonists had a special affinity for the
music: Spiegle Willcox had first played it with Goldkette sixty years
before.

The resultant album on the Circle label is called *Bill Challis' The
Goldkette Project*. It deserves the attention of students of arranging
and researchers in the history of jazz. The album should inspire a
re-evaluation of the place in jazz history of Bill Challis. Even without it, such a reassessment seems inevitable in the light the reissues
on CDs.

One of the discs in the Columbia Records release list is devoted
to Bix Beiderbecke, with emphasis on the band called Frankie
Trumbauer and His Orchestra, which recorded for OKeh in 1927.
Several charts are by Challis, including *Ostrich Walk*, from the repertoire of the Original Dixieland Jazz Band, Hoagy Carmichael's

Riverboat Shuffle, Three Blind Mice (Rhythmic Theme in Advanced Harmony), and two with the eerily awful vocals of Seger Ellis, *Blue River* and *There's a Cradle in Caroline*. The album also contains the famous *Singin' the Blues*, whose impact on musicians was comparable to that of Armstrong's *West End Blues*.

It is interesting to compare the original Trumbauer-Beiderbecke 1927 version of the tune on Columbia, a previously unissued take of a 1931 Fletcher Henderson recording of the Challis arrangement (with Rex Stewart reproducing the Bix solo) now out on Bluebird, and the version in *The Goldkette Project*.

The Robert Parker albums include a compilation of New York recordings from the 1920s, one of which is Paul Whiteman's *San*, another Challis chart, recorded January 12, 1928. The CD reissues should also cause a re-evaluation of Whiteman, a dartboard for jazz buffs for lo these many decades. That Paul Whiteman could not play jazz and merely stood there and waved a stick is not necessarily relevant. Dizzy Gillespie has repeatedly attested that Lucky Millinder, who was not a musician, was a first-rate bandleader. Cab Calloway, a singer, not an instrumentalist, had a crackling great band.

To be sure, Whiteman's band could be ponderous, but not always and certainly not in all its recordings. The personnel on *San* is only ten men: Charlie Margulis on trumpet, Beiderbecke on cornet, Bill Rank on trombone, Jimmy Dorsey on trumpet and clarinet, Trumbauer on C-melody saxophone, Min Leibrook on bass sax, Matty Malneck on violin, Carl Kress on guitar, and Harold McDonald, drums. The pianist is Challis, who didn't consider piano his instrument. *San* is a delight to this day, and one of the reasons is the quality of the writing. And it swings.

There is something else we should note at once about Challis. He was the man who transcribed the five Bix Beiderbecke piano pieces, *In a Mist, Candlelights, Flashes, In the Dark,* and *Davenport Blues*. Without him, we would not have those pieces, and perhaps not even Beiderbecke's piano recording of *In a Mist*.

We wouldn't have them without Whiteman, either: Whiteman made the deal with publisher Jack Robbins to put these pieces out, whereupon Bix and Challis went to work to get them on paper. Nor would we have the Challis charts for Goldkette without White- man, either. He was a natural target, with that rotund face with its pencil mustache, so easily caricatured, and he was later mocked by the jazz writers for that press agent's title "King of Jazz." He was privately modest on the subject of jazz, but he was a perceptive appreciator of the music, hired some of its best white players, arrangers black and white, and made the public pay some atten- tion to it.

I passed Scranton on Interstate 81, heading southwest toward Wilkes-Barre, which is nineteen miles farther down the Susque- hanna River. My father, who was English, worked briefly in one of the coal mines in this area just about the time Bill Challis left it to write for Goldkette. That was before I was born. My dad quit—he said the Pennsylvania mines were terribly unsafe, far below the standards of those in England—and went back to playing music for a living until the Depression and the arrival of the talkies dried up the work. My dad said that in those days, you'd see miners rest- ing on their haunches along the roadside, waiting for their buses to work in the mornings, the same posture you saw in the mining country of England and Wales. It's the only way to rest in a narrow coal seam. It occurred to me on that freeway that my dad may well have heard the Scranton Sirens.

You don't see miners resting easy on their haunches in Penn- sylvania any more. The pit mines are gone; the coal is extracted by the ruthlessly efficient process of strip mining.

It wasn't just the reissue of so many records with Challis charts that had set me on this quest into coal country. His name had been coming up more and more. Then Hank Jones expressed the view that Bix had exerted an influence on arrangers through Challis. And Benny Carter, who first wrote for Fletcher Henderson prob- ably in 1926, when Challis was with Goldkette, had said to me in New York that Bill Challis was one of his idols.

That alone gave him significance.

I pulled off at Wilkes-Barre, passed through the city, and

headed out into the country, following directions from Evan Challis, Bill's younger brother, keeper of the flame and family historian. Evan pronounces his name "Even". He says there are two pronunciations of the name in Wales. The family is Welsh on the mother's side, Huguenot on the father's. Thus the name Challis is French.

I arrived at Harvey's Lake. It is a little lake, ringed by a road and rows of summer houses and boat docks. It was deserted on this April afternoon, not a boat in sight. I could not find the house. Bill Challis lives with Evan and Evan's wife Elizabeth. I telephoned and at last found the address.

In a camel-hair topcoat, almost shyly holding up his hand to tell me I had come to the right place, he stood on the front porch, overlooking the road perhaps thirty feet below the house, and the lake that shone beyond it. As I climbed the steps and looked back, I saw, beyond the lake, among the houses that rim it, the skeletal form of a roller-coaster, from which no happy screams have emanated in years; it is abandoned. To anyone who grew up along the Great Lakes, as I did, a lake is a body of water you can't see across, and this one, Harvey's Lake, is a mere puddle, a postage stamp of water, narrow and a couple of miles or so long. Still, a sign by the highway as you approach it proclaims it the largest natural lake in Pennsylvania. It is not the largest in area but in terms of content of water: it is very deep.

Once upon a time, when you could get here on the interurban electric trolley from Wilkes-Barre, there were three dance pavilions around its rim, and two more between the two communities, five in all. You start to understand why Artie Shaw says that in the heyday of the bands you could play a month of one-nighters in Pennsylvania alone. But the trolley was long ago dismantled, and the pavilions died, and the sounds of bands no longer drift across this water in the evenings. Bill Challis played C-melody saxophone in bands that worked these pavilions. He was in high school then.

At the top of the stairs, I shook hands with him, having the curious sense—this happened when I met Rudolf Friml, too—that I was touching history. In Friml's case, the thought occurred to me that his hand had shaken that of Dvořák, which had shaken that of Liszt, which had shaken that of Beethoven, which had shaken that of Mozart. I was five handshakes from Mozart. In the case of Challis, I have no idea who all he shook hands with. Certainly with Fletcher Henderson and Bix. And no doubt Rex Stewart and Coleman Hawkins on the night of the legendary confrontation of the Goldkette and Henderson bands at Roseland. I looked into a face with clear skin, thinning white hair and, inside the one lens of his bifocal glasses, a dark eye-patch. As I learned, the sight in his right eye is going.

The four issues from April to July, 1929, of the British journal *Melody Maker* presented an extended analysis by Al Davison of Paul Whiteman's recording of *Sweet Sue*, a Challis arrangement. Davison, whose prose was tortuous, wrote that "modern rhythmic music has arrived at a stage where at its best it is worthy of being considered as a form of music which is by no means valueless even when adjudged with the highest of artistic standards in mind. In fact, at such a stage has it arrived that it is plain to see that it is more than likely that shortly the influence of the general atmosphere of modern dance music, and more particularly perhaps the subtleties of interpretation which produce what we broadly term dance rhythm, will have a strong effect on the work of the great master composers of tomorrow." With notated examples, Davison analyzed the orchestrator's harmony, including minor ninth and thirteenth chords, intimations of the whole-tone scale, and his voice-leadings, going through the chart almost bar by bar. The tone of the article, which in total covered eleven pages of the publication, is ecstatic. Bix got a copy of the article. He brought it to Challis and said, "Hey Bill, read this." What Bix had noticed was that Challis' name was never once mentioned. Indeed Davison attributes the arrangement to Ferde Grofé.

Another man came out of the house to join us. This was Evan Challis, whom I had talked to several times on the phone. I apologized for the intrusion, but the brothers dismissed this and said, "We want to take you to lunch." And so we left immediately for a little family restaurant partway back to Wilkes-Barre and sat down amid a clink of dishes and soft string music from the Muzak. A Jobim tune.

Bill was born in Wilkes-Barre on July 8, 1904, Evan on August 29, 1916, the sons of a barber. There were two more boys and a girl in the family, but only Evan and Bill survive. You could sense immediately the friendship between them.

How did Bill get started writing?

"We had a band here called Guy Hall's Orchestra," Bill said. He spoke softly and slowly. "He wrote *Johnson Rag*. He wrote a couple of other things too. I was just a kid, in my junior year in high school. He had a guy who played tenor sax in the band. The saxophones were just new. I got a hold of a C-melody sax. I was a good saxophone player. Russ Morgan was around then, nine miles down the road from Wilkes-Barre. He played trombone. Jimmy Dorsey and Tommy too, their father was a teacher."

"They were from the lower coal fields," Evan said. "Shenandoah." Jimmy in fact was born the same year as Bill Challis. Evan said there had always been a strong brass-band tradition in this area.

"I think the miners and their gals used to like to dance," Evan said. "They'd dance at the drop of a hat. Every night, there was a dance with somebody's band playing. In all these towns, Plymouth and Nanticoke and Wilkes-Barre and Scranton. The outside dance pavilions and then, in the winter time the halls, there was dancing going on all the time."

"Where did you study arranging, Bill?" I asked.

"I didn't study. I more or less just picked it up. I was a faker, a real faker. I studied with a fellow here named Fritz Anstette. Czechoslovakian. He taught clarinet. Most of the guys around here that were talking saxophone at the time said, 'Go down to Old Man Anstette.' I went down to him. It was a buck a week or something like that. He had a son who was an oboe player, another son who was a trumpet player, and I think some of the girls played piano.

"He started on me, showed me all about the saxophone. I had a very good tone. I figure he was the one who taught me to develop a tone. Long whole notes and low tones. Sooner or later I came up with a pretty good tone. That's what got me my job with the Scranton Sirens. Russ Morgan was in the band, playing trombone.

"I went with Guy Hall's band. He had five guys. Sometimes he expanded to three trumpets, two trombones, three saxes, and the rhythm section, with string bass, piano, and banjo. Guy was the drummer."

Evan said, "Bill wrote an arrangement of *Blue Room*. That arrangement had a history. Guy Hall had all those men for an occasion. They'd play the top club in town, the Westmoreland Club, where all the coal barons were members. They'd have a ball there. Playing gigs around town, it was five pieces, but they augmented it for big occasions. Bill wrote the *Blue Room* arrangement for that larger band. Bill was still going to high school. He'd play summers with Guy Hall."

"We'd play the pavilions around here," Bill said.

"After high school I went to Bucknell, about 65 miles down the river at Lewisburg. I took pre-law. I was going to go to law school at the University of Pennsylvania in Philadelphia.

"At Bucknell I wound up with my own band in my second, third, and fourth years. As the band augmented—and I did my best to augment it—I had to write for the extra instruments.

"The guy who had the band before me had five pieces. In my first year I was the second saxophone. The guy who played trombone doubled on saxophone. When I got the band in my second year, it got to be six guys. Then I got another saxophone player and a trumpet when they came to school. The band began to build up. It got to be three saxophones and trumpet and trombone and piano. We had no bass. Then a guitar player came to school. We did a little rehearsing, putting some tunes together. I had to write out the extra parts for the three saxophones. I wrote for the C-melody, the alto, and the tenor. Then I got another trumpet player and a bass player. So I had a rhythm section, three saxophones and three brass. We wound up with eleven or twelve pieces. It was practically a complete band.

"By my senior year, we had some harmony in the band. It

sounded like a bigger band. If necessary, I would write the trombone, which was closest in the register, so that the guy had to play the melody. If we wanted four parts, the saxophones would play the other three. We always had a band that sounded like it had a lot of guys. Itzy Riskin wrote that I was the one who brought that around.

"We played mostly for the girls in the sororities. They squawked a little about raising the price on them, but they paid it, and we had no problem. Each time we got another guy in the band, I had to write the part."

Challis graduated from Bucknell, his mind set on going to law school. "I sent in my tuition money," he said. He returned home for the summer and played for Guy Hall, then joined a band led by Dave Harmon out of Williamsport, Pennsylvania. "Dave Harmon's band played battles of music with the Wolverines," Evan said.

"I heard Bix then," Bill said. "I liked him. I didn't know him."

"Jean Goldkette had a lot of bands out in Detroit, including the band at the Book-Cadillac. When I was with the Dave Harmon band, I visited Detroit. I had a brother there, Lew."

Detroit was a different city in those days. Its initial prosperity had come from the automotive industry. But the Volstead Act vastly increased its wealth. In Canada, a short distance away across the Detroit River, the manufacture of liquor was still legal. A huge smuggling industry arose to bring this "good stuff" into the United States, so huge that the Canadian side of the river was soon deeply cut by countless small inlets to accommodate the motorboats that endlessly coursed the waters. A lot of the booze came across the river from Sarnia, in Ontario, to Port Huron on the Michigan side, to be carried into Detroit by car, hidden under the floorboards or inside hollow seats. Police and customs officials were able to interdict only the smallest part of this traffic. Detroit became a center of glamour and entertainment, largely run by the Purple Gang. Whereas "the mob" in St. Louis was Irish and Chicago's was Italian, the Purple Gang was Jewish. It has been rumored that the Purple Gang was behind the Goldkette bands, including the one that bore his own name and McKinney's Cotton Pickers. Certainly no one kept records, and we'll never know now, but Goldkette could not have functioned in the swinging entertainment world of Detroit without at least a nod of approval from the Purples.

"While I was there," Challis said, "these guys I'd played with in the Scranton Sirens, Fuzzy Farrar, Itzy Riskin, and Russ Morgan, were with Goldkette. I talked to Russ. Russ took me over to Charlie Horvath, who was the manager of the band. Russ said to Charlie, 'Why don't you have this guy make a couple of arrangements? He arranges, too.'"

The Goldkette band comprised three trumpets, two trombones, three saxophones, and four rhythm, including banjo. For recordings it used a violin-guitar duo. Goldkette did not lead the band and only occasionally appeared with it. He was a concert pianist by training who organized bands as a business. Whiteman too had several units.

Bill returned home to Wilkes-Barre, still intent on law school, but he turned in a couple of charts to the Goldkette band. "I made an arrangement of *Baby Face*. They sorta liked it. They asked me to make another one, so I gave them *Blue Room*. It was pretty much the one I'd written, updated. The Goldkette band came through Wilkes-Barre. A friend of mine and I went down to the Cinderella Ballroom to hear the arrangements. Bix and Frank Trumbauer had joined the band. The band sounded great. They'd leave open a space for the cornet and saxophone and Bix and Trumbauer would fill it in like you wouldn't believe."

That *Blue Room* chart is in *The Goldkette Project* album. Let's note that Bill said he'd updated it for Goldkette. But in its essential outlines, it was written when Bill was in high school. He was graduated from high school in 1921.

"About a week or two later," Bill continued, "I was going to go down to the University of Pennsylvania." He had spent four years at Bucknell, and this was September, 1926, the opening of the school year. Bill was twenty-three. "I got a call from Ray Lodwig. He wanted to know if I wanted to join the band. I said, 'I'm going to go to school.' He said, 'Well, we'd like you to join the band.' They wanted me to be the fourth saxophone. They told me to come up to a place in Hillsborough, Massachusetts. The band was staying there. I went up there. I knew a few of the other guys besides Bix and Trumbauer. Spiegle Willcox had joined the band."

In fact, the Goldkette personnel was now remarkable: Fuzzy Farrar, Ray Lodwig, trumpets, and Bix Beiderbecke, cornet; Bill Rank and Spiegle Willcox, trombones; Doc Ryker, Don Murray, and Frank Trumbauer, reeds; Itzy Riskin, piano; Howdy Quicksell, banjo; Steve Brown, string bass; Chauncey Morehouse, drums; Joe Venuti, violin; Eddie Lang, guitar; and Paul Mertz, arranger and at times pianist.

Bill continued, "Charlie Horvath told me, 'I can get a million saxophone players. They're a dime a dozen. I only have seven arrangements.' One of the things wrong with the Goldkette band while I was with it, they never had anyone to say, 'I want you to make an arrangement of this or that.' Horvath didn't do it, Goldkette didn't do it. Goldkette didn't even conduct. Ray Lodwig handled the band on the road. We didn't have a systematic way of building up any arrangements."

The 1926 New England sojourn of the Goldkette band has been well documented by Richard Sudhalter and Phillip R. Evans in their biography of Beiderbecke, as well as in other books. The promoter, a man named J.A. Lyons, had lodged the band at a place called the Hillcrest Inn, a country house—perhaps what would today be called a bed-and-breakfast establishment—at Hillsborough. The band arrived there September 21. It was to play gigs around New England and get ready for an opening October 6 at the Roseland Ballroom in New York, opposite Fletcher Henderson. Spiegle Willcox has a photo of the band on a wall in his home. The men are seated on the roof of a mini-bus on the side of which a banner proclaims: *Jean Goldkette Orchestra New England Tour J.A. Lyons Mgr.* Wherever the band played during that New England tour, the place was packed with musicians, such was the band's reputation—and Beiderbecke's.

"Up at Hillcrest, Bix and Trumbauer and I used to take some walks together. I went out on one or two dates to hear the band." Bill Challis, I was coming to realize, was a man in whom modesty amounted almost to a serious defect of character. That laconic statement about his stay in New England was how much he claimed for himself. But Richard Sudhalter's father, also a musician, several times heard the band during the New England stay, and said that the arrangements "that really knocked us out were *Baby Face* and *Blue Room*, both of them advanced, beautifully written, and played with enormous spirit." Chip Deffaa, in his book *Voices of the Jazz Age*, wrote, "Virtually no one had heard this new Goldkette orchestra; it had not yet cut any records; but on [the] New England tour, the band dazzled listeners night after night. And with the hiring of Bill Challis as a full-time arranger, all the pieces came together. Challis's work was downright inspired. His music was graceful, ahead of its time, and he knew how to showcase Beiderbecke and Trumbauer. They played Challis's charts with panache."

Bill said, "We gradually worked our way down into New York and the Roseland Ballroom.

"They said, 'You'll have plenty to do when you get down to New York.' Jesus. It was all, 'Have this out by eight o'clock.' Most of the tunes I got to do were lousy. Then we'd go down and record. Things like *Hushabye*. It was quite a while before we got a lot of arrangements together."

Lunch ended. Evan and Bill and I left the restaurant to drive back to Harvey's Lake. Bill continued talking in the car.

"When we came to the Roseland, I had made a few arrangements for Goldkette. Fletcher Henderson was opposite us. The story about what kind of trumpet player Bix was was put out by the trumpet players in Fletcher's band. They were sitting in Fletcher's band, Bix was sitting in the Goldkette band. They would have their time up on the stand, and then the Goldkette band would have its set.

"I was there the night it happened. Fletcher had a hell of a band. Don Redman was the arranger and first alto. Rex Stewart was in the Henderson band. Fletcher wanted to exchange arrangements. Ray Lodwig exchanged a few. They listened plenty to Bix. Matter of fact, they tried to get some of our players. They copied a lot from Goldkette."

There was more to it than that. At first the Goldkette band played its commercial material, eliciting titters. Trumbauer, according to Sudhalter, cupped his hands around his mouth, and called to the band, "Okay, boys, let's give 'em the business." They went into *Tiger Rag*, then the Challis charts, one after another.

Rex Stewart wrote in his *Jazz Masters of the Thirties*, "We were supposed to be the world's greatest dance orchestra. And up pops this Johnny-come-lately white band from out in the sticks, cutting us . . . . We simply could not compete . . . . Their arrangements were too imaginative and their rhythm too strong . . . . We learned that Jean Goldkette's orchestra was, without any question, the greatest in the world . . . .

"You can believe me that the Goldkette band was the original predecessor to any large white dance orchestra that followed, up to Benny Goodman. Even Goodman, swinger that he was, did not come close to the tremendous sound of the Goldkette repertoire, not in quality and certainly not in quantity . . . ."

And in an interview, Stewart said, "It was pretty humiliating for us, and when the time came for us to go back on, we didn't really know what we should play. They'd covered it all, and they were swingin' like mad. Everything. Bix, for Pete's sake. You know, I worshiped Louis at that time, tried to walk like him, talk like him, even dress like him. He was God to me, and to all the others cats too. Then, all of a sudden, comes this white boy from out west, playin' stuff all his own. Didn't sound like Louis or anybody else. But just so pretty. All that *tone* he got. Knocked us all out."

Fats Waller sat in with Henderson's band that night; Miff Mole sat in with Goldkette. *Orchestra World* wrote, "Most everyone who is anything at all in the music business was present . . . . Whoever is responsible for the Goldkette arrangements should be elected to the hall of fame. They are nothing short of marvelous."

The Goldkette boys were anxious to record the Challis charts. It wasn't to be. If we owe it to Whiteman that those arrangements still exist, we owe it to a man named Eddie King—the archetype of the tin-eared record producer—that we do not have the Goldkette performances of them. King didn't like jazz, and he specifically disliked Bix, objecting to his harmonic innovations, his "wrong note" playing. His attitude foreshadowed one that Dizzy Gillespie and Charlie Parker would encounter.

Challis was working hard, turning out charts on tunes King thought would sell, material Bill referred to as "crap."

"Fletcher began to play at Connie's Inn up in Harlem," Bill said. "I was living in Greenwich, Connecticut, then. When I'd go back home to Greenwich, I'd stop in at Connie's Inn. Fletcher and I became good friends. He began to commission some arrangements from me. I wrote a lot for that band. They paid me well. Buster Bailey and Coleman Hawkins and Don Redman and Jimmy Harrison were in the band. It was a great band.

"Don Redman had been the music director of McKinney's Cotton Pickers. He'd been writing for that band and for Fletcher. He also wrote for the Goldkette band, and also the Whiteman band.

"Fletcher said, 'I want you to hear this piano player sing.' After the band played a set, they would have this guy play organ or piano and sing. It was Fats Waller.

"After I had been with Goldkette about a year, the word got out that it was going to break up. Whiteman came down to Atlantic City with Bing Crosby. Bix and I were in the band room. Bix asked Whiteman to conduct the band. Whiteman said, 'I don't know any of the arrangements.' I said, 'You don't have to know the arrangements. Just give a down beat.'" Bix went up there, and said, 'What do you want to hear?' Whiteman said, '*Tiger Rag*.' He turned around to the band, and said, 'One, two . . . ' And Bix started it off. He played the lead. And while he was doing that, who was down at the door? Goldkette. He never stood in front of the band. Very very seldom. I didn't see him, but I was told he was down there watching the whole thing." Since Spiegle Willcox similarly remembered the sudden apparition of Goldkette, the experience was obviously traumatic.

"That was our first introduction to Whiteman," Bill continued. "He said, 'You can join the band now, if you want. Or you can wait and see how it goes.' Fuzzy Farrar and some of the guys wanted to wait around New York, do records, and make money. Farrar was a great trumpet player. He could read anything, play anything. He had no trouble finding work. He worked with several bands. But other guys, guys like Ray Lodwig, didn't work much at all.

"Trumbauer and Bix got into a band called the New Yorkers, which was run by Adrian Rollini. That band played at a place called the Whiteman Club, but they were together only about ten days. I went to see Trumbauer and Bix. They were going to join Whiteman when the band got to Indianapolis. They were in the band within a couple of weeks—a very short time. As far as I was concerned, I wasn't in the band yet, but I was traveling around with them. They were playing theaters. While we were in Indianapolis, I think, Jimmy Dorsey took Paul out to wherever Hoagy Carmichael was. They brought Hoagy up to my room. I had a little organ. It belonged to the Whiteman orchestra. They always dumped it in my room, in case I got any ideas. They said, 'I want you to hear this.' Hoagy sits down and plays *Washboard Blues*.

"Whiteman was taken by it right off. Hoagy sang it and played it on the organ. Hoagy traveled around with us. We got together fairly often, talked. I got to know the tune. Two weeks later, we were in Chicago, and we recorded it. That was my first arrangement for Whiteman. That was the number, and *Changes*, both my arrangements, that we recorded that day."

We arrived back at the house on Harvey's Lake and settled in a sun porch that overlooks the water. I asked Bill about the Whiteman instrumentation. As he recalled, there were seven brass—

four trumpets and three trombones, and six saxes. Bill used three baritones on *Changes*.

Bill continued, "After that Ferde [Grofé, Whiteman's chief arranger] gave me a couple of arrangements to do. He gave me *Old Man River*. I began to get good tunes, nice tunes. And they began to get some nice results. With Goldkette, we weren't an important enough band, it seemed, that we'd get nice tunes to do.

"Bix and I were good friends, but he was a drinker. And I didn't drink. So you got a guy who didn't drink and a guy who did, so I didn't pal around with him." Bix began playing his little piano fantasias for Challis, who was impressed by them.

"He had a very creative mind," Bill said, "and when he played his own music, the second time he played it, he played it differently.

"Paul went to Jack Robbins, the music publisher, about publishing Bix's pieces. Robbins told Bix, 'You have to have this written down, so you have to play it the same way.' Even *In a Mist*, he played a little differently on the record. I had to insist, when we went over anything, that he play it again, play it again, the same way. We went through all the things that he did, and I'd say, 'Play it the same way again.' We got the things out."

Challis transcribed *In a Mist, Flashes, In the Dark, Candlelights*, and one he took off a record, *Davenport Blues*. They are all that remain of Bix Beiderbecke's piano inventions.

"The harmonic thinking was radical," Bill said. "It fit in with what I expected from him. Our thinking was very much alike, harmonically.

"Ferde was a very good friend of Eastwood Lane's. Bix used to play parts of some of that music over."

I asked, "Is it true that Bix couldn't read? Or that he just read very badly?"

"I think he read badly. I don't say he couldn't read. He'd just sit down and he had to work it out. I would write a chorus for him, or a half chorus. I'd write the harmony. Harmony didn't bother him at all. He could certainly hear it. He knew everything. What the next chord was. And I supplied it to him. The same way with Trumbauer. He could read really, I would say, a little better than Bix. But Bix could read. When he sat down alongside of Fuzzy Farrar and Ray Lodwig, he had no problem following those guys.

"He'd come to a rehearsal. He'd go over the thing. Ferde would be there. If another trumpet player was there, they'd go over it together. He could read that. No problem reading that. Especially if he was doing it with another guy who could read. He could read some. Some."

Bill made an interesting observation. He said that he had never been too swift a reader, either, adding, "I can't read too well *now*." I have known several composers who wrote with facility but could not read well; Gary McFarland was one of them. Resuming on Bix:

"There was always a gin bottle alongside the chair. On the bandstand. Usually a bottle. He didn't get loaded or anything like that. He'd have a nip. Like Harry Barris. He'd take the cork off, put it back down. He'd do that how many times, Jesus.

"He liked guys he could drink with. Frank Trumbauer didn't drink much. Trumbauer was quiet. Bix was a quiet guy too. He certainly was not a talker." (Trumbauer's widow, Mitzi, once amplified on this point. She said, "Frank was an Indian and would never use one word where none would do.")

Bix was listening to Debussy, Stravinsky, Delius, MacDowell, and Eastwood Lane, among others. "He could play most of them by ear," Bill said. "He just did it.

"I'd listen to a couple of things of Bix's and put them in an arrangement."

I remembered what Hank Jones had said about the influence of Beiderbecke on arrangers by way of his influence on Challis. I wanted to verify the point. "He influenced your arranging?"

"Oh yeah!" Bill said. And you can certainly hear it in the chart on *San*. Even in the ensemble passages, Bill has the band phrasing and thinking like Bix. It is an early and classic example of an arrangement shaped to the abilities of the musicians who are going to play it, rather than generalized ideas of the character of instruments derived from European orchestration treatises. There was no precedent for what Challis, Ellington, Carter, and Redman were doing. They had to explore this form of orchestra, saxes, brass, and rhythm. In *San,* we hear true jazz writing, shaped to the idiosyncrasies of the players, and it's brilliant. And it swings.

Bill said, "In those days we did an awful lot with interludes, modulations, and Bix had the whole book, it seemed to me. I don't know where he got that stuff. He knew *Afternoon of a Faun* backwards."

"What do you think would have become of him if he hadn't died?" I asked. It is a question that has tantalized everyone who has ever given consideration to the short meteoric life of Bix Beiderbecke.

"We talked a lot about writing piano numbers," Bill said. "He wanted to put it down on paper. He wanted to do a lot more than the five numbers."

The days of Bix, Trumbauer, Bill Rank, Venuti, and Lang in the lush and largely happy traveling circus that was the Whiteman band were coming to an end. Whiteman did all that he could for Bix, keeping him on the payroll for many months when Beiderbecke couldn't even play. Whiteman was no puritan about booze, being a toper of proportions himself. But Bix was steadily destroying himself, abetted by hale fellows whose assistance was bitterly resented by Louis Armstrong, among other friends of Bix. "Ain't nobody played like him yet," Armstrong said when Bix was dead. Long afterwards, musicians who knew and admired Bix were protective of him when they were asked about his alcoholism.

"Whiteman started to play a different kind of music," Bill said. "When we went in the band, we made a lot of records. As much as the band played theaters, whenever we'd get the chance, we made records. When we were doing so much recording, Bix and Trumbauer and a lot of the guys were in the band. But when the band started to play concerts and things like that, Bix's spot wasn't so important. It was a lot of written music. And Bix was a great faker. You'd write the background for him, and all he had to do was hear the harmony and know the tune.

"Oh. He was the greatest. All the way around."

"The band broke up in 1930, wasn't it?" I said. "The Depression was on, and Whiteman was having financial problems, and fired a whole bunch of guys."

"I was one of them. That was while we were in the Roxy. The band appeared there with George Gershwin. Eight of us got let out. There was Lennie Hayton, Joe Venuti, Bill Rank, me, a lot more.

"Then Bix died. When Bix died it was . . . too bad. We were in New York, the guys who got let out. I was freelancing. I was working a lot with Nat Shilkret, Willard Robison, Don Voorhees, different guys like that. They'd call me. And I always had the Casa Loma I could write for.

"The Casa Loma was a band that came out of Detroit, patterned after the Goldkette band. But they picked up a few things of their own. Gene Gifford was their chief arranger. They were well managed. Cork O'Keefe was their manager. He and Spike. Spike Knoblaugh. That was Glen Gray's real name, Glen Gray Knoblaugh. We used to call him Spike when he played with the Orange Blossoms in Detroit. They were on the stand opposite the Goldkette band. They were the relief band. Most of their guys were from around Detroit."

In 1927, Goldkette had formed the Orange Blossoms, which soon became the Casa Loma Orchestra. Given the collective influence of the Goldkette band, McKinney's Cotton Pickers, and the Casa Loma Orchestra, a case could be made that the swing era began in Detroit.

Bill said, "I remember I was on the street when I heard Bix was dead. I heard it from the trombone player Boyce Cullen, one of the guys in the Whiteman band. I was up around Seventy-second Street on the west side. I ran into Boyce. He said, 'Did you hear that Bix died?'

"It shocked me."

Bill stayed on in New York, writing for studio orchestras and the Casa Loma.

As an arranger, Bill was largely self-taught, although this term is dubious: formal teaching to a large extent involves steering a student to the right books, and some of them find their way without that guidance. He said, "I was looking at the orchestration books, particularly Forsythe. I could find a lot of material there. If I wanted to find out how to divide fiddles, of what the fiddles consisted, I found it out of the Forsythe book. Later on I went to Schillinger. Over at Columbia they had practically a Schillinger group. Several of the guys, Glenn Miller, Lyn Murray, Gus Levine, studied with Schillinger.

"Schillinger changed everything around. He was very arithmetical, and I could understand that. Most of the other guys could too."

A lot of musicians were making transcriptions—sixteen-inch records containing a number of tunes—for distribution under pseudonyms to 400 or so radio stations, Benny Goodman and the Dorseys among them. Bill recorded as Bob Conley and His Orchestra. In 1983, the Circle label issued two albums of this transcription material recorded in February 1936, by Challis. The string section comprised ten violins, three violas, and a cello. The sax section, which included Artie Shaw and Larry Binyon, was five men, including a baritone. Charlie Margulis and Manny Klein were in the trumpets, and Jack Jenney and Will Bradley among the trombone players, with Frank Signorelli on piano, Dick McDonough on guitar, Artie Bernstein on bass, and Chauncey Morehouse on drums. Not even that illustrious group could make the Challis chart on *Clarinet Marmalade* swing: the orchestra was too big. The music might be described as pre-Muzak, thick and sweet. It was what the radio stations wanted. The time is four-square and corny. The writing is intelligent, the playing fully professional. But it is bland stuff.

"That's what we did for a living," said Artie Shaw in 1988, listening to this material. "The Challis sessions were better than most. They were coherent. At CBS all the jazz bands were incorporated into the Howard Barlow Symphony for an hour of music by something called the Columbians. That was impossible music. When you have a hundred men playing *You're My Everything*, you know you're going to have a least twenty-five guys playing doubles. That is irrational music, man. On a break, after we'd been doing *You're My Everything*, which was the song of the week, we heard this strange sound, you couldn't tell where it had started. It began '*Myaaaaaaaah . . .* ', this weird keening noise, and it was Jerry Colonna, who was in the trombone section, going 'Myaaaaa're my everything . . . ' and all the guys in the band cracked up. It was the thing he used to do later on the Bob Hope show.

"Another time I was in a studio orchestra playing these dumb, square eighth notes, and I couldn't stand it, and I fingered the high F key without using the octave key, which produces a kind of duck sound on the alto saxophone, and I was going quack-quack-quack. The orchestra was so big and loud that the conductor couldn't hear it. This was live radio, remember. At the end of it, the conductor held up his thumb and index finger in an O, to indicate 'Perfect.' Larry Binyon, who was sitting beside me, could hardly finish the tune for laughing.

"We did things like that to keep from going crazy. And we went up to Harlem to play jazz."

Challis freelanced through the rest of the decade and into the forties, writing for Charlie Barnet (for whom he arranged, improbably enough, *Ave Maria*), Mark Warnow, Nat Shilkret, Willard Robison, Lennie Hayton, Raymond Paige, and Glenn Miller. The chart on Miller's *Guess I'll Go Back Home This Summer* is Bill's. He went on staff with Artie Shaw, who formed his first band not long after the Challis transcription sessions. Bill arranged *Blues in the Night, This Time the Dream's on Me*, and *Make Love to Me* for Shaw.

"With Artie, you seldom made an arrangement by yourself," he said. "He usually worked on the tune with you. He was right there."

The cordial and even casual mixing of black and white musicians that went on in private and in the recording studio and certainly for arrangers—with Don Redman writing for Whiteman and Bill writing for Fletcher Henderson—still was unacceptable in public performance. Bill said, "The trumpet player we had—Hot Lips Page—Artie cancelled a whole trip through the south because they didn't want to have Page. Guys in the band told me that Page once walked around all night because he couldn't find a place to stay." Shaw too tells of the hardships endured; traveling with a white band was hard on Roy Eldridge, too, and particularly Billie Holiday. The segregation of bands came not from the musicians but from the public and, more to the point, the people who booked the bands. The bigots of the Bible Belt would ultimately get Nat Cole's TV show knocked off the air.

In 1936, Bill returned for a time to the Whiteman band, but there was really no place for Whiteman in the Swing Era, when the public expected each bandleader to be an instrumentalist, ideally a hot jazz player. The last of the 185 arrangements Bill wrote for Whiteman was *Sittin' on a Rainbow*.

He continued with the Casa Loma, by now billed as Glen Gray and His Casa Loma Orchestra. He said, "We got Bobby Hackett in the band for a while, and Red Nichols. Red was a great studio man. If he had a chorus to do, he'd even write the notes out and play them exactly. He was meticulous about what he put down for records. I liked Red. He was a great guy to work with. A great studio man. He wasn't a Beiderbecke, by any means."

The war years came. Bix had been dead ten years. Trumbauer, who had been in the navy in World War I, was now a test pilot. He went back to music briefly after the war, then gave it up and returned to aeronautics. He died in 1947.

Something sad happened to Bill Challis along the way. He was married for a time. How and when his marriage ended I do not know. And I sensed, in my conversation with Evan Challis, that the subject was a sensitive one. I pressed no questions about it.

I stayed overnight at Harvey's Lake, then had lunch again with Evan and Bill. We drove into Wilkes-Barre. Evan and Bill still own the building on a street corner in which their father had his barber shop. Where the barber chairs and mirrors once were are filing cabinets and shelves holding the memorabilia and some of the music of the life of Bill Challis that Evan has collected. Among other things, Evan has saved the many volumes on orchestration Bill studied at the time when he "just picked up" arranging. I felt strangely moved as I examined charts written in Bill's young neat hand in the early 1920s on printed score paper laid out for three trumpets, two trombones, three saxes, and rhythm section. Bill seems almost indifferent to his place in history. Evan, a salesman by profession and archivist by default, is not.

We shook hands and parted on that street corner in a modest neighborhood where these two soft, gentle men had grown up.

Not long after I got back to California, I received an envelope from Evan and Bill. It contained the transcriptions of *In a Mist* and the other piano pieces that Bill had made for Bix so long ago. I copied them and sent them to Hank Jones.

Once more I was talking to Benny Carter about Bill. I asked him again about Bill's influence. He repeated what he said in New York, his voice inflecting italics, "Bill Challis was my *idol*." And he added, "Will you be talking to him?"

"Yes."

"Please give him my love."

I did.

A Day with Herb Ellis

One afternoon a few years ago, I found myself standing behind a red-haired musician in a line of people waiting to check into a hotel at a jazz festival. At the time I knew him about well enough to say hello. I leaned close to him and sang, very softly:

> It was many and many a year ago
> in a kingdom by the sea
> that a maiden there lived
> whom you may know
> by the name of Annabel Lee.

The words were the opening stanza of Poe's *Annabel Lee*.

Herb Ellis turned, startled, and looked me in the face. "Where in the world did you learn that?" he said.

"In some club in Toronto that you and Lou Carter and John Frigo played when you were the Soft Winds. I can't remember the name of the room. It was probably not long after you guys set that to music."

"You must be the only guy in the world besides us who knows it," Herb said. "I don't even have a lead sheet on it."

"I do. Frigo gave me a copy in Chicago."

"Would you send me one?"

"Sure," I said. And subsequently I did.

The song is a memento of a superb trio that is now almost forgotten, as well as a phase in the career of Herb Ellis that few of his admirers even know about. I knew the song well not simply from casual hearings in a nightclub but from sitting at the piano, analyzing it, impressed by the way Ellis, pianist Lou Carter, and bassist John Frigo had turned a piece of classic metric poetry into song. The ability to lift poetry off paper and into persuasive fluent melody is far rarer than is generally realized. And they had done that to Poe's dark poem.

Nat Cole had established one of two classic trio formations, piano, bass, and guitar; the other being piano, bass, and drums. And a number of trios had been formed on the Cole pattern, including the Page Cavanaugh Trio, whose pianist leader, like Cole, sang. The Soft Winds used the Cole instrumentation, but there the resemblance ended, for the singing too was in trio, and they did adventurous things. They never became a famous recording group and, except for some of their songs, the group is all but forgotten, except by those who heard it.

There are five phases to the career of Herb Ellis, whose name would turn up on almost every guitarist's list of his favorite guitarists. After he left his native Texas, there was a period of working with bands about which, until recently, I knew absolutely nothing. Then there is the Soft Winds phase, followed by the period that made him famous in the jazz world, a six-year tenure with the Oscar Peterson Trio. After that Herb worked in the studios of Los Angeles, emerging to play in clubs and at festivals. Then he walked away from the studio work and has in recent years been touring, devoting himself entirely to playing jazz.

A high percentage of the finest jazz guitarists have been from the south and southwest, including Charlie Christian and Barney Kessel, both from Oklahoma, Tal Farlow from Greensboro, North Carolina, Freddie Green from Charleston, South Carolina, Jimmy Raney from Louisville, Kentucky, Mundell Lowe from Laurel, Mississippi, and Wes Montgomery from Indianapolis, Indiana, although northeastern cities have contributed a few too—Kenny Burrell from Detroit, Gene Bertoncini and Chuck Wayne from New York City, Jim Hall from Buffalo and Cleveland, George Benson from Pittsburgh, and Bucky Pizzarelli from Paterson, New Jersey. With his Texas roots, Ellis is solidly in that south-southwestern contingent, and his playing has an incomparable earthiness and swing.

Even Herb's approach to the instrument is somehow uniquely his. He sits low in a chair, right ankle on left knee, the instrument at a slant as it rests on the raised leg. A lot of piano players sing what they are playing. Herb seems to chew every note he plays. As one bites one's tongue in threading a needle, Herb works his jaw in a way that bespeaks a total physical involvement with the music. He seems to make music with his whole body.

The instrument called the guitar in jazz should probably have another name. The true guitar is an unamplified flat-bodied instrument strung in earlier times with gut strings and later, after Segovia made them acceptable even to purists, nylon. It descends from a family of instruments developed primarily in Spain. A guitar with steel strings evolved comparatively early, and it is this instrument that is widely used in the folk music of the United States. The steel-stringed guitar has more volume than one strung with gut or nylon, but not enough to make it competitive to horns in jazz groups. Not until the development of amplification was it possible to play long-lined solos that you could hear over the surrounding din, and it was then that the instrument took its place as an important jazz voice. The credit for pioneering the instrument usually goes to Charlie Christian, although Alvino Rey played an amplified instrument before Christian. But Christian was the first great creative soloist on this instrument, as Alvino Rey, who is now active as a classical guitarist, is the first to insist.

The character of the "amplified guitar" is as different from that of the historical guitar as that of an electric organ from a piano. Although they have the same tuning, E A D G B E', which forms an E minor seventh chord with an eleventh added, they are different in all other ways. The classical guitar has a strongly contrapuntal character. It is even built differently, the fingerboard being flat with the strings fairly far apart. The amplified "jazz" guitar has a slightly convex fingerboard and strings set closer together. The tones produced on a classical guitar decay rapidly; those produced on an amplified guitar have a long life, which lends to the instrument some of the nature of a wind instrument. Charlie Christian's great contribution was his perception that this was a new instrument, not simply a louder one, and his exploration of its possibilities through the exercise of a wonderful melodic imagination that made him a harbinger of bebop. This much the two instruments do have in common: as the late Hugo Friedhofer, who loved it, used to put it, "The guitar is an unforgiving instrument." There is no instrument on which it is easier to play a little, and badly, than the guitar—and no instrument on which it is harder to play a lot, and well.

It is common now for guitarists to play both instruments. Herb has remained devoted to the jazz guitar alone, although he has played other plectrum instruments in the studios. He is at the pinnacle, one of the great jazz guitarists and one of the most powerful jazz players on any instrument.

Mitchell Herbert Ellis was born August 4, 1921, four miles south of Farmersville, Texas, a hamlet of two thousand souls when he came into the world, about forty miles northeast of Dallas. This is astonishing, in view of the vigor of his playing and the cherubic youthfulness of his appearance. The red hair has faded and thinned a little now, but Herb has an eternal boyishness about him. His coloring is that of his Scottish and Irish forebears. His skin has that clear texture of one who does not smoke or drink.

Herb has been a member of Alcoholics Anonymous for more than thirty years. "I still go to meetings," he says. "It helps me keep a focus." His lapses have been few, although, as he said a few years ago, "When I fall off the wagon, the crash is heard around the world." No doubt this is because Herb seems like a pillar of sanity to those who know him, a man who has conquered a flaw, whether of heredity or habit being irrelevant. One could say of Herb what someone said of his late and much-missed friend Shelly

Manne: I never saw him in a social or professional situation to which he did not contribute something positive. Herb is a joy to play with, a joy to be with.

His two children are long since gone from home, and he and his wife Patti gave up their condominium in Studio City, California, to move to Fairfield Bay, Arkansas, next to a golf course. It doesn't matter where they live, providing there is a golf course handy, because he is away so much of the time, playing. Not long before they left California, I spent a pleasant laughing afternoon filling the gaps in my knowledge of him.

"I played the harmonica first, when I was about three," Herb said as we sat in his living room, the conversation accompanied by the slow tick of a big clock. "I have not too much recollection of that, but I can still play it. They thought I had some musical talent, so my sister bought a banjo for me. I learned to play the banjo. I got a little book, learned how to tune it, and I played the banjo. I must have been about six or seven. Then, a little later, a cousin—one of my city cousins—left a guitar at our house. My older brother wanted to play music with me. He tuned this guitar, but he tuned it incorrectly. He tuned it in a way that you could just hit all the strings at one time and it would make a major chord. He'd just bar across, and get all major chords."

"What did he do about the two top strings?"

"Well, it just sounded, parallel triads. I knew this was not right. So I got a book from Sears, Roebuck and learned how to tune it and play it, and then I showed him how to play it. So then we played together, banjo and guitar. Then I learned to play the guitar, and I played the guitar more, because I liked it a lot better. I just played. I listened to the radio. We had no recordings out there except a couple of things by a singer named Gene Austin."

"I remember him. I remember him well."

"Well he had a guitar player with him who sounded terrific. I can't think of his name. And so I learned to play a little of his stuff. I don't know what I was playing. It wasn't jazz, it wasn't hillbilly. Some country tunes. Then I went to high school. I got a little amplifier from Sears Roebuck, and another guitar. And I'd play

for the high school assemblies. Then I went to college, to North
Texas State University."

"You must have been one of the first musicians to go to North
Texas State!"

"Ever," he said.

"There was no jazz program then."

"No. I was there at the same time Jimmy Giuffre was. I'll tell
you who else was there—Gene Roland and Harry Babasin. Shortly
after I had been there, majoring in music, I played on the Satur-
day night stage show. They had a stage band, and Jimmy Giuffre
was in it, and Harry Babasin. And I played *Back Home Again in
Indiana*, and I played it pretty fast. I had a lot of technique. I could
play fast, play a lot of notes . . ."

"You still can."

"They heard me, and then they came to me, and asked me to
move into a house where they lived together. Two-oh-four Normal
Street was the address. They said, 'You've got the talent, but your
music is meaningless.' They told me this. They said, 'You're really
headed in the wrong direction.' That hurt my feelings. And then
they said, 'Listen to this guy.' And they played Charlie Christian
for me. The Benny Goodman Sextet records, after I'd moved in
the house with them. They said, 'Now what do you think of that?'
And I remember what I said. Very childish. I said, 'Well, he sounds
good. But what's the big deal? I can play a lot faster than that.' I
said that."

"Oh no. You know, I once made the mistake of saying something like that to Red Norvo about Bix."

"Oh boy."

"Red is too much a gentleman to get nasty, but he quietly let
me know. I said something like, he didn't play very many notes. I
was about twenty at the time. And Red said, 'He didn't have to.'"

"When we're young we often have our priorities in the wrong
places. Well, they said, 'You haven't got the message yet. Listen
some more.' So I listened some more to Charlie Christian. I don't
know whether it was the same day or the next day, but it wasn't a
long time, and it really hit me, like a spiritual awakening, what he

was doing that I didn't do. How much depth he had. How great it sounded. And how scummy and shallow I sounded. His playing sounded deep and mine sounded shallow. I was very upset, very distraught. So I put the guitar underneath the bed, and said, 'That's it. I've just got too far to go.' It stayed there about one day. Then I got it out. Now I went from all notes to no notes. Each note had to drip with emotion and be sent from heaven. I went from one extreme ridiculously the other way. So that's how I got some of the direction. The other direction I got, which has been with me ever since, came from Count Basie. I loved Count Basie, and Lester Young was very appealing to me. They had a big influence. We had some records of Jimmie Lunceford. They were very meaningful to me. That was a great band. And Earl Hines had a great band. And I heard Dizzy Gillespie with Cab Calloway before he was playing bebop. I had some Coleman Hawkins. But the main influences were Charlie Christian and Lester Young. Then, later, when I heard Charlie Parker and Dizzy together, that was a big influence. So those are my influences, and that's the way I've always played. I've never tried to change it. I've just tried to get better. As you get older, you get deeper, more mature. I'm sort of suspicious of people who change styles.''

"Because the music obviously is not a manifestation of their own personality.''

"It's not a big commitment.''

"A guitarist friend of mine says that Django Reinhardt is more honored in conversation than in actual influence.''

"I believe that's true. However, during all that time, I did hear Django and I liked him, but not as well as I liked Charlie Christian.''

"Christian electrified me when I was a kid. And there was a guitarist in the Billy Mills Orchestra on the Fibber McGee and Molly program.''

"Oh sure, I remember that. He played a little break in the theme. I tell you who it was. Botkin. Perry Botkin.''

"I heard a young guy a year or so ago who played like Eddie Lang.''

"Eddie Lang was tremendous. But I never heard him until later. I'll tell you who else I listened to, and who was another influence on me. George Barnes. I used to hear him on the radio from Chicago. A program called *The Plantation Party*. He had a spot on that show, and I used to hear him every week. I was very impressed with George Barnes."

"Where did you go from North Texas State? Did you graduate?"

"No. I went a couple of years, and the money was very short. So I went on the road with a big jazz band from the University of Kansas, led by Charlie Fisk. That band lasted a few months, and then we had to give it up. Charlie Fisk, he was a trumpet player, and I both had offers to go with Russ Morgan."

"That ain't exactly your groove."

"It wasn't my groove, but the reason I was hired was to play in a quartet context—plus playing with the band—with Joe Mooney, the accordionist."

"Oh, dear dear Joe. I never knew Joe was with Russ Morgan."

"Yeah, he was there. So we played some little jobs together, Joe and myself and a clarinet player and a bass player who is now a priest. Russ Morgan just petrified me. He ruled with an iron hand. If you made a mistake, he just zeroed in on you, he just scared me to death. So we were playing a theater somewhere, and I got sick, so they had to go on to the next theater and I said I'll meet you there. I never met 'em, I just split. I went to Kansas City and stayed about a year. That was about 1941. I just got the tale end of Charlie Parker. That was right before he joined Dizzy. A friend of mine, a saxophone player I'd met earlier on the Charlie Fisk band, was in Kansas City, and he was always telling me about Charlie Parker. He called him Bird, and he was trying to explain how he played. So when I went to Kansas City, he said, 'I want you to hear this guy.' He was playing out at Tootie's Mayfair, or some little place. And he said, 'Get your guitar and I'll get my sax, and we'll go out, and we'll play, we'll sit in. They know me.' This tenor saxophonist had perfect pitch, and ears, a sensational musician. So we went out to this little dark club, and we got on the stand, and Charlie Parker was sitting 'way in the back. And the first tune that they played was *Cherokee*. And they played it fast. I'd never heard *Cherokee*. The rhythm section was just playing for two or three choruses. When they got to the bridge, it was very foreign to me, I didn't know what was happening. At that time, that type of tune was not played. So the saxophone player called out the changes. And now Charlie Parker started playing. I'd never heard anything like this. I hadn't heard Dizzy then, except with Cab Calloway's band. I heard this and it sounded beautiful, but I had no idea what this guy was doing. So he played several choruses, and when he got through, they looked at me and said, 'You got it.' Well young and dumb don't have to go together. So I said, 'No thanks.' I mean, what am I going to do after that? So the rhythm section played three or four more choruses, Charlie Parker came back in and played another fifteen choruses. And then later on, we played something I knew at a reasonable tempo. Then I played. But what a shock that was. One of the biggest musical shocks of my whole life. It was a unique situation. I just love the memory of it. I don't know whether I dug him instantly. I knew it was different, and it sounded good, I suspected how good it was, but I was still championing Lester Young. Which you always should. Guys would say, 'Bird is the new thing,' and I'd say, 'No, man, Lester Young is it forever.' But it did have a great impact, and later on I learned not only to like it but to love it."

"What happened after Kansas City?"

"Oooh . . . From Kansas City? Oh yeah, Glen Gray. Glen Gray and the Casa Loma came through. I went with them and stayed a couple of years, and then I went with Jimmy Dorsey. From '45 to '47, when I went with the Soft Winds, then from '47 almost until I went with Oscar Peterson I was with the Soft Winds."

"How did that group come about?"

"We were all with Jimmy Dorsey."

"Lou Carter and John Frigo were also with Jimmy Dorsey?"

"Yes."

"Then you were three-quarters of the rhythm section."

"And we left. Together. And Jimmy was very unhappy. We went

to Buffalo and played at the Peter Stuyvesant, then we went to Canada a couple of times and played at the . . . "

"At the Zebra Lounge! That's what it was called! It was right across from the *Globe and Mail*. That's when I first knew you guys."

"The Zebra Lounge! That's right. Ray Brown heard me there."

"That was a wonderful group. How did you get the idea for that group?"

"We'd been playing together, and we'd get together when we could, and John Frigo, the bass player, got this job at the Peter Stuyvesant Hotel in Buffalo for a trio. We really liked playing together, and we had some great arrangements, if you remember. Magnificent arrangements, not just little heads, not just little-bitty first and last choruses."

"It was an orchestrated trio. Both instrumentally and vocally. Very hip."

"Orchestrated. That's exactly what it was. And Oscar heard me with that group."

"That group really was ahead of its time. Harmonically, my memory tells me it was kind of like what Gene Puerling was doing later with the Hi-Lo's."

"Sort of. That's very close. Well I stayed with them, and John left, and the group was dissipating. It lasted about five years."

"You guys wrote some marvelous things. *Detour Ahead* and that wonderful thing on *Annabel Lee*."

"*I Told You I Love You, Now Get Out*. That was ours. Woody recorded that. We had another one called *Ninety-nine Guys*."

"' . . . have eyes for Liza, but Liza has eyes for me.' Do you still get any ASCAP royalties on it?"

"Yeah, I just got $121 day before yesterday. People still record it."

"You went with Oscar, and Lou did some albums on his own."

"He made some albums as Lou the Taxi Driver, with all his funny songs."

"Marvelous wacky titles. *If I Had a Nose Full of Nickels*, I'd sneeze them all atchoo."

"Funny and well written, the rhyme and everything. It was great. He was on the Perry Como show several times, and did very well. He moved to Newark and started a jingles business."

"And Frigo went to Chicago and worked with Dick Marx, and Dick went into the jingles business too."

"And John did a lot of jingles too."

"Do you ever see Lou?"

"I saw Lou when I played Gulliver's over in New Jersey. And I always see John when I play Chicago."

"So what happened after the Soft Winds?"

"Well I was going to go home to Texas. Oscar called me and said that Barney was leaving and going back to Los Angeles."

"Barney Kessel was only with Oscar a short time, wasn't he?"

"Just about a year. Oscar remembered me from the Soft Winds. He came over to Buffalo to hear us and played with us. And he remembered that, because he's got perfect memory."

"It's creepy. He's rattled me with it a few times."

"He's done it to me too. He's got total recall. It's eerie. So he asked me to go with them. So I went down to New York, to hear them play. It was awesome. They didn't have nearly as many arrangements as they did when I had been with them a while. But they had a lot of them and I could hear how hard it was going to be. But I just said, well, I'm gonna give it a try. So I went with them and I was there until 1958, I guess. Six years. That period was one of the highlights of my life and my career—playing with Oscar and Ray. The challenge that Oscar put on me and put on Ray and put on himself. So you couldn't have any qualms about it, he made it as hard for himself as he did for everybody."

"Ray told me that Oscar would say, 'Can this be done on the instrument?' And Ray would say, 'I don't think so.' And Oscar would say, 'Well I think it can.' And he would end up doing it."

"Exactly. You'd end up doing it, after a lot of sweat and practice. And Oscar would say, 'See, I told you.' It was very difficult, but the rewards were well worth it. Because we reached musical and emotional heights that you don't reach very often. We reached some musical peaks that I doubt I will ever attain again. It was a trio where we were totally involved with each other, musically and personally. There was a lot going for it."

"Oscar and I were talking about the difficulty of judging your own work. I've talked to Dizzy about it too. Oscar was putting down critics, and I said, 'Hey, just a minute, have you ever been wrong about your own work?' He said, 'Yes, now that you mention it.' And he told me about an evening when he came off the stand in a club, somewhere, and he was mad as hell. Ray Brown said, 'What do you expect of this group?' And Oscar said, 'Just a little music.'"

"Sure," Herb Said. "It was in Chicago. At London House."

"Oscar had tapes of it, and started listening, and then he called Ray. You and Ray were rooming together."

"Did he tell you the end of it? He called Ray about five in the morning and said that *Sweet Georgia Brown* was just great, and Ray said, 'We knew that last night,' and hung up on him."

"You know, Oscar has received so many rotten reviews . . . . "

"Oh man, yes."

"What did you think of them?"

"At present he doesn't get bad reviews, but then he did, and we were very conscious of them. They all said the same thing, in essence. It's cold, it's mechanical. Granted he's a technician of the piano, but he's got no definitive style. First of all, they're really not hearing him. They're not hearing the depth of it. They're only hearing the surface. They're only hearing a lot of notes. Because sometimes he does play a lot of notes. Of course I'm not saying that's bad. I think they arrive at the conclusion that if you have a tendency to play a lot of notes, it's got to be cold. They miss the point. They just miss the whole point. I've played with a lot of people, and a lot of piano players. I've never played with anybody who had more depth and more emotion and feeling in his playing. He can play so hot and so deep and earthy that it just shakes you when you're playing with him. Ray and I have come off the stand just shook up. I mean, he is heavy. If you're not up to hearing it, well that's your loss. I won't even discuss it with anybody, because there's nothing to discuss. If that's the depth of their hearing, then we don't have anything to talk about. You can listen to the first two or three choruses of some of his solos. Sometimes he plays very sparingly. And it's grooving, it's about as hot as you can get. Then later on he may play faster and double it up to give it some build and some flavor. You see, most piano players end where he starts."

"There's a bit at the start of *Our Love Is Here to Stay* that he did with Ed Thigpen and Ray, in which he plays . . . " I sang the little figure to Herb. "He bends the note up, or seems to. He creates the illusion of a rising glissando, like a trumpet. He delays the first note slightly until he's into the second, and it's like a doit. I have never heard anyone else do that on a piano."

"Yes. And his ballad playing is absolutely lovely. Harmonically, it's quite involved. It's Tatumish. And he's got a love for playing the melody. I hope I have that too. And the sound that he gets out of a piano is so lyrical. If you have to name the world's best piano player, I can't see that there is much competition. There might be somebody that somebody personally would like better. But as far as playing the piano, and I'm not just talking about chops, I'm talking about all of it, the feeling, the emotion, he's the man."

"Tatum to me never had the rhythmic drive that Oscar has."

"No. Art Tatum didn't have the deep hard swing that Oscar has. I'm not taking away from him. Oscar has that earthy, deep commitment of swing."

"What caused you to leave the trio finally?"

"Patti and I were married while I was with Oscar. I met Patti out here in California. She's from Oklahoma. First we had Kari, and then Mitch was on the way, and we moved out here."

"To stay in one place?"

"To stay in one place. I've made several moves in my life where I didn't know what was going to happen. Of course I had some name value, but how did I know I was going to get into the studios? I wanted to. And it happened. I did seventeen years of it. I went first with the Steve Allen show, with Donn Trenner, about 1960. Ella Fitzgerald called me, wanted me go with her, and she made me a really good offer. So I went with her for about a year and a half and then I did come back and stayed."

"What was that incident with the *Bell Telephone Hour?*"

"We did a Bell Telephone television show, with Gus Johnson and Wilfrid Middlebrooks. I was the leader and I was the only white guy in the group. So they told Norman Granz, 'Now we will want to use another guitar player.' And Norman said, 'What?' And he found out the reason."

"Because they wouldn't have a white and black on camera at the same time?"

"Right. And Norman found this out, and said, not only would I not do it for that reason, but they had to use me, because I was the leader. Well, they diffused the picture, with vaseline on the lens, so you couldn't tell who was back there. Norman took out a two-page ad in *Variety* about it. And he wiped them out."

"You had a good relationship with Norman."

"He was very good to me. He was very understanding at that time when I was struggling with booze. The problem had hit me and I really didn't know I had a problem. We didn't know about alcoholism, he didn't know, Oscar didn't know. But he knew that that I missed the plane to Europe and some incidents later . . . I was a periodic type drinker. And Norman and Oscar must have known innately that I wasn't a bad guy. That the sickness, when I would drink, would make me do those things. He stuck with me. He told Oscar, after the second time when I fouled up with that group, 'You know, I don't want to get into your business, it's your group, but I wouldn't get rid of him.'"

"What would happen? You just wouldn't make the gig for a few days?"

"I'd get so sick. We'd have time off and I'd start to drink. I never drank on the job. When I was with them, I hardly ever drank. But we'd have some time off, I'd start to drink, and it would be okay for a few days, and then it would get the best of me. One time I got so sick in New York that I just couldn't make the plane. I couldn't get the passport, I couldn't get the transformer I needed, I just got so screwed up, so sick, I just had to call A.A., and they put me in a hospital. And then it happened again a year or so later. Oscar was very understanding about it. And then the second time it happened, nobody knew where I was for a month.''

"Not even you?''

"I only knew I was in New York, just surviving from drink to drink and day to day. I couldn't make any moves, because if I'd stopped I'd have gone into D.T.'s or shock or something. I didn't know that, of course. I even made Walter Winchell's column.''

"For what?''

"'Where is the red-headed guitar player?' Because nobody knew where I was. My folks didn't even know.''

"Now what about the practical jokes? I've heard so many stories.''

"You didn't hear the story, did you, about Ray Brown and me dying our hair opposite colors? This was out here in California. We had a day off. Ray and I played golf, which we did frequently. On the way home from the golf course, late in the afternoon, we were walking from the bus, and we passed a drug store. And there was a new thing in the window. It said, 'Dye your hair any color, and if you don't like it, you can shampoo it out immediately.' I said, 'Hey, I got an idea. We'll buy some red dye and black dye. I'll dye my hair black and you dye yours red, and we'll call Oscar over to the apartment, and there'll be a lot of fun.' Ray said, 'Okay,' but he looked at me as if I manufactured this stuff, and he said, 'Are you sure this shit's gonna wash out?' I said, 'I don't know. That's what it says.' He said, 'It better.' It's late in the afternoon, and we dye our hair. Ray's is this flaming, sickening light red, and mine was jet black. We call Oscar. We said, 'How you doin'?' He said, 'Fine.' I said, 'We need to see you.' He said, 'Wha'dyou mean, you need to see me? You saw me last night, you see me every day. I'm on my way out to dinner with some people.' I said, 'Well there's something we gotta talk about.' He said, 'Well, we'll talk about it tomorrow.' I said, 'Well this can't wait till tomorrow. We gotta talk to you, man. It's semi-serious. Why don't you just drive by on your way out?' He said, 'What's the matter with you guys?' 'Just come by,' I said. He said, 'Okay.' Ray's in a chair, reading the paper, Oscar knocks on the door. I open the door, and he says, 'Hey, Herb, hey, Ray. Well, what do you guys want?' Looking right at us. He didn't crack a smile. He said, 'What did you want?' Ray said, 'Don't you get it?' He said, 'Get what?' He said, 'You guys detained me from my dinner.' He said, 'Get out of here. I'll see you tomorrow.' Next day we told him about it, and he maintained for a year that he never noticed anything. Now that's control, isn't it?"

"It sure is. What would he do to you in turn?"

"He would untune a guitar string during intermission, and get your attention when we went up to the point where you wouldn't even touch the guitar. He could do that. He could keep you talking like that, and then it would be, Here we go. Or sometimes he would look like he was retuning it, and then he would start the tune in another key, up a tone or half a tone down.

"In 1953, the first big jazz tour ever in Japan, Jazz at the Philharmonic . . . it started with Norman and Oscar playing a joke on Ray. Ray and I were in the wings. We played with Ella. We played with everybody. Ray was standing backstage, waiting to come on with Ella, and Norman introduced us all, with Ray last, right before Ella. And Oscar had tuned Ray's G-string down, a lot. Then he got Ray's attention while Norman was announcing, some way he kept Ray from hitting the strings. And then Norman introduced Ray Brown and then Ella, right on top of it, so we walked out, and bang! counted off and hit. And Ray started to play, and the string was just loose, dunk dunk. And Ella wasn't reacting too nicely to this. And she's giving him a lot of rays back there. And Ray looks over at Oscar, and Oscar and Norman are just guffawing. And Ray said, 'Okay, all right.' Ray can take a practical joke, but he's not one to play it on, because he can really pay it back.

"Ray went out between shows. There's a game over there called Perchinco, and if you win you get a lot of little steel balls, and when you have a hundred, you turn them in and you get packs of cigarettes or whatever. Ray played and won a lot of little steel balls, which he put in his pocket. So now we came back. Oscar, during that show, his hands were hurting a little bit. First time he made his entrance was when we did the ballads part. So he walks out to great applause. Bill Harris is walking out from the other wing to play his ballad. It's dark and I see Ray lean into the piano. I have no idea what he's doing. He's scattering these little steel balls right across the strings. It's Bill's ballad, so he says, '*But Beautiful.*'

"Oscar starts to take the intro, and every note is brrr, brrr, brrr, it sounds like a whorehouse piano. He knew that Ray did it and he's taking them out of the piano and flinging them at Ray and they're hitting the bass. And Bill Harris is suffering out there. So we finally wade through that. And Bill Harris comes over to the piano and says to Oscar, 'One day, one day.' And nothing happened during that tour. Not till we got to Rome the next year."

"The Rome Opera House, wasn't it? What happened exactly?"

"In those theaters over there, they serve Cokes and booze and beer and everything backstage. You can order them. Bill Harris overheard Norman talking to the trio before we went on. Norman asked Oscar to sing. Oscar was very hesitant. Norman said, 'Sing something. To them it's a foreign language. It'd be just right for you.' So Oscar said, 'Okay, I'll sing *Tenderly.*' So Bill gets the waiter and gives him some lire, and gets one of those big trays, and piles it up with glasses and empty bottles, and puts it up on a ladder, and just waits back there. Oscar starts, and it's quiet, man. I remember it was one of those true dramatic stages that slant down, a raked stage. Norman is standing right in the back, you could just see him. He's loving the trio. And Oscar, he was kind of nervous, he goes, 'The evening breeze . . . caressed the trees . . . tenderly,' and when he goes 'tenderly,' Bill Harris gives a push, and crash! Oh! It went on, forever! Crash! Brang! And it went on, and on, like it was never going to stop."

"Bill ran upstairs, so he could come down like he heard it. And nobody copped out on him. For a long time. Because Norman was so mad. Nobody told on him."

"What happened after you came out to California?"

"I became Mr. Television. I did the Steve Allen show, the Danny Kaye show, the Red Skelton show. At one time I was doing the Della Reese show in the morning, five days a week, and the Joey

Bishop show in the evening. I did all the movie calls and record dates, and played whatever they wanted, I was there to do it, from banjo to wah-wah pedal. Then I did Merv Griffin's show up until a few years ago."

"We talked once about what the studios do to your playing."

"The studios take a lot from your playing. It takes the stamina, the longevity, out of your chops. You can't play hard or fast or intense for a very long time after you've played a lot of studio work. I never stopped playing jazz. I'd play maybe once every two weeks. My ability to play strong jazz and sustain it did diminish, but not as much as with some people, because being with Oscar all those years, I had built up such reserve stamina and technique that it lasted me through those years. So the transition to coming back into playing wasn't that hard. And that's all I do now. I'm either home like this, or I'm out on the road, playing. And when I do play, most of the time, because of a suggestion of Ray Brown, I don't use a piano. I've liked it."

"You do have a conflict with a trio with piano and guitar, because you have two harmonic instruments."

"Yeah. Unless you get someone very sensitive. I love to play with Roger Kellaway, and I love to play with Ross Tompkins. There are a few piano players around that I do like to play with if I can get 'em, but when I go out to most towns and have to get a rhythm section, I just get bass and drums. I'm doing that, and I'm very happy doing it, and my playing seems stronger than it's ever been. Musically, and in depth."

"Does playing in studios get in the way of your inventive thinking?"

"Absolutely. The only invention you're doing is giving them the type of sound they want. They might say, 'Give me some kind of a swamp beat.' But that's not really inventing. It's coming up with the jive they want."

"The conception of a line, the development of a little piece of material into logical continuity, does the studio get in the way of that, your mental chops?"

"Sure. First of all, you're not creating. And the stuff you are playing is a deterrent to the creation of good logical music. You're on a rock date, and they want you to play the wah-wah, and you create a certain sound. Well who's going to use the wah-wah when you're playing *Stella by Starlight*? Or you have to play the banjo or the ukelele or the twelve-string."

"Did you do all that? Folk dates and all that?"

"Yes sir, all that. Rock and roll dates. I made a lot of money just playing that chick-tick-whack, chick-tick-whack. It's a funny way to make a living. And the music you're playing and the music you hear coming out of the orchestra, be it big or small, is for the most part very low-grade. Sometimes you'll get a Johnny Mandel date, but not often, and most of what you play is pretty trashy. And you hear that, if you have a big day, from eight o'clock in the morning until twelve at night. You hear that crap. So that's gotta sink in. Got to."

"I believe that if you do that enough and rationalize it enough, it'll destroy your standards of taste."

"Absolutely. I can name guys it's done that to, and so could you."

"When Tom Scott left the studios to put a group together, I asked him why he did it. He said, 'I got tired of playing music I didn't like for people I didn't like.'"

"That's right on it. And there's usually somebody in charge who knows far less than you do about music, and you have to do what they want."

"You did jingles too?"

"Yep."

"But you got your family raised."

"Got 'em raised."

"You stayed sober."

"Most of the time! Ninety-eight percent of the time. I'm sober today."

"Did you feel with the kids raised, you could now do that riskier thing of just going out and playing, fulfill your responsibilities to yourself?"

"Yeah, I just needed it. I did it kind of slick, if I do say so. I was

doing the Merv Griffin show. And I would take a week's engagement here and there. I'd go out for a week, and come back for a
month. I'd use a sub on the show. Pretty soon I'd be gone for four
weeks, I'd come back for three days, and I'd be gone again. And
I got a call from Mort Lindsay, the leader on the show, saying,
'What are you gonna do here? Are you gonna keep this job?' I
said, 'Well, if it's down to it, I'm not gonna keep it.' So then Mundell Lowe took it. Now they've got a rock player. Merv wanted all
youthful rock players.

"Of course. Get the young audience. The one that isn't there
any more."

"It was an interesting life, the studios, but I had to get rid of it,
because, you know, I never got used to it. I never got used to going
in and never knowing what they're going to put up in front of you.
It could be easy, it could be boring, it could be so-so, or it could
be absolutely straight fright. They put it up there and they want it
right now. And I never got to be a zippo reader like Tommy
Tedesco or Al Hendrickson or cats like that. 'Cause I started too
late."

"There are very few guitar players Roger Kellaway likes to play
with, you know. Except you. He says Herb's got grounded time.
He says guitar players have jumpy time."

"They do. They rush."

"Why?"

"I don't know. It must have something to do with picking a note
and fingering it at the same time."

"But bass players do that too."

"The only thing is that a bass player digs in a little harder."

"And also the clarity of the attack isn't as sharp, as bang! as it is
on the guitar."

"It's one of those questions I really can't answer. But they do
rush. And why do a lot of tenor players have good time? You can
get a rotten tenor player sometimes, and his time is grounded.
Why?"

"If you've got a piano with an even action, and you get used to
it, you know how deep that key bed is. But with the guitar, the split

second of releasing that string is very hard to judge. I wonder if the problem lies in the critical moment of releasing the string."

"It could be that. But I do know most guitar players rush."

"I've heard it argued that Oscar rushes."

"Well, we're talking about guitar players rushing within a phrase. The phrase is not steady. Oscar and Ray Brown and myself would push a tempo, we'd push, but it would take a long time to go up. That's all right in my book, because something is happening. It's just an edge you put on it."

"Yeah, there's a right way to go up tempo, but there's no right way to go down. It feels like it's going to sleep."

"Right, it feels like a weight on your shoulders. You can climb a tempo so long as everybody does it together. And the space between the beats will still be even. It's compressed a little bit. But there are all types of rushing. And the way Oscar does it, if indeed he does, I do it too and Ray does, and a lot of people do, and it doesn't bother me."

"I asked Oscar a question once. I said, 'If everybody goes on top of the time, doesn't the time itself change, and you're back in the center of it?' He said, 'No, not really.' And I said, 'This question verges on philosophy.'"

"Well . . . That's a great question. And I've got a pretty good answer for you. I don't think everybody does it really together. When I was with Oscar, and I was playing rhythm, when Ray would climb on top of the beat, I would hold it in the center, and I loved it. I love to do that! It wasn't a labor. I would be just under him, you wouldn't hear the difference. And that gives it the tension. You've got to play on top of something. If you're all playing together, you're not on top of anything."

"I think a certain amount of pull within the rhythm is part of the excitement."

"You've got to have tension. Of course, we all know when it goes past tension." And Herb laughed that big laugh of his. "God, those were exciting days with Oscar and Ray. Hoo! The Stratford album comes about as close as anything to what we sounded like."

We went out to the kitchen then. Herb opened the refrigerator to search among various fruit juices. "Do you want a drink? He said. "I mean, a drink?"

"No thanks," I said.

"How about some pineapple juice?"

"Perfect. When are you going out again?"

"Monday. Matter of fact, I'm going up to our old stomping ground, Toronto."

"Give everybody my best."

Driving home that day, I thought about the long arc of time since I first heard Herb with the Soft Winds. There is something exceptional about him that is evasive of definition. That expression "down-home" has long since been worn to a tatter but it could have been coined for Herb Ellis. His playing has the feeling of sun on warm dark loam, which quality is the direct expression of what the man is. There is no art in which it is harder to lie than jazz, although a few men have managed it. But Herb would never even think of trying. The candor is complete. In his casual admissions of weakness, there is enormous strength. This makes him and his music profoundly human and peculiarly comforting, and time spent with Herb Ellis always lingers sweetly in the memory, long after the conversation itself is forgotten.

Boy Lost:
Lenny Breau

Lenny Breau was an odd little guy, delicate, dishevelled, bohe-
mian, and shy. He had a raggedy mustache and slightly woolly dark
hair that was receding from his forehead, and he looked like what
he was, French by origin, probably Norman French. Chet Atkins,
whose conversation about guitar is liable to range from Charlie
Christian through Jim Hall to Segovia and Bream, once called him
"the best guitar player in the world today."

Country music has produced some remarkable guitarists,
including Hank Garland and Thumbs Carllile, that incredible
autodidact who used to sit there with his guitar lying across his lap,
playing with a combination of fingers and thumb pick in the right
hand and pressing down on the thing with the fingers of his left,
the strings set up in some sort of E-flat major tuning. To hear
Thumbs burning out bebop lines in the middle of a banal country-
and-western dance tune was very strange indeed.

Nor should one underestimate Jerry Reed, whose pursuit of hits
and a movie career has caused his early recordings to be forgotten.
But in such tracks as *In the Pines, Roving Gambler, The House of the
Rising Sun*, and his knock-out performance of *Georgia on My Mind*,
we hear how good he really was, and how much jazz had infused
his playing. The miscegenation of jazz and hillbilly has long gone

on in Nashville, and some of the best of its players are at ease in both idioms.

Lenny Breau came up through country-and-western music, his parents being professionals in the field, and it was Nashville that made him welcome. He is, like Garland, Carllile and Reed, the result of the jazz-country fusion, except that Breau took it a step further and brought into his work the full range of classical guitar technique. Chet Atkins was the first a&r man to give him his head, letting him record for RCA a milestone album in which he showed off his startling, for the time, jazz-classical technique. Gene Bertoncini, who is probably the best living exponent of jazz on the five-finger classical guitar, admires Breau; but then you'll search far to find a guitarist who doesn't.

Lenny was a heroin addict, which is one reason his career never blossomed the way it should have. There were periods when he was simply too unreliable to book, and others when he would disappear completely, either to sink into destruction or to withdraw himself from it. He considered himself a Canadian, although he was actually born in Auburn, Maine, on August 8, 1941. He spent much of his career in Canada, in Toronto and Winnipeg, and in the mid-1970s he was in Kililoe, Ontario, of all places. But he would turn up from time to time, playing exquisitely, because, apparently, he never ceased to put in his six or seven hours a day of practice, strung out or not. When I would encounter him, he talked diffidently across that great gorge that separates the strung from the straights, although I had more compassion for his problem than he could possibly have realized.

In earlier times, it was not possible to play jazz on the classical guitar. The sound of the instrument is too delicate to be heard in most jazz contexts; and the amplification in use in regular jazz guitars, a magnetic pickup system, functioned only with steel strings. Until the invention of the ceramic pickup, then, it was not feasible to play group jazz on the nylon-string guitar with that classical technique developed by Sor and Tarrega, among others, and brought to perfection finally in this century by Andrés Segovia. Charlie Byrd was among the first to experiment with the classical technique in jazz; but some pioneer work by Al Viola, including an album on Dick Bock's old World Pacific label, is usually overlooked.

At one time I suspected the technique would never be adapted to jazz. I thought that only the release of the string from a plectrum could place a note in that perfect moment to produce the swing without which it isn't—for me, anyway—jazz. I thought that the very nature of classical-guitar articulation militated against a strong rhythmic pulse. Lenny Breau demolished this theory in that first album for Chet Atkins which, at the time, flabbergasted me. Then came Brazilian guitarists like Oscar Castro-Neves to dispose of that theory forever.

Gene Bertoncini doesn't like the ceramic pickup, and will use the nylon-string guitar only in circumstances quiet enough to make it unnecessary. Otherwise he uses the amplified steel-string guitar. Lenny apparently felt the same, and when you hear him on the nylon-string guitar, it sounds unamplified.

There is something else the two guitarists have in common: Gene said years ago that we should think of the guitar as if it were a keyboard instrument, instead of in "grips"—the chord positions beginners learn from books published by Mel Bay and others. Lenny repeatedly pointed out that he approached the instrument as if it were a piano. Lenny told an interviewer, "My inspirations have been Ravel, Debussy, as well as Ravi Shankar. However, Bill Evans is my number one inspiration. He was the Bach of his age. I want to play his music on the guitar. Bill was 'way ahead of his time."

Lenny had developed a degree of control over the instrument that, with all deference to all the superb guitarists around, is unprecedented. His colorations are amazing. There's a chorus in Miles Davis's *All Blues* in which the melody is played entirely in harmonics. Lenny's facility, his unstrained ease, in their use were astonishing. Often toward the end, he played a steel-string instrument, a solid-body guitar on which he used a thumb pick, which gave him the advantages of the plectrum while leaving the four fingers free for use in chords and melody.

Lenny once wrote of his own playing, "A lot of my tunes aren't worked out. They're made up as I go along—and that's taking a big chance. It took me years to analyze the structure of the music, to be able to call up something fast and make it work. I've been listening to Keith Jarrett and his approach to playing the piano is like my approach to playing the guitar. I try for total spontaneity."

Lenny had an incredible lexicon of tone colors. Sometimes, for example, he'll play high-speed passages with damped strings. Other guitarists use the device, particularly in country music, but none I've heard can do it with such facility.

The rest of the album is more conventional—or as conventional as such virtuosic playing can be. In material such as *On Green Dolphin Street* and *Summertime* he might play linear amplified guitar, filling in with chords. Always the amazing thing is the independence of his various functions.

Yet Lenny couldn't read music. Not that this is unknown in jazz. Everybody knows the old jazz musician's joke: "Can he read?" "Yes, but not enough to hurt his playing." There's a truth in that, of course. Academic training is inherently at odds with the spontaneity and individualism that are at the heart of jazz, although the best players have managed to reconcile them. Nonetheless, good reading is a common skill in jazz musicians. The brilliant players who can't or couldn't read, such as Sidney Bechet, Buddy Rich, Wes Montgomery, and Ira Sullivan, are strange and special.

But Lenny sounded as if he had been steeped in the exercise books, playing Sor and Tarrega and the Segovia transcriptions all his life. There are times when his sound told you how closely he had studied Julian Bream's playing, with its tone-coloring placement of the right hand in relationship to the hole. Working the strings down at the back of the instrument produces a hard, metallic sound; over the hole gives you a warm sound; the farther you move the right hand up the neck the more the instrument sounds like a harp. And Bream will change coloration in the middle of a run. He employs color in his phrasing as a compensation for the small dynamic range of the classical guitar, although, he pointed out once that the dynamic range of the instrument is not as small as is commonly supposed. Bream uses tone to enhance the shape and contour of a line. Lenny too had that kind of command. "He could play anything he could hear," one of his friends, clarinetist Brad Terry, said. And he could, apparently, hear everything.

For the last few years of his life, he had been using a seven-string guitar—not one with a lower bottom string, like that of George Van Eps, but one with an additional A string on the top. He found that stretching an upper E-string that further fourth didn't work, the string soon broke. Brad Terry says that at the end he was using fishing line. This expansion of the instrument enhanced the pianistic effect he was always after.

Sometimes he would walk bass lines with his thumb pick, playing chords with his fingers.

Lenny died in Los Angeles at the age of forty-three in August of 1984 in murky circumstances. I had heard that he was straight at the time—had finally beaten heroin and everything else and was on his way to the career he richly deserved. At 8:00 a.m. on the morning of his last day, he called his mother long-distance, his voice full of fear, asking her to send him enough money for bus fare. At 11:00 a.m. the police found him at the bottom of a swimming pool, and called his mother. They said he was apparently the victim of accidental drowning. An autopsy proved otherwise: he had been strangled before being rolled into the pool. The police know who killed him. His mother knows who killed him. His friends know who killed him. But nobody can prove it, and Lenny's executioner walks around free.

And so Lenny Breau now is a figure of the past. The body of his known recordings is small, alas. But he did leave a few more, which are beginning to find their way to the public.

Drawing as he did on the styles and techniques of jazz, classical, and country-and-western guitar, Lenny Breau covered more ground than any guitarist I've ever heard. Superlatives are treacherous. None of us has heard every guitarist—or clarinetist or violinist—in the world. Nonetheless, Chet Atkins' evaluation of Lenny may have been on the mark.

Emily

Sometimes she wore a jump suit on the bandstand, playing with her eyes shut, rocking back and forth from one foot to the other, the guitar slung on a shoulder strap, her faced tilted up as if she were imploring a god unknown to send her ideas. Other times she sat on a chair with her legs crossed tailor-fashion, seeming to embrace the instrument, like a little girl cuddling a doll. She was improbable: white, middle class, a product of the affluent Englewood Cliffs area of New Jersey, and she was, before she turned thirty, one of the finest jazz musicians of her generation.

If you know her work only from her Concord albums, excellent as it is, you have not encountered the scope of her playing. The albums are moderately conservative, middle-of-the-road jazz. I was impressed by them as they came onto the market in the course of the last seven years. Then, on November 14, 1987, in Pittsburgh, I noted that she was working in a club there and went to hear her. I was unprepared for the sheer strength of her playing. She was an extraordinarily daring player, edging close to the avant-garde, and she swung ferociously. There was also a deeply lyrical quality to her playing. I returned to hear her on two more nights.

The jazz world is a very small one, and there were rumors about her. The story was out that Emily Remler had fallen victim to what has often seemed—from a time before Charlie Parker—like the endemic curse of the jazz profession. Heroin. People who had never even met Emily Remler were troubled by the stories about her. But she seemed now to be on the rather long list of jazz musicians who had beaten the problem.

A three-year marriage to the brilliant Jamaican pianist Monty Alexander ended in 1985. He had tried to help her break her habit, but in the end it was too much for him to handle. They remained close.

That's what she was doing in Pittsburgh, working it out it away from the familiar haunts, working on the fears and self-doubts that had given rise to the problem. She was studying composition at the University of Pittsburgh with Bob Brookmeyer and, after that, with avant-garde composer David Stock.

She was born in Manhattan on, she said, September 18, 1957, the youngest of three children, her father a meat broker, her mother a psychological social worker, both born in Brooklyn. Her sister became a lawyer and her brother entered the U.S. diplomatic service. Emily never knew financial insecurity. The legend of the poor boy forging his way to the top in jazz is not entirely without foundation, and Louis Armstrong was its classic exemplar. But the majority of jazz musicians, black and white alike, have come from the comfortable middle class. So that part of her story is not as strange as it might seem.

She got interested in music through the folk movement, and then rock. What was atypical is that she had gone on to discover jazz, and then not only entered a field that has severely discriminated against women even while its practitioners have been in the forefront of the demand for racial equality, but became one of its most masterful young players.

In her book *American Women in Jazz*, Sally Placksin documents the cases of women of genuine ability who have been driven out of the profession, or at least pressed to pursue it only as a sort of hobby. There have been a number of excellent women jazz play-

ers, including Melba Liston, Carol Britto, Patty Bown, Mary Lou
Williams, Margie Hyams, Billie Rogers, Patrice Rushen, and others whose names are forgotten because they succumbed to the
pressures put on them by the men around them and simply quit,
Lester Young's sister among them. The guitarist Mary Osborne
told me that she had never felt that she has suffered from discrimination, but she is the only woman jazz player I ever heard say that.
The fine alto saxophonist Vi Redd said she has suffered far more
discrimination as a woman than she has as a black. Anne Patterson,
who plays all the woodwinds from oboe on down, sometimes plays
baritone saxophone in the Nat Pierce-Frank Capp Juggernaut
band, and leads the all-woman band called Maiden Voyage, can tell
you endless tales of discrimination. Marian McPartland says that
when she has hired a woman, such as drummer Dottie Dodgion,
for her trio, male musicians would ask not "How does she play?"
but "What does she look like?"

Some years ago, Stan Getz played Donte's in North Hollywood.
Playing piano in his group was Joanne Brackeen. She was at the
top of her form that night. For some reason the place was full of
piano players. Her playing was powerful, propulsive, wildly inventive—anything but the deferential and delicate music women jazz
players are assumed to produce. And every one of those pianists
was seriously upset by her, genuinely disturbed, including some
highly accomplished musicians. So this phenomenon is real.

A few months after the Pittsburgh engagement, Emily played a
job in Los Angeles. I spent an afternoon with her. Her room was
on the second floor of the motel. Below it was the usual motel
swimming pool overhung by the usual California palms, and the
laughter of children rose in the usual California sunlight. There
were bottles of Evian water on the dresser. Emily was wearing
black slacks and a white blouse. She sat cross-legged on the bed.
She was not small and, as she pointed out, she had large hands.
The backs of them bore tracks—the scars left by needles, those
wrinkled lines looking like tiny railroad tracks that I knew all too
well from seeing them on Bill Evans. I suppose they bothered me
more because I had never seen them on a woman. She had a rather

large nose and she wasn't conventionally pretty, but there was something attractive about her. And something that made me feel protective toward her. She seemed so eager that day, looking to her future.

"You're one of those players who don't hold back," I said. "Jazz is not a holding-back music. Paul Desmond may have played delicately, but he didn't hold back. Bill Evans may have played with great sensitivity, but sensitivity is not an exclusively female quality."

Emily, who had a musical voice slightly colored by a New York City accent with softly dentalized d's and t's, said, "That's a point I was going to make. Music is sexless. I think everyone has something that is feminine, something that is masculine. I'm very confused about that as it is, now that I have opened myself up to having women as friends for a change, after hanging out with the guys my whole life and wanting to be one of the guys. I'm finding out how incredible women really are. When I see a woman that is good at what she does and is confident and does things with conviction—I guess 'confidence' is the key word here—I just admire her so much. Women inhibit themselves as a product of society, or what their mothers taught them, or whatever it was when you're coming up. Women get the message that they're supposed to get married, have children, that's their function, and that's it. My mother never gave me that message. It was always: Achieve. Do well. Maybe a little too much of that, which I drive myself crazy about. I grew up with this thought that anything I applied myself to, I could do."

Life expectancy at birth in nineteenth-century America was about thirty-five, not much different from what it had been during the Roman Empire. I pointed out to Emily that when a husband and wife had to have ten children in order that two or three might live to the adult years, there may have been some reason for the division of labor along sexual lines. But that has changed, and given the advancing destruction of our fragile environment by the effluvia of our own excessive population, women are gradually being allowed to do something other than breed.

"I'm not into sitting and crying about it," Emily said. "I'm into doing. I never was real bitter about the fact that there are so many bandleaders who have told me face to face that they couldn't hire me because I was a woman, or that there have been so many instances where I wasn't trusted musically, and drummers handled me with kid gloves because they figured my time wasn't strong."

"Yeah, but Emily," I said, "realistically, a lot of guitar players have got flakey time."

Emily said, "It just so happens that I don't. That's something I'd like to talk about—the holding back thing that you mentioned. It seems that a lot of women don't get into the time, really hit it. That's a very big psychological trick. You have to be confident to be into the time like that. You have to know where it is. Herb Ellis said to me once, 'If you don't know, you don't know.' He meant someone who doesn't know that they're off, and that they don't know that they don't swing. And that's a huge subject. There are some people I play with that you can't not swing, it's so wonderful.

"You have to have your innate sense of the time, and you have to believe in yourself that your sense is correct. Especially when there's some big burly guy at the other side of the stage who doesn't like the fact that you're there anyway. And he's not going to give you an inch, he's not going to acknowledge that you're correct. You have to believe in yourself. In some ways I have a lot of belief in myself. I just know that women are going to come out more and more with this conviction, as soon as they work on themselves properly. Women can do anything, anyone can do anything. It never did occur to me to stay in one place and bitch about this, about how I wasn't given a chance. I think it gives me more merit—to get really good, so good that it doesn't matter. Okay, it sucks, being in this position. But: get so good that you surpass it.

"It's not going to hurt you to be a great player. That's what I wanted to be anyway. If that's part of the motivation, fine. But it's not part of the motivation any more. It was when I first started at Berklee. I'll show these guys!"

And she did. Emily was graduated from the Berklee College of Music in 1975. She said that she still played very badly at that time.

"I had a boyfriend, a guitarist from New Orleans. The plan was that I would move down to New Orleans. On my way to New Orleans, I stopped in Long Beach Island on the shore in New Jersey, and rented a room, and proceeded to quit smoking cigarettes, and learn to play. In that two months, I lost twenty-five pounds. I was just on a discipline trip. I could have been a Spartan! I want to do that again! I know I'm capable of it. Will power is not the question. I have a tremendous amount of will power.

"After that I went down to New Orleans. I still wasn't very good, but I had a lot of ideas. The boyfriend, Steve Masakowski, was an incredible guitarist, and still is, and still lives in New Orleans. He's a monster. The competitive atmosphere was still there, because I'd hear him practicing through the wall. I started to play all the shows at the Blue Room of the Fairmont Hotel, all the Vegas acts, Joel Grey, Ben Vereen, Robert Goulet, Nancy Wilson. I got a gig with her. Besides that, I was doing bebop gigs, Dixieland, and traditional New Orleans stuff. I had this thing, which I still have, to do it right. Don't sit and put this type of music down until you can do it as good as the best person who does it. For instance, I can't play country music like Roy Clark. Not that I would want to. But I have no right to say that that is invalid music. I like bluegrass a lot. And I'm into the Irish music that it comes from. I'm not, thank God, one of these snobby jazz musicians who put down everything except jazz.

"The reason I am so eclectic is that I get such satisfaction out of doing different types of music that sometimes I'm not sure what my true stuff is. I have confidence that the more I work on myself as a person, the more that the music is going to open up. I'll notice progress in sounding like my own voice and in my satisfaction in music by doing other things than practicing or playing. By figuring out things that have been bothering me for years, that clutter me up and make me have limits, and make me worried. Clearing me out of all sorts of things. For example, when you have a resentment against someone, let's say in the band, it clouds your ability to be creative, to be happy that evening. Sometimes you can turn it into so much anger that you can get into a weird I-don't-care stage, and sometimes you play good then. But if you work on those things, you can clear them out to get to your own voice. It's occurred to me in the last few years, it's not even the notes and the chords so much any more, it's the person. I never said more than two words to Bill Evans, I talked to him once, but I know what he was like. I know it. I'm positive. I never met Wes Montgomery, but I knew what he was like before I asked every person who ever knew him. I knew what Joe Pass was like. He is exactly like he plays. Things come out in the playing. If the person has intelligence, and humor, and creativity, or is introverted."

"I know an outstanding exception, though," I said, and Emily said, "If you mean . . . "And she named a man the beauty of whose playing and the perversity of whose personality have always presented an irresoluble contradiction to other musicians. We both laughed hugely. "Actually," she said, "I've watched him over the years, and he's changed. There's a lot of good inside."

"The relationship of personality to playing is very strong in jazz," I said. "Jazz musicians, generally, even talk the way they play. They sing like they play."

"Yeah, I can see that, that they play the way they talk." Then she said, "What was Coltrane like?"

"Soft and gentle. A very sweet man. I liked him a lot. Tell me, how did you get from folk music to jazz, from Englewood Cliffs to Berklee in Boston?"

"During the Black Panther movement, we were bussed to the Englewood high school instead of the nearest one. We grew up with Italian and Jewish kids. I hadn't been exposed to black people. I was already listening to a lot of blues music. I just wanted to be friends. They didn't want to be friends with us. They beat us up, they stole our money, they burned white girls' hair—I had very long hair. It was very frightening. For that and a few other reasons, I cut school constantly. I just wasn't into it. I was into having parties and being a hippy, a very young hippy. So I was sent away to boarding school, but it was a hippy boarding school, an experimental school where you could do anything you wanted. It closed after the year I was there.

"During boarding school, I played folk music. I listened to rock music, Jimi Hendrix and the Beatles. I was about fifteen years old when I came to dream that I wanted to be a blues player, so I listened to B.B. King and Johnny Winter and all these people. I played my brother's Gibson ES 330, which I still play today. I have a few other guitars, but I keep coming back to that one. I played with my fingers, I did all sorts of strange things, but now I realize I was always working on my music. I was always singing along with things. I would sing along with Ravi Shankar's music for Bangla Desh, this whole raga piece, I could sing it from beginning to end. Weird stuff that my friends couldn't do. I had a weird ear. There was something different between the way they listened to music and the way I did. I remember we were listening to the Rolling Stones, which I loved. I was singing the saxophone solos and the guitar solos, I wasn't with the lyrics. I started playing some of the guitar things, the very repetitive rock things where they stay on three chords forever. I'd get off on that. I'd sit in my room, discovering that that was a way of leaving the planet. I loved that. Until this day, I've found that that's the best way for me to practice—just jamming. I realized when I was about twenty-one that I knew how to get better. There are a lot of people who study who don't feel they know how to get better. I was just out of Berklee, and it came to, 'Why don't I practice what I'm going to play?' From then on, I'd tape myself playing some backgrounds for the songs I was going to record. I put the metronome on to make sure I'm right. And then play over it. I still do it to this day. I'm getting a four-track for my bedroom.

"Schubert supposedly used to play guitar in bed," I said.

"I do that!" she said. "I used to sleep with my guitar. I'll just sit in my room and play a phrase over and over until I feel comfortable. And if I can't do something, I stop the tape and do it twenty times until I am comfortable."

"If you started out playing folk and rock things, when did you get beyond the phase of the grips and begin to see scales across the fingerboard?"

"That didn't happen till I was at Berklee."

"I've watched the way your hands work," I said. "You think a little as if you were playing a keyboard instrument."

"That really makes me happy that you can hear that. I think like a keyboard so much that sometimes I think it's bad. With me, I don't know about anybody else, if I can't hear the phrase, I won't be able to execute for anything. I play everything that I can sing or can hear, and I always was that way, and always will be. There are many people who play by rote. I don't look at the neck because I don't relate to patterns. I hear, I hear. I've tried to do guitaristic licks, and I screw them up. Even ones that I could get easily. Because I don't hear them right there in the music. George Benson said to me, 'You're great when you're playing what you believe in.' I cannot force myself to do what other people want me to do. It's very confusing, it's the way we're taught as we're growing up—that you do things the way that's acceptable to do, in some many aspects of life. You don't jump on cafe tables and yell. And all of a sudden, with what we've chosen to do in the arts, you're supposed to do what you really feel like doing. You live in a double life. You still don't jump on cafe tables and yell, but in your work you are supposed to do what you feel. So it's very common for musicians to be eccentric, and not conform. Because they can't just all of a sudden change. If I were to conform to the masses, I would have been a rock-and-roll guitarist, wearing silver suits." She laughed at herself. "Instead of red jump suits. I could have been very successful and rich doing that.

"In New Orleans, I learned to play. By the time I got back to New York, I was pretty good. I met Herb Ellis in New Orleans, and he recommended me for the Concord Festival, where I got to play with Ray Brown. I was twenty. Carl Jefferson told me that he was going to sign me [to the Concord Jazz label]. I thought, 'This is it, my future is set.'

"They wanted me to be straight ahead. Since I want to do everything well, I decided that I would write tunes that were more like standards, learn a lot of standards, learn how to play within the limitations of jazz tonal progressions, get my chops up in bebop.

I needed a guide. And the people that I liked in those limits, straight-ahead mainstream bebop, were Wes Montgomery and Joe Pass and people like that. I pretty much copied them. I learned a new Wes Montgomery tune every day. I copied his phrasing. Above all, I copied his timing. He was unbelievable. But I didn't hear from Concord for a while, and I proceeded to move to New York, and I got a gig with Nancy Wilson. I also worked with Astrud Gilberto, and in Washington D.C., I ran into Herb Ellis again. I was a better player by then, and I got a contract with Concord."

"Back to that position of the transition from playing in that folk way, how did you do that? Through a teacher?"

"I never took a guitar lesson in my life, not really. I noticed that people who do things well do them with a minimum of effort. I learned basic scales and melody patterns so that I could vary in that vertical way. I decided, 'Why move up and down?' I watched people, I watched myself in the mirror. I did scales and arpeggios, but I started right away doing melodies and finding the ways that other guitar players did them. You can, if you get good at transcribing, find from the timbre which string they're using. So I copied Pat Martino's way of doing things. He's a master of the instrument, his technique is astounding, you can count on him doing everything in the most logical way. And maybe I copied some of his fingerings, due to transcription. There's a lot of illogical stuff that I do, though. I have to play everything that I hear, and there sometimes isn't time to work it out, and there's a lot of reaching for stuff in ridiculous positions that, I realize if I review it later, I could have done some other way. But I just have to get it somehow, and my will to get it is stronger than my knowledge of the guitar.

"For instance, I play solo guitar and try to back myself up with chords, like Lenny Breau did. But I do not have Lenny Breau's knowledge of the guitar."

"You do know," I said, "that Lenny was a totally intuitive player. He played entirely by ear, he'd had no formal training, and no knowledge of formal theory."

"We're talking about two different kinds of knowledge."

"Of course. His knowledge of the instrument itself was enormous."

"I agree. And I don't know the instrument the way he did. The thing I do best is . . . " She laughed. "I'm resourceful. I'm a good hustler on the guitar. I'll hustle the phrase that I want. I'll work until I get it. It's the same thing I use to win at pool and pingpong without being the greatest pool or pingpong player. When I call on myself to put extra energy into a tune or a phrase, it's from the thing that makes me win at pingpong. It's just a will to do something."

"Now. We're onto a characteristic that is not generally considered feminine. Overt will. And throughout history, women's will has been suppressed and thus driven underground. Sometimes, when it isn't destroyed, it becomes devious. In order to get around men, many women will lie if necessary to get their way. Women are supposed to be submissive, but they have as much will as any man. They just hide it."

"You're right! I like that. It's something I am admiring more and more in women: will. I don't know. All I know is that the more I be like I'm supposed to be, the more I be like me, the better I get at music. I believe I have a tremendously strong will. I don't know what masculine or feminine is. I can tell you that I like the way dresses look, but I can't wear them onstage because I can't sit with my legs crossed all night. I don't deny that I'm a woman. And people say stuff about this, and have been doing it for years. Why don't you wear something more feminine, something flowing? It's just that I don't want a dress swaying when I move. The rest of the time, I like to be stylish, I like a lot of modern things. I'm split between two things. I love flowing, very sophisticated, very simple dresses. I don't like flowery or lacy things. I love dresses. But I love baggy pants too. It's strictly a matter of comfort. I don't identify masculine or feminine by what you wear. But people do. And how can you change millions of people?"

"I think it already is changing. Ever since Marlene Dietrich wore a pair of slacks in a movie. Look at the Scottish kilt, and the traditional old battle dress of Greek soldiers. Now, about this self-destructive business . . . "

"We've noticed," she said, "how people of great creative talent often have a dark side that wants to destroy it and themselves. I'd say that the biggest fear for an artist is that if they stop destroying themselves, they won't have that other, good side. It's very easy to see the good side when you're doing bad. It's the one pure light that you have. You get to be afraid of a balance, of mediocrity, you get to be afraid that you won't get these brainstorms. How much more precious is it to succeed coming out of the gutter than it is to be comfortable and balanced and healthy. It's the misconception, but I have a feeling that a lot of musicians have problems with this—a feeling that they will not be able to create unless there's havoc and chaos."

"Well, a friend of mine said, 'Confronted with order, the artist will create disorder. Confronted with disorder, he will create order.' All creative people are perpetually trying to shake up the pick-up sticks: Let me create chaos so that I can create something out of it. Let's see if I can do that trick again."

Emily laughed. "So then, maybe I really should clean my apartment! Maybe if it was totally orderly, I could write better."

"No. That's not the point. When I am writing heavily, the room becomes a disaster area. And when I am through, I have to clean it up, because I can't go into the next phase of disorder without having cleared away the disorder from before. The artist needs raw clay to make the statue. If the only piece of clay I have is the statue I just made, which already bores me, then I will tear it apart to have the clay to make the next one. The process interests the artist more than the result, though he has to sell the result to make a living."

"So what's you're saying," Emily said, "is that this is totally normal. That's something to think about. I've been trying to get rid of it, and it hadn't occurred to me that maybe it's needed."

"Well there's a balance to be found, to be sure. I do know that many artists consider their neuroses are part of their talent, and cling to them. And sometimes they may be right. I know that depression goes with the creative process, and most psychiatrists know it too, and there assuredly is a manic quality about the compulsion to create art."

"What my therapist says is, Why am I creating this guilt and pain to create?"

"Nobody wants unhappiness. If you can get rid of it, get rid of it. On the other hand, if you get a good tune out of your guilt, play it. The artist is just that selfish and just that ruthless. It's like William Faulkner's comment in his Nobel acceptance speech, which shocked everybody. He said that the *Ode on a Grecian Urn* was worth any number of little old ladies."

Emily giggled. "It's unbelievable, isn't? After Monty and I were divorced I played great for a while on that pain. I really did. I also tried to destroy myself as fast as I could.

"You know, I had a strange experience in Michigan about ten years ago. As you might imagine, I've had a lot of requests to play with all-female groups. And when I was twenty-one, some very good musicians had this band and asked me to do a gig in Michigan, good money and just one set. I was going to get out of New York for a couple of days and be in the Michigan lake country. It was a very enlightening experience. It was eight thousand gay women. They have a different language to desex the language. Woman, singular, is womon. Women, plural, is womyn, for example.

"It's one thing to accept that sort of thing, but it is quite another to be in the severe minority. I felt weird. But there were some things I really loved about it. There was no bullshitting. There was no manipulating with charm. It didn't matter what you wore, whether you combed your hair even. People were taken for what they were, not what they looked like. And the view on beauty was a lot different than Hugh Hefner's standard.

"I was with one of the girls in the band. A woman we would consider fat walked by and I heard a girl say, 'Isn't she beautiful?' Look, I personally know women who stick their fingers down their throats to try to lose ten pounds. And there are a hell of a lot of schoolgirls developing complexes about being thin. I had that problem.

"There is a psychiatrist here in Pittsburgh who says that the people with the lowest self-esteem are the ones with the most gifts. This psychiatrist says that 99 percent of the problems he deals with, even to psychosis, are based on distorted self-perception, low self-esteem. I was raised to think that if I was thin, people would like me more. And the truth is that I'm not built that way. My body has a tendency to be a certain weight, but I have not accepted it my whole life. To me, I seem overweight. It was very interesting at that gay thing in Michigan to see that they don't have that perception, they canned all that. I'll tell you something else: there are a lot of women in this world who are using drugs to stay thin. They're killing themselves, their bodies, their souls, their minds, to be fifteen pounds lighter and please American society."

"What else has it done to you, being a woman in the jazz world, and a nonconformist in a conformist society?"

"Well, some musicians didn't trust me to be able to comp, which I love to do, and I feel I'm very good at it. If they want to play up the woman thing, women are trained to nurture people, make people feel good. I comp well. I can put my ego aside, as opposed to some other people who comp so loud and pushy, 'Look-at-me.' I know how to comp to make someone else sound good. I love to do it. It gets me out of myself. But I've ended up being a leader, more than a side man. Even at nineteen years old, the minute I could play a blues, they used to push me out front, because of the novelty. So I feel a little deprived. I wish someone would take me under their wing and teach me further, because that's how I get better, playing with great musicians. At this point now, I am ready to be a leader."

"You may be in the position," I said, "of having no choice but to be a quote star. I think Bill Evans passed beyond the possibility of being a side man."

"Yeah, but he was a side man with Miles. Do you think Miles would hire me?

"I wouldn't be surprised if he would."

"If I played with Miles, I would have to play some rock-and-roll and I wouldn't want to. But that's a matter of taste.

"I hear a lot of music that fuses rock and jazz together. And I find myself listening to Led Zeppelin and Jimi Hendrix. I'd rather hear the traditional rock-and-roll.

"The thing that makes me play with conviction is the same thing that makes me swim extra laps in the pool. It's from your gut. But I don't play from I'll show this guy. I notice that anybody who wants to cut anybody is not playing in the creative vein, and is not going to reach the peaks I want to reach. It's about letting go of yourself and becoming a channel—of love and God. That's what I believe. You can't do that by saying 'I'm going to show them this or that.' If I want to become a channel for God, which you can consider to be a lot of different things, you have to get rid of stuff, and be free."

I said, "I have to go and do my work in a cave, silently."

"That happens to me. I tune out as a protection. I tuned out for years as a protection."

"Well, look at Bix Beiderbecke, at Charlie Parker, there are all sorts of people who put up a chemical shield."

"Sure, because that makes you not care if the guy in the front row doesn't like you. That's why anger sometimes works, you can play better because you don't care. But it all comes down—I'm hoping this will take care of it—to feeling okay about yourself, that you deserve to be there, that you have something valid to say, that you have a lot of love to give, and you have a gift, and you have a right to be up there, and if somebody doesn't like it, that's his loss. That's the attitude I want. This guy can't make me or break me, this musician telling me to play this or that is not valid— it's what I feel. If I could get to that, I'd like to achieve it. I'm getting a little of it now.

"I was with a group in Europe last summer. Some drummers lack a little subtlety or they just prefer music that's loud and rau- cous. The feeling of aggression and speed is more what they're interested in. This isn't all drummers. This drummer said to me and what a lot of drummers have said to me, and that I bought and accepted, 'You gotta play louder, I can't hear you, you've gotta play harder. My favorite guitarists are Hendrix and McLaughlin, you oughta play more like them.' And I thought, 'Okay, I'll turn up my amp tonight and I'll play more rock and roll.' And then I stopped and said to myself, 'I can't believe I'm buying this package for the thousandth time.' And you see it's easier for him to tell me what to do because I'm a woman, and more important, it's easier for me to take it. And for the first time, I said back to him, 'Why don't you start listening to where I'm at? Why don't you come up to my level? Why don't you learn how to be romantic and subtle a little bit.'

"I couldn't believe I stood up for myself like that. So it's getting better, and the better it gets the better I'll be as a musician and the better I'll feel about that guy who doesn't like me.

"You should be a woman for a while and then you'd see. It's a hell of a lot different than you think."

Some time in the course of those days in Pittsburgh I asked Emily if she planned to stay there. No, she said. When she felt she was ready, she planned to move back to New York.

A month or so ago a pianist friend called me. He mentioned in the course of the conversation that he had joined Alcoholics Anonymous. "I never knew you had a problem with that," I said.

"It was mostly on the job," he said.

Somehow Emily Remler's name came up. He had never met her, and yet he said, in a voice soft with concern, "How is she doing?" And you knew exactly what he meant.

So I called her number in Pittsburgh. I was given a referral number, the area code being that of Brooklyn. I called it. After a year and a half in Pittsburgh, she was back in home terrain, living near Sheepshead Bay.

She had just completed a new album for Concord with Hank Jones. She was full of plans and the enthusiasm in her voice told me the answer to the question before I asked it. "How are you doing?" I said.

"I'm doing just fine," she said.

I was pulling for her. I wanted her to make it. Al Cohn and Zoot Sims and Gerry Mulligan and Hal Gaylor and many more I know made it.

In May of 1990, I got a call from a friend who told me Emily had been found dead in her hotel room in Sydney, Australia. Whatever the proximate cause of her death, I could not help feeling there were other and underlying factors. Perhaps she died of being a woman in a profession dominated by men. Perhaps she died of the contradictions she lived with, her confusion about her own femininity. The sensitivity that makes it possible to produce good art makes life painful for those who possess it. Chemicals may not enhance the creativity, but they dull the pain, or seem to, for a little while. In the end they add to it.

Emily Remler was a superb musician, and on her way to being a great one. I will always see her sitting cross-legged on the bed, reaching out for life and looking like a little girl. She didn't make it.

Escape to Freedom:
Bud Shank

No doubt every biography of an artist, from Rembrandt to Gauguin, from Beethoven to Miles Davis, has tried to relate the subject's character to his art. The connection is implicit in the term "self-expression." It is assumed that the subtlest choice of colors or tones is an expression of the inner self, that everything the artist does reveals him as surely as his handwriting. In general this is true.

The expression of personality is far more obvious in jazz players than it is in "classical" musicians, although they too are capable of the imposition of self on a traditional repertoire. It has been said that Toscanini conducted Beethoven as if it were Verdi. And Glenn Gould so infused his work with his own character that he drove people to polar extremes of adulation and fury. There are those who loathed Glenn's approach to Mozart and Beethoven. I found it all interesting, because Glenn was distinctly odd and offered fresh views of everything he did, whether it was "correct" or not.

Jazz playing, however, is a creative art, as opposed to an interpretive art, and therefore acute individuality is not only tolerated, it is expected. To be sure, this freedom is compromised by those who would politicize the art and insist that this approach or that is the truth faith—what Paul Desmond called McCarthyism in jazz. It would make for a tidy equation if we could say that this folly is restricted to critics, but some of the musicians have been equally culpable. In general, however, musicians and critics alike have looked on jazz as, and to it for, individual expression. If you're familiar with his playing, you can identify Benny Carter in about one bar. Nobody in the world phrases like him, no one inflects notes the way he does, no one has that urbane, gentle, aristocratic tone.

But there are mysteries in jazz. One of them is Bud Shank. In general, jazz musicians find their styles early and, while their art may evolve within that style, stay with them. There are exceptions. The evolution in his fifties of the Montreal pianist Oliver Jones has been startling. And Dizzy Gillespie's tone changed when he altered his embouchure a few years ago. There is early Gillespie and recent Gillespie, and they are different. And although he does not, by his own statement, have the physical stamina, the capacity to burn at full throttle for hours on end, that he once had, his powers of invention and his fattened, burnished tone keep him one of the soaringly inventive, one of the half dozen most creative artists, jazz ever produced.

No jazz musician's work has changed as conspicuously as that of Bud Shank. It was reasonable to speculate that the change occurred because he gave up life working in the recording studios of Los Angeles, moved to the state of Washington, and went on the road again to play jazz, and only jazz. But that is only part of the explanation, and the change in Bud's playing is one of the most interesting examples of the relationship of personality to art that I have come across.

Bud was for many years a fixture of West Coast jazz—a somewhat imprecise term used with condescension if not contempt by those East Coast critics and musicians who believe that the purpose of art, jazz in particular, is political polemic. As such, Bud became a focus of hostility, the handsome and successful white studio player with his swimming pool, sports cars, and sailboats. His playing was pretty and lyrical but, according to the eastern orthodoxy, it lacked balls. The trappings of success, however, concealed a tortured spirit.

There was indeed a softness about his playing in the old days, a tentative quality. But no one—at least no one with open ears—would today characterize Shank's playing as tentative. On the contrary, it has a kind of ferocity about it now, and you hear tales told with a chuckle about musicians going into concerts or recording sessions expecting to dominate him and coming out of them with their asses kicked.

This change has manifested itself in his saxophone playing, not in his flute work. It is not yet generally known that a man who was considered one of the premier flutists in jazz has given the instrument up entirely. Nor is it known that Shank's standards for the instrument were so high that he despised his own playing. He hasn't played the instrument at all in several years. Bud has put aside the flute forever to concentrate on the saxophone, and only one of the saxophones at that. He no longer plays baritone. He plays only alto. And he is opposed to doubling.

Bud and his petite blonde wife Lynn stopped off to spend a couple of days with my wife and me in Ojai when he was traveling down the coast to a gig in Long Beach, California. I have known Bud about thirty years, but never as well as I do now after those days of conversation. Indeed, now I wonder how well I—or any of us, really—ever knew him at all.

One of the first things we discussed was his abandonment of the flute. Bud said, "Giving up the flute came after a great deal of thought, when I decided to make a break for it out of the studios. It was a long drawn-out decision. I had really concentrated on the flute, and I really practiced. I used to go over on my boat to Catalina Island for two weeks at a time just to practice the flute. I was really getting more and more into the classical thing and learning how to play it, realizing that the reason I was bugged with my jazz on the flute was because I really couldn't play the damn instrument.

"I knew I could not play the flute as well as I play the saxophone, so it was a matter of finding out how I'd feel really learning the instrument. I spent a couple of years doing a really concentrated thing. I did some recitals. Bill Mays wrote a suite for me for flute and piano, we made an album in 1980.

"All the stuff I did with the L.A. Four was mainly based around the flute instead of the saxophone. Finally I reached the point around 1984 or 1985 when I said, 'This is not what I want to do. I want to be a saxophone player and I always wanted to be a saxophone player.' I was not getting very far either. Even though I was becoming better and better and better on the flute, it was still, as far as playing jazz music is concerned, not making any sense to me. It was still not what I could do on the saxophone.

"So I took a long look at my life and what I had to do. I was in the position that I could say I'm here because I want to be and I'm doing what I want to do. And as long as I'm doing what I want to do, lets find out what I *really* want to do. And what I really wanted to do was to be a saxophone player. I look through my life back to the very beginning and that's all I ever really wanted to be, a good saxophone player. So I saw that the problem with the saxophone was really the flute, because the flute was taking all the practice time."

I asked Bud if there was a problem of embouchure, or was he talking about something much deeper—the very conception of playing. He said, "Flute will not bother the saxophone playing, but a lot of saxophone playing can bother the flute, at least until you get to the point where you are so strong that nothing is going to bother you. And that's just a matter of practice time and that's what I was doing. I could play saxophone all night and still pick up the flute and play one of those little classical things. I had gotten myself to that point. But the satisfaction wasn't there. It was called, So what? The satisfaction I'm getting now from my saxophone playing is total and complete. But I was trying to be two persons.

"I am a Gemini and I'm double enough things as it is, but I could not master two instruments. It's physically impossible. Nobody's done it yet. I was trying to and didn't make it, and I think I was adding to the insult to flute playing. Most other people who are trying to play both are also insulting the instrument.

"I don't know what it's going to take to produce jazz on the flute at the level I want to hear it. Maybe there is some kid out there somewhere who has dedicated his life to the flute and done nothing but play the flute. That's what it's going to take to make the breakthrough and make it make sense. Hubert Laws is getting closer. But Hubert spent a lot of time playing the saxophone too. Finally threw away the saxophone, as I've thrown away the flute, and concentrated on flute. Hubert is close to doing it. Dave Valentine is close, but the guy to me who is the closest is Steve Kujala. He worked with Chick Corea. He stays around L.A. and does some studio work, but he is a bitch on the flute and I see more promise in him than anybody. He grew up more in the fusion world than the straight-ahead jazz world. There's nothing wrong with that, but it's going to take someone like that, maybe another generation.

"Doublers ain't going to make it. There isn't enough time. You can be a master of the doublers but you're not going to be a master of anything else. That also goes for the writer-players, or arranger-players. Dave Grusin has gone on playing, but I'm sure Grusin doesn't think of himself as a master pianist. He is a great piano player but he is not a master. But he sure is a master writer. Even now I don't know of anybody who is a great writer and a great player. People try, we all try, I tried, but I had to go back at the age of fifty-eight and practice the saxophone again like a teenager. Actually I've enjoyed it—as much as you can enjoy practicing."

Art Farmer's experience, I said, seemed to verify Bud's position. Art got from the fluegelhorn the sound he wanted, and after years of playing two instruments, he finally gave up the trumpet, at least for public performance. I named several other musicians who doubled instruments, or indeed, played more than two of them—Jack Zaza in Toronto, who plays studio sessions on seemingly any instrument whatever, and Don Thompson, who records on bass, piano, and vibes.

Bud said: "Look at Bobby Enevoldsen. He was a clarinetist with the Salt Lake Symphony, but he's most known as a valve trombone player. And back in the 1950s most of his jobs were playing bass.

With his talents, he should have been one of the heavyweights in this art form. But it's because of that thing where people say, 'He's a great bass player . . . No, no he's a great trombone player.' You get into that thing with the categories, people don't know what to do with you, they can't handle it. People who are your market, your audience, can't handle all that. This new kid from Australia, James Morrison, trombone player and a trumpet player, he's something else on both those instruments. The one that kept up playing and writing most of all is Roger Kellaway, But he plays now all the time. He didn't when he was in Hollywood."

The next question was about Bud's years of studio work. He was one of the most successful players in Hollywood. He said,

"I didn't stop playing. I was just not able to improvise all the time, there wasn't any place to do it. My ears had deteriorated, what I could hear. After just doing studio work. I have pretty good pitch and I'm able to hear things, but from not using them all those years, my ears started to deteriorate. Now that I'm playing all the time, they are better than they ever were. Even though they are supposed to deteriorate with age, mine haven't.

"I was not playing much jazz for ten years, not improvising, just playing in the studios. Who cares in the studio as long as you're in tune? Not using your hearing from an improvisational standpoint, that's what all the guys face coming out of the studios, the loss of their ears. This has never happened before where jazz musicians were forced to—or chose to—go into another form of the business, and then come back out as jazz musicians past the age of fifty, fifty-five. This is a unique situation in history. All of a sudden there's a chance to be a jazz musician again, there's a market out there, and a chance to record. You're not going to make as much money as you did in the studios. But I got out of the jazz world and into the studios not because I wanted to but because there was no place to play. And I came back to jazz music because things have turned around the other way.

"There was nowhere to work in the early '60s. Some guys went to Europe, some guys went off into never-never land with some form of chemical assistance and avoided facing reality. In my case,

I ended up doing studio work because that was what was going to pay the rent. But as soon as I saw a spark out there, I left. Same thing with Ray Brown.

"We saw that spark in 1975 when we put that L.A. Four group together. We did it very cautiously, we even had a very cautious sound. We were one classical musician, Laurindo Almeida, and three jazz musicians, myself, Ray, and Shelly Manne. Theoretically that can't work. To a certain extent we made it work, and it is amazing that we were able to keep it together as long as we did. We had to do a lot of give and take so we would not get too hot for the audience. The instrumentation made the drummer really lay back. A drummer could have pushed a flute and guitar almost into silence. So that automatically gave the group a light sound.

"We broke up the L.A. Four in 1984. My wife Lynn and I already had our house up north in 1980. That's the time I stopped doing studio work, weaning myself away from it in the middle '70s. I would maybe fly down to Los Angeles to do a movie call or something. It happened so gradually I can't put a time on it except when I made the decision in 1983 that I did not want to participate in the L.A. Four any more. That's when I decided that I really wanted to be a jazz musician. The L.A. Four group was almost like being in the studios.

"I got my first clarinet when I was ten and my first saxophone when I was twelve and I knew I was going to be a professional musician some way or another. My love was the sax, even though clarinet was my major instrument up through college. That stopped as soon as I left, after three years. The clarinet never came out of the case again unless someone made me take it out.

"The most important band for me was at the University of North Carolina, Chapel Hill, when I was a student, Johnny Satterfield's band. I started playing with that band in high school. It was a marvelous band, those guys are the ones that really made a musician out of me. Then I went to L.A. and was struggling around, doing the usual parking cars and cleaning houses and all that.

"I got a job with Charlie Barnet at the end of 1946. That was the first big-time band I went with. I was with Barnet in '47, '48, then went back to L.A. in '49. I stayed in L.A., worked with a small band Al Viola had.

"That's when I met all the guys from Kenton's band. They were in L.A. also. When Stan put that Innovations in Modern Music band together, they recommended me for the job, and I had my only audition of my whole life. I got the job! Stan needed a saxophone player who could play the flute. I had just started with the instrument, so I had to bullshit my way through it. I guess I got the gig cause he couldn't *find* anyone else. I had and still have a lot of respect for Stan. He really encouraged the guys in the band to do whatever their thing was. I was hired to be lead alto player, not to be a soloist. That was Art Pepper's job. Whatever your position in that band, Stan encouraged you to do your thing.

"But that band was too clumsy to swing—because of the instrumentation and the voicings. On the other hand the sounds that came out of it were really big noises, really impressive. That's what that band was all about, making these really big noises. As far as swinging, it never did swing. Maybe it wasn't supposed to, I don't know. There sure were some players in it who swung.

"The *Contemporary Concepts* album, with those Bill Holman arrangements—that's one of the best big-band albums I've ever heard, I really enjoy listening to that album. That's probably as good as Stan ever got. I feel bad that I was not around then, I was long gone from the band by the time that album was made. That was some marvelous writing and some pretty good playing.

"I left Stan," Bud said, "because I got drafted. He kept me out of the army for two years. I had been 4F since I was eighteen because of my eye problem. When I became twenty-four and the Korean war was under way, they decided they were going to take me anyway. Stan's office kept me out up until January of 1953. Then I got drafted into the Marines, of all things, and they said, 'We don't want you in here, we don't want any one-eyed people in the Marine Corps. Get the hell out of here.'"

I was slightly startled by this bit of information, so casually communicated. I wasn't sure I'd heard Bud correctly. What was this about one-eyed?

"They discharged me," Bud continued. "I went home and turned twenty-five and then nobody could touch me any more.

"My military career! Six weeks, it took them six weeks to straighten it out. Which is ironic because my father is career army and my brother went straight out of college into the navy and here's old Bud being a saxophone player who did not want no part of none of that shit.

"So, that's how I got out of Stan Kenton's band, went to L.A., went back with Charlie Barnet for a couple of months and then I wanted to stay around L.A. for a while, and I started working with an R&B band that played jitterbug. That was one of the best things that happened to me. I always wanted to be a soloist and with Stan's band I never got the chance. I was the first alto player, so getting to be a soloist never happened, I was held back. By now I was twenty-six years old. I got this job with this jitterbug band playing tenor. We worked five nights a week around town. Every night there was a different jitterbug concert around. George Redman was the name of the band. Maynard Ferguson and Bill Perkins and a lot of other people played in that band. I started bringing in my friends, but the rhythm section always stayed the same, it was always horrible. I just went on honking, and it got rid of some of my inhibitions.

"Then an opening came up at the Lighthouse with Howard Rumsey's band. I started with them in '53, and I left in January of 1956 to form my own band, recording for Dick Bock and World Pacific. That's when Laurindo Almeida and I made that first Brazilian album. I keep hearing that story that we started bossa nova with that album. That's bullshit.

"If bossa nova is a combination of Brazilian folk melodies and jazz music, then maybe. But there are a lot more elements involved than that. The rhythmic parts of what we were doing on that first album had hardly any relation to the samba. A couple of the tunes were baions that were somewhat related but the melodies were

most certainly melodies that Laurindo remembered and brought
up from Brazil with him. Maybe that album might possibly have
helped in the evolution of bossa nova, but I'm not even sure about
that. Those guys were quite capable of evolving what they did without the help of Laurindo or anything else. Those early albums
were good and there were some valid things that came out of
them. But we most certainly did not invent bossa nova, by any
strange twist of the definition.

"I worked with my own quartet starting in 1946, with Claude
Williamson, Don Prell, and Chuck Flores. Did a lot of tours
around the U.S. and Europe, back and forth, back and forth. Then
in '60 I started to stay in Los Angeles more. By this time Gary
Peacock was working with me a lot.

"I formed another group in 1961 with Gary Peacock, Dennis
Budimir, and various drummers, an endless flow of drummers. We
worked at a club out in Malibu called Drift Inn for a few years.
Then it sort of petered out and then the studio years began."

Bud and I were far into our conversations when suddenly, unex-
pectedly, the explanation of his life came out. If you remember
what Bud looked like in his twenties, when he came out of the
Kenton band, you have an image of a tall, notably handsome
young man who seemed to have it all. He didn't see it that way.
Born Clifford Edward Shank, Jr., May 27, 1926, in Dayton, Ohio,
he had grown up convinced of his own ugliness.

"When you said you wanted to write this," he said, "I thought,
'What the hell does he want to write about me for? Hell, I've never
done anything. I'm middle class, Midwest, middle everything.' I'm
finding out what I sound like and who I am, and what I am, and I
like what I'm finding in here. Not that I'm satisfied with it, but I'm
liking what I find inside me. Down inside there all those years of
practicing in the woodshed to find the facility to get it out at last.

"You see, I was born cross-eyed. And I lived with that all my
life. When that isn't corrected, the brain compensates. It will not
accept two visual signals that it cannot co-ordinate. It shuts one of

them off. The weaker eye goes blind. I went blind in one eye early in my life.

"I was cross-eyed till 1976, when I was fifty. I went to an ophthalmologist because I had developed glaucoma. If you catch glaucoma early, it can be treated with drugs. But while I was seeing this man about that problem, he said, 'You know, I can straighten that eye by surgery. It's not going to help your vision, you still won't be able to see out of it. But it will stay straight.' I didn't know what to do about it.

"I went off to Catalina for a couple of weeks and thought about it, because it would be such a change, and there would be surgery. I came back and said, 'Okay, lets straighten it.'"

I said, "You know, Bud, all these years I've known you, I had no idea you were cross-eyed."

"No, you sure didn't, because I had ways of concealing it, and that was part of my problem.

"We went ahead and did the surgery, and it changed me all around. I had confidence I didn't know I could ever acquire that came from down inside me somewhere. All of a sudden I could look at people and talk to people where before I was always looking with my head down.

"And I played like that, I had always played as if I was walking around with my head down.

"I hope I'm still a lyrical player but I hope I'm playing with a lot of confidence and with a lot of strength and conviction. All those things I didn't have before. I was following other people, and following what they expected of me. And now I don't give a shit. If you don't like what I do, that's tough, 'cause I feel like I'm doing it right and doing it good.

"It didn't happen overnight. It has come about over the last ten years. It really changed my life around. I gave me the courage to get to where I am now, to get rid of the flute and get to this plateau of my playing. I was always a follower, following somebody else around, following what the West Coast sound was all about, you know, like a little sheep.

"This thing of being myself didn't happen till I was nearly sixty years old. There has never been a real me, and now there is a real me. I think I was always a good player in spite of the inhibition. But it was never a zap! I'll go this way. I was waiting for somebody else to go and then okay I'll go this way too. I don't feel this way at all any more.

"I'm involved with just being a jazz musician and improviser, and creative in my own way. The funny part is that I'm having more depressing moments than ever before. I didn't realize it until I read that article you did in the *Jazzletter* about Emily Remler, and you were talking about depression as a part of the creative process, and all of a sudden I realized I was having some really down periods. I could talk my way out of them but I was having them, and this was something I did not have when I was a studio sausage, with no ups and downs. I started to get bugged at these things happening.

"When you're a studio musician, they don't want you to be individual. That's how I got into sailboat racing. I didn't care about that music, just play it and take the money, and racing was my creative release.

"But since I stopped being a studio sausage, I care about what I'm playing and sometimes I'm up about it and sometimes I'm not."

Bud and I talked about the exodus of great musicians from Los Angeles, especially those who were involved in studio work, either as composers or players. With the rise of the synthesizers and one-keyboard film music, such as the dreadful moaning that passes for music in Oliver Stone's *Wall Street*, a great many brilliant musicians have paused to re-examine their lives. J. J. Johnson, Roger Kellaway, and Benny Golson, all have given up writing music for films and television. Or else they were ignored as yuppie producers raised on rock went after swoosh-moan-and-ululate. Whichever the reason, they went back to playing, and all three are playing better than ever before in their lives, because they have applied all the years of experience in composition to playing, and have rebuilt their chops. J. J. had doubts as he built up his chops for a return to playing, but they were groundless, and his playing has passed beyond brilliance now into grandeur. His playing now is awesome. Golson too had doubts, and he said it took two years for him to rebuild his saxophone chops. The labor was worth it: he too has exceeded himself.

Ray Brown has checked out of the studios, as has his longtime crony and partner guitarist Herb Ellis. Many of these people have left Los Angeles. Ellis now lives in Arkansas, Kellaway in New York. J. J. Johnson moved back to his home town, Indianapolis. Meantime, there is a growing jazz community in the Pacific Northwest. Dave Frishberg and Bill Hood now live in Portland, Oregon. And Bud Shank lives in the little fishing town of Port Townsend, Washington, with the Strait of Juan de Fuca before him and the great jagged blue wall of the Olympic Mountains at his back.

"We discovered Port Townsend," Bud said, "when I went to play in Seattle in a club called Parnell's and the piano player was a guy named Barney McClure. Barney told me about this little town he lived in, which was Port Townsend, and it fascinated me the way he described it. Lynn and I had been looking for an alternative place to live since 1975 and had been spending some time in Maui, in fact we had a condo there. Not a place to live permanently, just an alternative to L.A. Then that too got crowded and we looked for somewhere else.

"Two years later I went back to Seattle and learned that Barney McClure had been elected mayor of Port Townsend. Bebop piano player becomes mayor, right? In 1979 Barney was involved with a very small jazz festival and a one-day workshop they were having. He invited the L.A. Four to play there. I fell in love with it. Came home and told Lynn; Barney invited us back next year and Lynn came with me and we bought a house there in 1980.

"Barney's story was he had come up from L.A. with a bass player and drummer in the car, ripped out of their nuts, hippies, Barney with a beard and an ear-ring. They got to Olympia and went the wrong way and ended up in Port Townsend. Barney decided to stay there.

"Port Townsend at that time had been abandoned by the regulars and had been taken over by the hippies. A lot of kids from Berkeley had come up and found paradise and beautiful old empty houses. Meanwhile the establishment had rediscovered Port Townsend and the hippies were out on the street again. There was terrible conflict and Barney ran for mayor and won. He opened a music store and became very successful. The ex-Berkeley kids opened all the restaurants and art galleries, and the Establishment from Seattle came in and restored the old homes.

"Barney became more and more involved with politics and the Democratic party started grooming him for the governorship. And all this time he is playing piano every night—and he's a damn good piano player. He decided not to run for governor. He was a member of the state legislature. Eventually we may have our first bebop heavyweight politician. I think he has a very bright future in politics and he really is a great pianist.

"I sort of inherited this little festival in Port Townsend, run by something called the Centrum Foundation, funded by state, federal, and private donations. The foundation also does a chamber music week. There's a week for writers, and a week for poets, and a week for the Seattle Symphony workshop, a folk music week, a bluegrass week, and a jazz workshop and festival.

"What I like about the Pacific Northwest is the weather, the freshness of it all. It's a very inspiring place to live. There are a lot of artists and arts-minded-people—arts-conscious versus money-conscious."

I asked Bud where he'd met Lynn. He said,

"I think my first wife introduced us in L.A. in the mid-'50s. Strangely enough it was through my other hobby, which is sports cars, racing Formula One cars. I used to go to sports car races and Lynn's first husband was a sports-car driver and that's where our paths crossed. My first wife went off into a film career. We got divorced, and Lynn and I got married in 1957 and we've been at it ever since. We don't have any children, by either marriage. Not by choice, it just happened that way."

I suggested to Bud that a new situation has arisen in jazz, the return to the art of its old masters, men such as J. J. Johnson, Ray Brown, Herb Ellis—and Bud Shank. There is always much talk about the new young talents. What about the return of the old masters? It is bound to have an effect. Bud said,

"There are more opportunities in jazz now than there ever was before, certainly more than in the '60s. The clubs come and the clubs go, but the records are selling fairly well right now and there are a lot more small record companies out there, there are more opportunities. At least there are for me. There are a lot of festivals, but I don't do a lot of them. Most of the festival operators still think I'm a studio sausage, but I'm working on that. It's just a fact that there are places to play and there weren't for so long.

"I see a lot of younger audiences and that's really healthy, and I'm not talking about college tours. When you book into clubs, I'm really amazed at the younger audiences. I'm pleased and I think it's really healthy. There is a great number of jazz camps around in the summer. There may be a hundred students at each one and maybe one of those will become a star. What you have left is ninety-nine jazz fans out of each camp, and not all of them will become great players but they will have an appreciation of jazz and they will go their way and have careers and get married and then for each one you'll have two people with an appreciation of jazz, and on it goes. I think this is the only way to perpetuate this thing."

Bud Shank remains very handsome, but the prettiness is gone. He now has a beard which, like his thick head of straight hair, is gray. He is full of maturity and good sense and he looks a little like a mountain man.

At the end of the two days, he and Lynn got into their car to leave. We were sorry to see them go. We waved good-bye to them from the driveway.

I'll never view him the same way again. I'd been hearing him differently for some time, and now I knew why.

Trombone and Tulips:
Al Grey

Al Grey has been pushing jazz through a trombone for more than forty-five years. By the age of sixty-six, men in most professions are in retirement, either voluntary or enforced. But people in the arts rarely retire, either because they are doing what they do not out of necessity but out of passion for the work, or because they have never accumulated enough money to retire. Al Grey's motivation is more the former. Early in 1988, after a seven-year partnership with his friend Buddy Tate, Al launched a group whose front line consisted of two trombones, the first of that configuration since the group of J. J. Johnson and Kai Winding. The second trombonist was Al's son Michael, who plays a lot like his father. The guitarist was the late Al Cohn's son Joe.

Al Grey's career has been rich, despite times of frustration, and he has interesting—sometimes funny and sometimes startling—things to say. How many musicians played their way through the bands of Benny Carter, Lucky Millinder, Jimmie Lunceford, Lionel Hampton, Dizzy Gillespie, Duke Ellington, and Count Basie?

Albert Thornton Grey was born in Aldie, Virginia, June 6, 1925. The family moved almost immediately to Pottstown, Pennsylvania, where Al still lives.

"My father was a musician," Al said on a sunny afternoon in

Boulder, Colorado. "He played trumpet. I kept wanting to get into his case. Eventually I did and I got the horn out, and I'd try, and nothing would happen. One day I took his horn out and didn't get it back right and bent the second valve. He came home and started beating me until my mother had to run up and grab him and hold him to stop him. He just went off. He didn't mean to. All he could think was that he had a job that night. It's nothing to get a valve fixed today. My mother went out and got a job washing the floor of Lamb's music store. This is in the days when you had to take a pad and brush and get down on the floor and wash it. She washed that floor until she bought me this trombone, a King trombone, Tommy Dorsey model, with a rimless bell. It took her a year. My father began to give me lessons. But by then music wasn't as interesting to me because the kids were out playing baseball. He'd come home and I'd get a whipping then for not practicing. He didn't allow me out. I had to practice until the other kids went in. I found out many years later why. He told my mother, 'Well, if he's going to play, I don't want him to get hit in the mouth.'

"I played in the band in junior high school. Then the teacher said, 'You're a pretty big boy, we need a bass player.' So they put me on the E-flat tuba. Everything was different."

Pearl Harbor came when Al was nineteen, and he joined the navy.

These many years later, Al, who is tall, carries not a trace of fat on his lanky frame. He has a wide warming smile, bracketed by deep lines from the nostrils almost to the chin. He has pouches under the eyes, like those of Duke Ellington. He has a loose mustache that is traced with gray, and that fringe of hair that some brass players allow to grow to protect the lower lip. He is of that older school of jazz musician that did not draw a line between entertainment and art and believed in amusing as well as moving an audience. Therefore he is animated on stage, moving with a kind of awkward grace, a little like Pinocchio just after shedding his strings or Ray Bolger as the Straw Man in *The Wizard of Oz*. He wears curious little hats like smaller-brimmed variants on an

English bobby's helmet. He has them in several colors, including solid white, solid black, and brown tweed. He wears them onstage, and they go curiously but somehow effectively with his suits, which are beautifully cut, dark, and formal, his blue shirts, and his neat, usually red, ties. His playing is as loose and joyous as his movements.

He is the master of the plunger mute, and he uses it a lot, shaping tones into vocal sounds in the manner of Tricky Sam Nanton who, he says, refused to show him a thing. The attitude was common among the generation of jazzmen ahead of him. Ray Brown tells of asking one of the noted bass players of his youth about the instrument and being told curtly, "We figured it out. You figure it out."

Mutes change the resistance in the embouchure. A harmon or cup mute pushed into the bell makes the instrument a bit sharp, the solution to which problem in a long passage is to push the tuning slide at the top of the horn out a little. But when the rubber plunger is used (sometimes with a small straight mute in the bell) it alters the intonation from note to note, and sometimes within the same note. Thus means the compensation must be made from tone to tone or within the same tone. "Using the plunger is an art in itself," Dick Nash, himself one of the master trombonists, said. "When it comes to the trombone, Al Grey can stand up to anybody."

He never uses the slide for vibrato. He gets the vibrato with the lip. The slide flicks to a position and stops dead and this lovely even vibrato sets in. Al uses the slide for vibrato only in orchestral section work, when he is blending with other players. The measure of Al Grey as a superb player of the instrument can be taken from a 1984 Pablo album he made with J.J. Johnson, titled *Things Are Getting Better All the Time*. It contains some stunning trombone by both men.

The brass instruments amount to lengths of pipe with mouthpieces attached. You sort of spit into the mouthpiece, with the lips tensed, rather as if trying to get a bit of lint or tobacco off the end of your tongue. The resultant buzz resonates through the pipe.

The tones available are a consequence of the overtone series, and limited. The bugle is the basic brass instrument, and in theory cannot play all the notes. The bugle calls are selected from the limited group of notes in its vocabulary, essentially the tones found in the major triad, repeated in the octave above. For example, the melody we call *Taps*, heard at military funerals, is built of the second inversion of the major triad. So is the tune we sing to "baby by, see the fly." So are the opening four notes of *For All We Know*.

In Mozart's time, brass instruments could play only the tones of that small vocabulary, and in the key of that vocabulary. To alter this, extensions, or crooks, could be added to the piece of pipe, but the player still was limited to the new key that this lengthening of the tube created, and he was incapable of chromatic playing. The valved trumpet was developed in 1813. In effect all the crooks were added to the horn and connected by valves, which instantly cut these extensions in or out. That's essentially what a trumpet is, a form of bugle with all the extension crooks added and linked by a valve system. When you depress different combinations of the buttons, the action lengthens or shortens the resonating air column.

The trombone differs from the valved instruments in that one lengthens the resonating brass column by pushing the slide out, which drops the pitch. There are seven positions, which lower the tones—all the tones of the bugle-call repertoire—by half steps. Seven half-steps, as you can work out at a piano keyboard, add up to tri-tone or flatted fifth (or raised fourth) and thus the positions of the slide exactly divide the octave into equal portions. And they make it possible to play all the notes of all the keys, with the slide in one position or another. Some notes can be played in different positions, though not equally easily.

The trombone is far older than the trumpet. Paintings from the late fifteenth century show the trombone—known then as the sacbut—with the essential characteristics of the modern instrument, but, surprisingly, it was not used much in orchestras for centuries. Beethoven introduced it into symphonic music in the Fifth Symphony, but it really was not part of the orchestra until Berlioz and

Wagner began using it. And they had no idea of its potential. Traditional textbooks say that because of the time it takes to move the slide, true legato is not possible on the trombone. That's because their authors never heard J. J. Johnson or Jack Teagarden.

Teagarden said that you should be able to play virtually any note in any position. Trombone players say that that's carrying things a little far, but nonetheless Teagarden, who could do amazing tricks on the horn, once sat at a table in a nightclub with me and played a major scale in closed position. He had begun playing when he was quite small, and his short arms couldn't get the slide down into the lower positions, and so he worked out ways to play many of the tones in positions where they weren't supposed to be.

Al said, "Melba Liston taught me a lot—like alternate positions where I was playing legit. This is when we were with Dizzy. I discovered why J. J. played so fast—he used those alternate positions. I used to hang around Melba's house. With Mary Lou Williams and Thelonious Monk and Tadd Dameron. They would get to the piano and play things. Melba and I were very dear and close."

Another, if inadvertent, influence on his playing was the writing of Thad Jones. He said, "You see, Thad didn't know how to write for the trombones at first. We were fighting the slides." The charts Thad wrote for Basie extended Al's chops.

Jazz has expanded the scope of a number of instruments, but none more than brass and, in recent years, the string bass. It hasn't done much for the piano, and jazz pianists have had to tag along behind in the control and scope on the instrument of major "classical" virtuosi; most of them will tell you honestly that they haven't yet made it. But on brass, it's different, as it is in pizzicato string bass. Nowhere has the expansion been as spectacular as in the vocabulary of the trombone.

The use in jazz goes back to the tail-gate kind of playing associated with New Orleans marching bands. The bluesy dirges on the way to a funeral followed by the hot soaring numbers afterwards are part of the legend of the music. But the instrument really began to grow in the 1920s. One of the important figures is Teagarden, and then there is a series of great trombonists, including J. C. Higginbotham, Trummy Young, and Vic Dickenson. The way Tommy Dorsey opened the way to the highly lyrical use of the horn is a significant element in the expansion of twentieth century instrumentalism.

"I loved all of them," Al said, "but you left out a couple—Jack Jenney and Turk Murphy. I loved Tommy Dorsey's smoothness, but the solo Jack Jenney played on Artie Shaw's *Star Dust* impressed me, and Jack Teagarden's *Sophisticated Lady*."

Then came J. J. Johnson, whose significance usually is seen to be his adaptation of bebop to the trombone. To do so required extending the high-speed technique that Teagarden had demonstrated was possible, and J. J. played—and plays—the horn with almost the speed of a trumpet player. J. J.'s facility at this, not to mention his harmonic command, inspired a generation—by now two generations—of brilliant players. After J.J. you get Curtis Fuller, Carl Fontana, Frank Rosolino, Jimmy Knepper, Phil Wilson, Bill Watrous and others who would blow Richard Wagner's brassy mind if he could return to hear them.

I guess I've known Al Grey nearly thirty years, but I never knew him well until April of 1988, when we were room-mates for a week during the annual Conference on World Affairs on the campus of the University of Colorado at Boulder. There is a surprisingly large contingent from the jazz world, and among the panelists that year were Leonard Feather, Dave and Don Grusin, Johnny Mandel, Les McCann, Ben Sidran, Al Grey, and myself. Don Grusin and Les McCann kept everyone in laughter. The panelists were farmed out to various homes. The jazz contingent was at that of Betty Weems, a hospitable architect and jazz lover. Al, Ben Sidran, and I shared an exquisite guest cottage at the bottom of her garden out of whose door we could watch the tulips coming into blossom, a rabbit taking his toll on them, Boulder Creek running full with snow melt, and, on a sidewalk beyond the swift waters, students jogging or strolling or pushing baby carriages. No more than a mile away, the first great wall of the Rocky Mountains rose suddenly out of the prairie. That week Al and I talked often and at length.

Al Grey's experience in the navy would shape the rest of his life. He was assigned to the Great Lakes Naval Training Station, where a number of bands were in training, some of them under the direction of Sam Donahue. But Al didn't get into one of those bands: the armed forces of the United States were strictly segregated, right down to the level of the bands.

"Camp Small was the black camp," Al said. "On our side we had players like Clark Terry, Soupy Campbell, and the Batchman brothers from St. Louis, who had been with George Hudson. We had arrangers like Luther Henderson and Dudley Brooks and Jimmy Kennedy, a guitarist who had played with Benny Carter. We had Pee Wee Jackson who had played with Jimmie Lunceford, and Gerald Wilson. Osie Johnson was my bunk-mate, him up above and me down below, and he would tell jokes all night until they'd come in and threaten to put us on the slackers' squad for not going to sleep. He was a funny, funny man. And played good rhythm.

"But I couldn't get into that band because they already had so many great famous musicians—plus I had been playing tuba. Obsolete. But we had a trombone player that was very famous, Rocks McConnell, from Cleveland. He was playing with Lucky Millinder's band and got a hit, on a song he wrote, *Sweet Slumber*. The royalties started coming in and he just went over the hill one day, and we never saw him again. So I started covering for him in rehearsals when they'd come for inspections. That's how I got into the band, fourth chair. Then they sent us to Hingham, Massachusetts. After boots, I became a musician third class.

"Hingham was another all black camp, an ammunition depot, where everybody was just about illiterate, from the south, Mississippi, Alabama. These guys could not read. I had to write letters home for them to some of their parents and I knew that some other person, it always sounded like some white person, had to write the letters back, and I would have to read them to them. I showed a few how to write their names. They had to write X for their pay.

"Our job was to practice every day and go out to the shipyards when ships were commissioned and play *The Star-Spangled Banner* and a couple of tunes and then get off. We had a good dance band there, a good reading band. I'd learned to read from my father and from school.

"The band was so good we auditioned for Major Bowes radio program. We went down to New York and they put us up in the Teresa Hotel. When it came time to go down and play, it was the greatest thing in the world for us. And they gave us a week's liberty behind this.

"Because of those guys being illiterate, they didn't allow them to go on liberty but every other day, whereas the band was allowed to go on liberty every day. They got angry, saying that we never had to work. Somebody decided that maybe the musicians should work a couple of days. Everybody wrote a letter to President Roosevelt to complain. So they decided to break the band up. They sent us all to different places. I got shipped out to Grosse Isle Naval Air Station, near Grosse Pointe, Michigan. It was great for me, because we could go in to Detroit. And this is where I got a lot of training from great musicians. This was around 1943, '44.

"We would hitchhike in. People were very friendly about picking up the sailors and taking them in to Detroit. First we'd stop at Stroh's Brewery. We'd have a couple of beers and then be on our way to sign in for our rooms at the U.S.O. And whatever passes you needed for whatever show, especially the boxing matches, the U.S.O. would give them to you for free. You didn't have to pay no transportation, because you could go free on any public transportation.

"We did have one problem. There was prejudice. Right next to the U.S.O. there was a bar that didn't allow blacks. And eventually some sailors came back who had been to the war. And they really knew that they had no business to be treated like that. They went into the bar one night, and they started to get called names, and they wrecked the liquor stock. Smashed it all. The navy punished everybody black. They kept us on the base for fifteen days. We weren't allowed to go in to Detroit. This was a big hurt for something you had nothing to do with.

"There were so many clubs in Detroit, the Twelve Horsemen, the Three Sixes, the Bluebird, where Milt Jackson played. He was like the kingpin out there, till he went with Diz. So many musicians. Mostly black clubs. And there was the famous Paradise Theater. This gave me an opportunity to sit and play.

"Duke Ellington came to town. I was so fascinated with Tricky Sam Nanton. I would go to the Twelve Horsemen, where he hung out. He was a very heavy drinker. I said, 'Well, I'll buy you the drinks, just show me what you're doing. He said, 'Uh-unh, I'll play.' I heard what he was doing. But I didn't take no mind—it was many many years before I fooled around with the plunger.

"We had such a good band at Grosse Isle. I would get people to replace me so I could sit in with other bands. If you didn't want to eat on the base, they would pay you subsistence. And at the U.S.O. you'd get all this free food. That's how I was buying war bonds and sending them to my mother.

"I had a problem with my feet that they couldn't fix, so they gave me a medical discharge.

"Lanky Bowman, who was a great alto player of Detroit, led a great band in the pit at the Paradise. A lot of times his band would jump on popular bands that came through. He knew all the best musicians, and he was in with George Clancy, who was on the board of the musicians' union. George Clancy really loved the black musicians and used to give them a break. Give guys a chance. A lot of cities had two locals, black and white, but Detroit had one, Local 5.''

"Unlike Chicago," I said.

"Local 208 in Chicago," Al said, "had accumulated a lot of money and built apartments for musicians. So when it came time to join the white local, they didn't want to. They had so much money. They were *forced* to merge. I know a musician who even today lives in one of those apartments.

"Anyway, when I got out of service, Lanky Bowman went and got me a card in the Detroit local that day.

"I found out my mother had saved all the money I'd sent to her, and she told me, 'Here it is, you better get yourself a car,' and I bought a station wagon.

"The day I got out of the service, Benny Carter was losing J. J. Johnson, and gave me his job. The next day I left with the band for Louisville, Kentucky. This is when they had the girl trumpet player, Jeanne Starr. And Max Roach and Sonny White and Bumps Meyers and Willard Brown and Jimmy Kennedy. That was a powerful band.

"We went to the Swing Club out in Hollywood for a month, and then the Trianon Ballroom out at Southgate. We'd play for a week at a time. The places would be packed. We'd be in California for three months at a time. We played on V-discs, plus we'd go out and jam. Benny played a lot of jobs for the government. We'd get on these C-27s and C-26s and fly to the military bases. We played a club in North Hollywood, the Casa Manana, and then the Swing Club, and the Suzie Q on Hollywood, and the club where Art Tatum worked. Billy Berg's, where Bird and Slim Gaillard—who used to run it—played. Jackie Cooper and Mickey Rooney and all the movie people would come in and want to play. Kay Starr and Lana Turner wanted to sing. Kay Starr became a star, but the guys wanted to jam. These were guys like Teddy Edwards.

"We took a trip with Benny Carter cross-country. That old raggedy bus would get on the hills and we had to get out because it wouldn't make it with all of us on there. We finally got to the east coast, and Benny was just so sick of going on, he said, 'Fellows, that's it, I'm going into the studios.' This was 1946.

"Jimmie Lunceford selected out of Benny's band me and Reynald Jones to go with him. Joe Wilder came with Lunceford. Lunceford made me play Trummy Young, all his parts, exactly like Trummy played them. Trummy was my idol, so it was no problem, I could play those things.

"It was such a great band. Jimmie Lunceford would have you

on the bandstand fifteen minutes before hitting time. *He* tuned
you up. You didn't take your ear and tune your self up. That was
a must every night with him, whereas with Basie, you'd come on
the bandstand five minutes before you hit.

"The music with Lunceford was so different than all the other
music I had been playing. With Benny Carter, everything was long.
Lunceford would make a dotted quarter maybe a quarter, while
Benny Carter might extend it." Al sang two bars of melody evok-
ing Carter's lyrical style. Then he sang the same phrase very drily
and with the notes given short value and punched, in the exact
manner of the Lunceford band. He said, "It was a drastic change.
I'm supposed to be hitting that sucker short, and that took some
time.

"Jimmie Lunceford played the black universities and colleges all
over the country. We couldn't get to play downtown in New York.
We always had to play at the Renaissance and the Apollo in Harlem. We predominantly played for blacks, and that was one of the
bad things, we thought—we had such a great band. Sy Oliver was
writing for the band, and then Edwin Wilcox came in.

"I stayed with that band until Jimmie died, out at Seaside, Oregon. We were playing at the resort at Seaside. They didn't allow
blacks in. We were waiting for Lunceford to come back from a
record shop where he was signing autographs. He never got back,
and that was the end of it.

"After that I went with Lucky Millinder."

I said, "You know, Dizzy told me that although he didn't even
play an instrument, Lucky Millinder was a very good bandleader."

"Oh yeah!" Al said. "And he selected the best of musicians. And
the best arrangers. And this was on a fair basis. If you were white,
it didn't matter. If you were good, you could play in that band. It
was a mixed band, and he *made* it so. We had Freddy Zito on trombone. Fact, Lucky used to think that blacks couldn't play the trombone. After Tommy Dorsey, Lucky Millinder didn't think blacks
could come up with it. Basie thought that for a long period too,
until J. J. Johnson came along.

"I'd been singing all of Trummy Young's tunes in the Lunceford band. So Lucky Millinder wanted me to sing too. And I *hated* singing. It was bad enough to sing *Margie* and those tunes, and it was marking me. Lucky made me sing.

"After Lucky Millinder, I went with Lionel Hampton.

"Jimmie Lunceford was a professor of music at Fisk University, and most of his musicians came out of Fisk University. We had to sit up straight all the time, and no clappin' hands and moving your feet.

"So I went from that to Lionel Hampton, where we had a lot of routines where we had to clap our hands, to do all kinds of things. They would turn on fluorescent lights and you'd see all our hands moving in white gloves in the dark. Coming from Lunceford to clapping your hands with the white gloves, I really just didn't think that that had anything actually to do with the music, or the playing. It got to me. I'm a real northerner who went to white schools and lived around whites all my life. Pottstown is one of those really mixed towns. They've really integrated fabulously. So to do the white gloves and all that, I thought it was Uncle Tomming and the minstrel scene. But then we'd do *Air Mail Special* and things like that and the music was good. The band would swing. We would get up and walk around the whole block and the rhythm section was still swinging. But it used to kill drummers, wear them out. Even George Jenkins, who was a *powerful* drummer. Then we had acrobats who would go out in the audience playing their saxophones and walk the edges of the seats, jump from the balconies on the stage, and all like this. And, yes, Lionel Hampton had them standing in line waiting to get in. We went on Broadway for two weeks and stayed something like nine weeks.

"All the guys felt like I did. Milt Buckner felt we had so much musical ability that we didn't have to do all that. Hamp eventually cut it out, because he was getting complaints from the NAACP and other people. The era was changing.

"Hamp stopped all that and changed drastically. That's when he got political. Look what happened to him in Madison Square when he came out for Reagan to help him get the black vote. The black people threw tomatoes at him. At that time his greatest friend was

George Bush. We had to get on trucks and go play for the Republicans. Although we did that in Count Basie's band for Nelson Rockefeller. That's how Basie got his club established up in Harlem. It made Hamp a big man. He has all these houses now.

"I'll never forget the year we played the inaugural ball for Eisenhower. They had the *Tonight* show band, and James Brown, who had a record out called *I'm Black and I'm Proud* and here we were playing to an all-white audience. And they didn't even want Lionel Hampton's band to set up. The musicians complained and Tony Bennett spoke up for them. So they let the band play for the review for Eisenhower—and the Marriotts and all like this.

"After all those trying times, we lucked up with Hamp and now we were playing just about only in white clubs. We're talking about 1948. It was great that Hamp had changed. There was no more handkerchief-head. Some white players came into the band.

"I got fired from Hamp's band. We were playing at the Latin Casino in Cleveland. Hamp had been working an hour or so over each night. This night we had been on overtime an hour and twenty minutes. And we hadn't even gone into *Flying Home* yet! And *Flying Home* meant another half an hour. Dinah Washington walked in and he was playing for her and another singer, Bill Farrell.

"I had a lady I was supposed to see back home, and now the last bus was about to leave. I got off the bandstand, and the whole trombone section got off with me—Benny Powell, Al Hayes, Jimmy Cleveland, and a Japanese guy we had, Paul Hagaki, from San Francisco, who could hit high notes on the trombone that I have not heard anybody else do to this day. The whole section got off! Now Hamp don't even see this, he's doing a trio thing, and then he goes into *Flying Home* and he needs the band, and this thing for the trombones, and there's no trombones." Al sang the passage. "Gladys, his wife, was the *boss*. She said, 'Al Grey's a bad influence on the band, get rid of him.' And so she fired me. Fired the whole trombone section, but they needed some 'bone players, and they let them work out their notice. But I was gone that night.

"I went into New York. I went to Beefsteak Charlie's bar, and ran into Sy Oliver, and he said, 'Hey! What're you doin'?' I said, 'Nothin'.' So that's how I went to work in the studios. I went to work for Sy Oliver and Dick Jacobs, recording. In those days, there weren't many black musicians in the studios. They were accused of not being able to read. I remember that first date, I arrived, and Sy said, 'Hey, where are your mutes?' He say, 'Boy, you get outa here and get yourself a cup mute, harmon mute, and all that.' That day I recorded on Decca with Ella Fitzgerald, *Early Autumn*. I had eight bars on it.

"I stayed in the studios for a couple of years. But then I knew I would never be a studio musician. Maybe if I hadn't played on the road with a band, I might have settled to it. But I found that playing to four walls every day would never do it for me.

"After that I became the musical director for Bullmoose Jackson, who had been with Lucky Millinder, and then I went with Arnett Cobb, who had a great small group. He had several hits like *Too Old to Dream* and *Dutch Kitchen.*

"But the greatest thing was next, to go to Dizzy Gillespie's big band. This would be '49 to '52. What a band! Come on! We'd come to work twenty minutes before time, warming up getting ready to hit. In the trumpet section we had Lee Morgan, Carl Warwick, we used to call him Bama, Lamar Wright. The trombone section was Melba Liston, Chuck Connors, Rod Levitt, and me. The rhythm section was Wynton Kelly, Paul Wess, and Charlie Persip. The reed section was Benny Golson, Billy Mitchell, Ernie Henry, Rudy Powell, and Billy Root on baritone, who came from Stan Kenton's band. For a while we had Phil Woods.

"This is what I admired about Diz. And Lucky. They didn't care what color anybody was.

"What a band. But Dizzy was losing so much money. To play in that band we all had to take a *drop* in fees. We all got $135 a week, and you had to pay your hotel and all your expenses out of that. I ran into a big, big problem.

"One night we were playing in Birdland. I come off the bandstand. Two white guys came up and said, 'Oh, you're so great! You're a fantastic trombone player. We like your playing!' And then one of them opened his coat and here was a badge. 'We've come to pick you up tonight for domestic problems, and we have to take you to jail and you have to go to court tomorrow.'

"I wasn't sending enough money home to my wife and kids and she had to go and get relief, and she told him that I worked for Dizzy. And these two guys said, 'You play so much. We're going to let you play out tonight, and trust you to be down in domestic court tomorrow morning. We want you down there at seven o'clock tomorrow morning. And sit on the bench until they call your name.' I says, 'Oh my goodness, I have a recording date tomorrow morning at ten o'clock with Sarah Vaughan.' He say, 'You find somebody to play in your place, we don't want to have to come back here tomorrow night, because we know you'll *be* here.'

"So I got a lawyer, Maxwell T. Cohen. He's the one who got the law changed about cabaret cards. He was the lawyer for Dizzy's band. Max went down to represent me. Dizzy had just come off one of those State Department goodwill tours, and it was in the newspapers that he had made a lot of money. Max told the court that my salary was only $135 a week, and I was sending her $25 or $30 a week and after Max got through the court awarded her $15 a week, which wasn't as much as I'd been sending. The court said I should get together with her and get it taken off the record.

"So I said, 'Why would you do something like that, Tina?' I said, 'Let's try to bury the hatchet and I'll try to do better. But I was just trying to become a real great musician.'

"You see, I had a job at home playing bar mitzvahs where I would make $175 to $200 a week. So she wanted to know why I would give this up to go out on the road and pay your expenses out of $135 a week. Then she said she'd tell the domestic court that we were back together and everything was fine.

"Playing with Dizzy, we all loved it. But Dizzy was losing money and finally, in 1952, he had to go back to the small group. We didn't want to leave.

"Lee Morgan and Benny Golson and Billy Mitchell, they were

playing, and that enhances you, that inspires you to try and play too. That enabled me to get much faster with my horn.

"From Dizzy I moved to Basie and I was with Basie on and off for almost twenty-one years, from '51 to '76. I did some television with Duke Ellington and recording. We'd be in Birdland in New York and I'd be recording every day.

"I came into Chicago in 1961 with a band that won the *Down Beat* new group of the year, and you wrote about me in *Down Beat*. We had such a great group. I had signed Bobby Hutcherson and we had Billy Mitchell and the drummer was Eddy Williams, from California, and Doug Watkins, who was a great bass player."

"By the way," I interrupted, "whatever happened to Doug Watkins?"

"I'll tell you about that. We played the Jazz Workshop in San Francisco. Doug fell in love with one of the waitresses.

"We came across the country by car. Doug's Peugeot broke down in Texas. Billy Mitchell took all our little money out of our pockets to get it fixed. We went into Birdland in New York. And Doug says, 'I'm in love, and I'm going back to San Francisco with Philly Joe Jones.' And we'd struck it good. We were going into the Apollo from there. And we hadn't received that money back. The night before he left, Billy Mitchell and I almost got into a fight, because he hadn't wanted to bring Doug Watkins to New York, he said New York had so many great bass players. And we were short on our payroll because we had lent this money.

"Doug left for California, and he got out there on the highway and fell asleep, and one of these tractor-trailers wiped him out. We got a telegram at the Apollo that morning.

"Anyway, we came into the Sutherland Lounge in Chicago, to cover for Ahmad Jamal, who was sick. The people lined up around the corner in the snow to see us. We had a hit, *Salty Papa*, and in the *Down Beat* critics poll, we beat out Sonny Rollins for new group of the year.

"Soon's you get a good group, it seems like all other groups try to get that musician away from you. Herman Wright was now our bass player—a cousin to Gene Wright. Terry Gibbs offered him more money to come with him, so we started getting friction there. Miles Davis wanted our drummer, Eddy Williams, and he was threatening to leave. So the overhead ran too big. It was really sad, because we had such a group, and people like Quincy Jones and Gene Roland and Ernie Wilkins were writing for us. Everybody can't write for tenor and trombone. Billy and I broke up the group and I went back to Basie."

He stayed with the Basie band until Basie had a heart attack, formed a group with Jimmy Forrest, returned to Basie when the band was re-formed, then went out with Forrest again to work all over Europe. The strains of the jazz life finally undermined his marriage, and Al and his wife separated, she to live in a house they own in Philadelphia, he in another house they own in Pottstown, or, more specifically, Stowe, Pennsylvania.

"I've been a freelance player since '76," Al said. "I was with Jimmy Forrest for a long time, and the past seven years with Buddy Tate. And now my own group with my son Michael and Joe Cohn. Michael was given a chance at study, and he loves it. The family is really together when it comes to that.

"I have four boys. Albert is the oldest. The second son, Ernest, takes care of our house. Mike and Robert are both musicians. Mike plays trombone, Robert plays valve trombone. Like me, as a baby, hearing the sounds, they were determined that they really wanted to be musicians. Michael had a scholarship to Westchester State Teachers' College, but he wanted to go to Berklee. He became so good that in his last year he had a half a year's scholarship.

"We started music in our basement. We had a three-story cobblestone home in Philadelphia. We fixed up the basement so we could play pingpong and have rehearsals. Around the corner from us we had Kevin and Robin Eubanks. They would come over and play with my boys.

"My oldest son, Albert, put together a little band playing rock-

and-roll, with Michael and Kevin Eubanks. They got only a dollar a night and put the rest in a kitty. They ended up with so much money they bought a second-hand bus, drums, a whole sound system. Michael went off to Berklee, Kevin went to the Academy of Music. One of them had to go into the service, and Albert inherited the sound system, and now he's a very famous rock disc jockey in Philadelphia, and he calls himself Captain Boogie and he has a partner they call Astro Boy, and they make more money than I could even think of making. Just for one night at the Athletic Club in Philadelphia of playing discs they can make $4000.

"I'm really excited by the new group I have with Michael and Joe Cohn.

"Michael and Joe Cohn were working around Boston with Alan Dawson. Phil Wilson was Michael's trombone teacher. Mike does something I can't do—circular breathing. Phil taught him that. If he gets hung up, and he thinks his old man is playing too much on him, he'll string me out by hitting on a note and holding it and holding it until the people start to applaud. Then he'll turn his head, 'You see, Dad?'

"And we have a wonderful drummer, Bobby Durham, who hasn't had the recognition he deserves because he has worked so much with singers.

"I really believe so strongly in this new group that I'll go down the drain with it.

"Johnny Mandel has written some things for me. We have some things that J.J. Johnson and I recorded together in 1984. Frank Foster has written some for us and I have and Joe Cohn too.

"Joe Cohn has been overshadowed by his father, and no one knows him until now. I have made up my mind that we're going to record an album of Al Cohn's tunes. Al and I were close. We used to break bread together. This group just has to be heard and I will go all the way with it.

"When you've been out here playing with jazz musicians like Louis Bellson and J.J. Johnson and Oscar Peterson, it makes you want to stay in the business for life. Roy Eldridge came to hear

Buddy Tate and me one night at Sweet Basil. This was after his
heart attack. We came off the bandstand and he had tears in his
eyes because he couldn't play any more.

"Just think. I'm so happy Roy can sing a couple of numbers and
pacify that desire."

Al and I were sitting at a table near the door of the little cottage
we were sharing. Ben Sidran had just returned, and he was sitting
on the corner of the bed, listening to us talk. I was looking out the
open door. The air was perfect, and it was too early in the season
for insects. There was that little brown rabbit, out there among
the tulips in that springtime Colorado garden, making his living. I
had seen him a lot in the past several days, and it struck me that
he had a lot of nerve to be out there doing that in broad daylight.
Had he no sense of danger?

Al heaved a sigh of a sort, and his face suddenly took on a deep
sadness, a weariness of all the years on the road. And what he said
next made Ben Sidran's eyes meet mine and hold for a moment.
Al said, "I'm just out here trying to be a great musician and make
a little peace."

And then the smile returned.

Boy with Drum

Is he, I wondered as I drove into Los Angeles that evening, as marvelous a drummer as I remember? Or have time and personal affection colored my impression of his playing? I had not heard Edmund Thigpen play in person in twenty years, excepting in Dusseldorf, when he worked on a Sarah Vaughan album for which I wrote the lyrics, doing a journeyman job in a huge orchestra that offered no room for his personal expression—and left me no time to listen to what he was doing in any event. The reason is that he had been living in Copenhagen, part of the enclave of American players there that included Kenny Drew, Thad Jones, Richard Boone, Ernie Wilkins, and Sahib Shihab.

"There are as many reasons for living over here as there are musicians doing it," he wrote to me from Denmark a few years before. "Race is only one of them. In my case it was love of a woman." The girl was Danish. Her name was Inga-Lisa. She became Ed's second wife and bore him a son, Michel, and a daughter, Denise. She died of the complications of cancer. "She'd been sick a long time," Ed said gently. He stayed on in Denmark to be, as Shihab and others told me, mother and father to his children. The children began to ask him, "When are you going to take us home to America, Daddy?" Then he brought them on a visit. The journey was a landmark in their lives. Until then, their impression of American blacks had been obtained largely from television, and they knew little of the black American middle class.

Ed began coming home more and more, playing and, particularly, teaching. He was always a natural and intuitive teacher, and I, for one, learned a lot from him. That was back in the early 1960s, in Chicago, his native city, although I for a long time thought he was from St. Louis. His real home is Los Angeles.

He was born September 28, 1930, the son of Ben Thigpen, himself a superior drummer best known for his work in the Andy Kirk orchestra. In 1951, Ed joined the Cootie Williams band at the Savoy Ballroom in New York. He was in military service from 1952 to 1954, first as a drum instructor at Fort Ord, California, later with the Eighth Army Band in Korea. After his discharge, he returned to New York and worked with Dinah Washington, the Johnny Hodges band, Gil Melle, Jutta Hipp, and Toshiko Akiyoshi, and recorded with many of the best young players of his generation. He worked with Lennie Tristano, with the Billy Taylor trio, then for six years with the Oscar Peterson trio. He went on the road with Ella Fitzgerald in 1966 and in 1967 returned to Los Angeles where, in a short time, he worked with Pat Boone, Andy Williams, Peggy Lee, Johnny Mathis, Oliver Nelson, and Gerald Wilson, and in the studios. He is a particularly excellent drummer for singers because of his sensitivity, the delicacy of which he is capable, and in 1967 Fitzgerald lured him back onto the road. He stayed with her until 1972, when he settled in Denmark and began playing the European jazz festivals and teaching at the Conservatory in Aarhus. And he gradually began to be forgotten in America.

I also mused, as I drove in to see him that night, on the reasons we had become such close friends. I liked Ed Thigpen the moment I met him, which was in mid-1959. He joined the Oscar Peterson trio January 1, 1959. I joined *Down Beat* a few months later, and came to know Thigpen when the trio played the London House, that excellent restaurant at the corner of Wacker Drive and Michigan Boulevard, looking across the Chicago River at the mad

Gothic architecture of mad Colonel McCormick's Tribune building and the equally improbable wedding cake architecture of the
Wrigley building. It was a historic club that brought in superb jazz
groups, treated them royally, did first-class publicity on them, and
served them and the paying customers some of the finest steaks to
be had in all the American Midwest. It's gone now, its location
become a Wendy's or a Burger King or one of those. A friend in
Chicago told me that when Art Farmer saw what it is now, he got
tears in his eyes. The London House was a classy joint, and the
Peterson group played it at least twice a year, which meant that I
saw a lot of Edmund Thigpen in the years from 1959 to 1962.

Sometimes he and his first wife, Lois, would stay with me and
my then-wife in our apartment on a street with an appropriate
name—Bittersweet Street. It was at what Chicagoans call forty
hundred north, in the block between Broadway and the lake in one
of the most beautiful city fronts in the world. I have lovely floating
memories of that time, the four of us at the beach down at the
Indiana Dunes, going to openings, laughing in the night, talking.
Always talking. Ed and I had interminable conversations.

He was a notably polite young man, quite good-looking, of middle height, dapper, with a resonant clear voice and literate enunciation. His manner with people was serene, direct, open, and
devoid of suspicion.

One day as we were driving home we heard a clanking under his
car, a small European station wagon. We got out, looked, and
found the exhaust pipe and muffler dragging on the pavement.
We took the car to a garage in my neighborhood. A young
mechanic, with that kind of stringy blond hair, wiping his hands
on an oil rag, asked what seemed to be the trouble. I winced at his
accent—that of a cracker, whether from Tennessee or Kentucky
or Georgia I couldn't tell, but a cracker—and anticipated hostility.
This was only three or four years after Selma and Montgomery and
Bull Connor and the cattle prods.

The mechanic ran the car up on the hoist and looked at its
underside. He told Ed he didn't have a pipe to fit it but thought
he could make one. Ed told him to go ahead. He fired up an acet-

ylene torch and began cutting the broken pipe away, close to the
gas tank.

"You can stay here and get blown up if you want," I told Ed,
"but I'm standing across the street." And we watched from a distance through the open garage doors as the mechanic tried to
bend a pipe to fit Ed's car. At the end of an hour, he said he just
couldn't do it.

Ed thanked him and said, "What do I owe you?"

"Nothin'," the young man said. "Ah didn't fix it, did ah?"

But Ed insisted on paying him something.

As we drove off (in a very noisy car) I told Ed of the twinge I'd
felt when I heard the man's accent. "You can't judge people like
that," Ed said. "You can't judge them by their accent." Which tells
you something about Ed, who majored in sociology at Los Angeles
City College before deciding that his life lay in music.

But judging people by accent, I have realized in the years since
then, is just what America does—as England does. American big-
otry is rooted perhaps as much in speech as in color. His accent
contributed to the destruction of Jimmy Carter. And Lyndon
Johnson's didn't do him much good either.

Another insight into Edmund came through an incident involv-
ing a butcher. My wife had made a connection with a butcher who
gave us very good cuts of meat. He turned out to be a jazz fan.
When she mentioned that Ed Thigpen and his wife were staying
with us, he was overwhelmed. When she got home, she told us that
he had asked if he might come by and meet Ed. I had misgivings
but Ed saw no reason why he shouldn't, and the next afternoon
the man turned up. In a rapture bordering on mesmerism, he
hung on Ed's every word. Ed was patient with him, even as the
afternoon turned into evening and he showed no signs of leaving.
Finally, we made it obvious that we had to get dressed to go to the
London House, and, reluctantly, the man left. And we dressed.

As we were descending the front steps of the building, the man
returned, carrying a large tray covered in aluminum foil. He said
he had a present for Ed and Lois, and removed the foil, like an
artist unveiling a painting or a sculpture. And a sculpture indeed,

or at least a sort of bas relief, was what it was: a great red heart made out of ground beef, pierced by strips of steak or veal, the whole strange thing surrounded by smaller hearts shaped out of filet mignon. He had made it, he told Ed and Lois, "as a tribute to your great love." I never forgot the phrase—or the tribute. It was one of the most astonishing things I had ever seen.

And one could not laugh. I remember vividly the graciousness and sincerity with which Ed thanked the man, who almost glowed as he went home, no doubt to listen to his Ed Thigpen records. We took the tray into the house, set it in the refrigerator, and left. In the taxi, we began to laugh. Although I am not sure whether Ed laughed.

He was under a lot of pressure in those days. So was I. Although he already had a solid reputation, joining Peterson had propelled him up to a high national visibility. And I, just having become the editor of *Down Beat*, was in a somewhat similar position. Maybe that had something to do with the relationship. We were both in hot seats, and I for one was scared.

Oscar puts pressure on players. I think it made Ed nervous, but he survived it, and pianist Eddie Higgins, who led the house trio at London House during those years and thus probably heard the group in person more than anyone else on the planet, excepting its own members, has argued that it was the greatest piano trio in jazz history.

There are in one's life those relationships wherein conversation seems to resume where it left off years ago. As Ed and I settled to dinner in the restaurant at the Sunset Hyatt hotel in the Sunset Strip area of Los Angeles, I said something about that pressure.

"Geniuses have a tendency to do that," he said with a smile. "Buddy Rich is like that."

"Do you consider Buddy Rich a genius?"

"Yes. Definitely. He's just incredible. He's a great, fantastic, player. If it can be done on a drum, he can do it. He's absolutely incredible. I've heard people say he doesn't swing. I think he swings. I used to practice with things he does. I've heard it said he's not subtle. I've heard him be so subtle, so gentle. The man can play. I told him—and I'd tell Oscar—that geniuses don't realize that what they do is hard. They just do it. They're hard on themselves as well, though. Extremely. If they're not fair, in such cases, it's debatable what's fair. So far as the pressure is concerned, it's what one allows oneself to be subjected to for what one's personal goals are.

"I had pressure, a lot of it, but a lot of it was due to myself. It doesn't mean that a person won't apply it, because they certainly will, but if I sat there and took it, I had my reasons. It was a great honor, and I learned a great deal. Certainly in the long run, I made it work. I benefited from it. And my contribution, which I found out many years later, was obviously worth all of it. The performances we did had a lasting impact. It took a long time for me to realize what my contributions to that group had been.

"Well," I said, "a classic example of what you did with that group is *Con Alma*. You recorded that twice with them, including the *Swinging Brass* album with Russ Garcia and that big band. Take out what you did with the tymp mallets on cowbell and tom-tom, see what a difference it would make." We sang the rhythm figure together.

"You know," Ed said, "many people still associate me with that group."

"They still call me the former editor of *Down Beat*. I was there not quite three years, and left more than twenty-five years ago. But you read what Eddie Higgins said about the group. You hear arguments from people who think the trio with you was the greatest and the ones who think the trio with Herb Ellis was the greatest."

"The same way with Ahmad's group with Israel Crosby and Vernel Fournier. That was an incredible group. They were unique. I didn't listen to our records for about ten or twelve years after I left in 1965. It's been twenty-one years."

"When did you join the group?"

"Officially, '59. January 1, 1959. I was called right before Christmas of '58. I had been called earlier in '58 for the job, when I was with Billy Taylor. It was a matter of how much bread. It seemed I asked for a little bit too much, and Norman Granz decided to get someone else. I could have kicked myself. But, as they say, the Lord provided, and the call came anyway five months later."

"How did you happen to be chosen?"

"I first encountered Oscar in Japan. I think Ray had something to do with it. I was in Korea. I had gone down to Tokyo on R. and R., right before I came home. Jazz at the Phil was there. Naturally, I knew Ben Webster and most of the guys because of my father. And I knew Ray from New York. I was very young when I first met Ray, and he was very kind. He took me out and gave me a milk shake and sent me home.

"I started doing a lot of Prestige and Blue Note things, some dates with Coltrane, some things with Art Farmer and Kenny Dorham. I was recording just enough to get reviews every couple of months, and they were always very favorable. And I started moving up that way. And then I recorded Toshiko's first album in America, and Lee Morgan's first album. It was the young new ones coming around. Then, Ray, Kenny Burrell, and I recorded with Blossom Dearie.

"I always wanted to be with Oscar's group, even when Herb was with that band. I told Ray in Japan, 'The only thing wrong with this group is you need a drummer.' Ray said, 'Well, y'never know, kid.' I said, 'I need to play with this group. I love this group.' And they went out and proceeded to swing so hard I thought, 'Well, maybe I'll miss it, but I still would like to play with the group.' So it was four years later that I joined them. Yeah, it was a lot of pressure though, back to that. It was. Because whatever insecurities I had . . . I was in awe of those guys, I loved them, I really loved them, and when it's like that, you give everything you have. They were so heavy, so fantastic and, obviously, so acclaimed, that I was in awe of both of them. Ray was very kind. All the time. He just took me under his wing and saved me."

"I don't think Ray is as moody as Oscar. Oscar's told me stories that . . . "

"Well, let me put it this way. Like I said, geniuses are different.

Oscar's just as kind as Ray. He knew what he wanted. There are certain things he looks for. He was just as hard on himself. He was a perfectionist. One thing you learn with people like that, and you never lose it, and I'm very grateful for it, is a standard of performance. It was so high. He had a thing where he said, 'On our worst night, we've got to sound better than most people on their best night.' And so consequently, every song was an opener and a closer, there was no skating, no nothin'—never. You never cheat, ever. When you come up under that kind of discipline, it stays with you, man. So wherever you are, man, something must happen.

"There are other great artists, actors or whatever, when they place this kind of demand upon themselves, to get the optimum that they can do, whatever that extra something is—outside of our gifts from our good Lord—that extra effort is what makes the winners, the real ones. It's like that's the whole thing, that's your life."

I have always wondered how people chose their instruments. There are only two instruments that I can imagine appealing to a child, the piano and the guitar, since they can function both melodically and harmonically and thus in complete independence of other instruments. I am always amazed that someone somehow in his past endured the anguish of learning to play drums or bass or trumpet or saxophone, the practicing of which in the early stages must be singularly unrewarding if not downright agonizing. I am both bemused that they have done this, persisted in it long enough to attain that mastery that has given me a lifetime of delights, and infinitely grateful. I mentioned this to Ed, adding, "Ray told me he took up the bass because it was the last instrument they had left in his high school band." Ed chuckled, as if he were not quite buying that story from Ray. I said, "Of all the instruments, there is none that I can imagine would be harder to get started on than drums."

"It's relative. Piano is very difficult. You've got four limbs, and the problem of co-ordination. It depends on the teachers, the motivation. Certain people have certain little gifts. Some people just do it."

"Did you have a good teacher? Or did you just start?"

"No, I just started. I took little lessons. The first real teacher I had was just a joke. He wasn't teaching anything. You learned on your own. He was giving me a press roll while he was practicing his piano lessons. It was during the Depression."

"But why did you choose drums? Because of your father?"

"Partially because of that, I guess. I didn't grow up with him."

"You're from St. Louis, aren't you?"

"No, I was born in Chicago and they brought me up in St. Louis until I was four."

"But he was from St. Louis."

"No. He moved there when he left Andy Kirk's band. People associate him with St. Louis because most of the later years he was there. East St. Louis is actually where he went."

"That's where Miles is from."

"Miles's father's dental office was right around the corner from my father's house. My father's and Rosemary's. My spiritual mother. I guess you'd say step-mother, I don't like that word, I think of her as my mother reincarnated. They had a house around the corner from Miles's father's dental practice. I lived there for one year exactly, from my nineteenth to the middle twentieth year, then I went to New York and on the road."

"The rest of the time you were in California with your mother. Didn't you go to high school with Vi Redd?" Vi remembers him as very shy and polite. She says she was surprised when he emerged as a major drummer in the 1950s, having had no idea he was even involved in music when they were young.

"No, junior high. Actually, I went to junior high school with Vi's brother Buddy. They were with the Hightower Orchestra. My mother brought me here in 1935. I grew up here, on the east side, 48th Street. I had most of my schooling here. I had a beautiful experience here last week at the National Associaton of Jazz Educators convention. I saw some of the guys down at the union, and they said you should call Mr. Browne, Samuel Browne. He was our music teacher. I called him, he's retired now, and he said, 'What are you doing here?' And he was about to receive an award at the NAJE convention."

"Where did he teach?"

"The Jefferson High School swing band. Dexter Gordon went through that band earlier. Art and Addison Farmer. They were from Arizona, but they grew up here. And one who came up after me, Frank Morgan. He was playing everything in the tenth grade."

"Due to Samuel Browne?"

"Due to their talent, they were all great players, but he nurtured it. He encouraged us to go on as far as we could go."

"Did you know Art all that way back?"

"Sure, and his brother too."

"Yeah, I knew Addison. Fairly well. What a shock his loss was."

"They were one year ahead of me. They graduated with the Prometheans. I graduated with the Carthaginians."

"What were they?"

"High school class names."

"Well, I didn't grow up among you Americans. I don't know all your strange folkways."

Ed laughed, then said, "We had a lot of good players. Good arrangers too. When I was in junior high school, we had a drum battle in the assembly. There were three players, including Buddy Redd, Vi's brother. I came in third. It was a good lesson, I didn't even know how to use a high hat. They played good. But I remember walking in the hallway, and a girl saying to me, 'Thig, you didn't win, but we liked what you did.' I've never forgotten it, all my life. It showed me that, in the United States, in America, with all the negative things you hear about it, we were taught as a credo that it doesn't matter who wins, the thing is that you were able to participate. There may be only one winner, but as long as somebody cares what you do, you're still in the ballgame, and you always had the chance of getting better. Whatever your limitations today, if you continued, maybe tomorrow the limitations would be gone."

"I saw something on the news the other day, a young black kid, nineteen years old, had won some athletic award, and the interviewer asked, 'Is this what you're going to do with your life?' and he said, 'Oh no, bio-engineering is my direction,' and I thought that twenty-five or thirty years ago he might not have been able to say that."

"That would depend on who it was. It depends on what your talents are, and when you were coming up," Ed said. "As I come back to this country, I see so much progress in the society in some ways. I see other things where it's standing dead still with the intent of going backwards. I come back to my America, if you want to call it that, my people—you, and people I know that you don't hear a lot about, people who are busy just trying to do the right thing. I refute the idea of the so-called silent majority."

"You're right. It's not a silent majority. It's a mouthy minority."

"In many ways, yes. This country is sick, in many areas. But it's sick all over the world. We were brought up to believe you have to do what you have to do. It's a matter of courage. We were brought up with the Christian ethic, and taking it to heart. Not the misuse of it, but the fact of forgiveness as a very very powerful force. Jo Jones, my mentor, used to say, 'To hate makes sickness.' When you hate, it makes you sick. The longer I point out, the more my finger starts curving, until it's pointing at me. It behooves me to carry myself well. There but for the grace of God go I. It could be me just as well as them—acting stupid.

"It's interesting, coming back here. Seeing the changes. Time moving on. The changing in styles. The changing of the guard, so to speak. Youth must be served. All the cliches which, in later life, you begin to find out have a definite meaning. The young, many of them, they want the truth. Here I am coming back into the big pool, so to speak, the United States, re-establishing myself for the last four years or so, not so much in playing as in education. Many of these kids haven't a clue who I am, not that it matters, many of them don't know who Duke Ellington is, either.

"So who am I to complain? At the NAMM convention today"— he referred to the National Association of Music Manufacturers, gathered that week at Anaheim—"I was with a very fine young drummer, doing a lot of recording, very visible, one of the people who are very strong. A young man came up to him and wanted to pay him a compliment and have his picture taken with him. And he said, 'Do you know this gentleman here? This is Ed Thigpen.' And the guy didn't know me, and he wanted to almost push me out of the way to take the picture. It's like watching the fighters, the new breed coming in. And you're out here still trying to do your thing, too. But the music has evolved into another thing that is popular. And you can't go into all the business of why it is, whatever it is. The point is: What is your worth in this whole scene now? And how do you compete in it? Because you have to compete to make a living. What role do you play? You're not as visible, so everybody doesn't know who you are at the moment. And you're trying to get back on the magazine covers so people will know your presence. So it's like starting over in some ways. Then somebody walks up to you with a salt and pepper beard and says, 'Hey, I know everything you ever did,' and he's raving. And you're leaving and all of a sudden a young man—a *young* man, one of the up-and-coming people—walks up to you and says, 'I have your brush book, and it's helped me so much,' and so on and so on. And he is doing contemporary things. So you could have been down because of that lack of recognition on the one hand, and you turn around and it all balances out. So the recognition is coming not through some record you just made, but on another plane, because your contribution now at this point in your life is through a brush book, and a video cassette I made. This is what I wanted, and this is what I went after. And then when they hear you play, with Tommy Flanagan or somebody, and you can present the music, then it becomes something else.

"It's a very productive area. It's like watching your kids grow up, the way they had to watch us grow up. He—or she—is looking you dead in the eye, but you may be looking up to them, because what they're talking about is valid. The trick is where you can become truly the extension and share this learning experience of life together. You take your experience or my experience—the experience of the older ones—youth can use that. But there must be mutual respect for them to accept it. By the same token, you can take what they have to offer and add it to what you have, because that's valid. There are certain things that I have in mind to do, but physically I can't do them. I can hear 'em. But this young cat's got the technique that he could pull it off. Like a good athlete. You need that extension of you out there, with that physical thing, to bring it forth. And it's quite rewarding. When it happens, boy, the joy! I can readily understand the joy and importance of a coach, of a choreographer, of a director who is sympatico with the artist who can bring it off. They become extensions of each other."

"Are there, then, some of the rock drummers you like?"

"Yeah, loads of 'em!"

"To me, they are the essence of non-swinging."

"It's a different kind of swing. The groove. It's different. The epitome was the English drummers, until Steve Gadd came along. Harvey Mason. Some of the English kids are the best, at what they do. So much of it has to do with marketing, labeling, promotion, a lot of hoopla and brain-washing that doesn't have much to do with the music. I've been trying to put it into words. You mentioned swing. Somehow it clicked today, the difference. There's a groove. To get a funk groove—that's more jazz-oriented, with the twelve-eight, whereas with rock they're basing it on the eighth note. Now you can get a groove on it. You can pop your finger on it, you can get a groove. An eighth note is not a swing groove. But it is a groove, and you can get down with it. It's like salsa. Like marches, in some instances. You put those other minipulses in there. That's the part that comes from the swing, that kind of two-four lilt."

"You know, Kenny Clarke's playing amazed me. He could boot a big band playing comparatively quietly."

"He was playing music. It's the pulse. You let the music come through the rhythm—through the swing, through the ride rhythm. It's like punctuation. When you phrase, you don't always use an exclamation mark. You're enhancing what's already there. It's like spice. At the same time, you lay a foundation that can function properly, secure."

"I can't believe what Klook could do with a cymbal. I've heard Elvin Jones do wonderful things with different tones out of a cymbal, with where the stick is placed. Klook was so so subtle with the way the tone shifted."

"Playing with Thad Jones, I learned that very well. It's a very interesting thing. It's what do you hit, what you don't even have to hit. If you have good arrangers and if you play the music, let the music play itself, almost, if they're good arrangers . . . you have to love the music, love the people. It's not your own little personal ego trip. You know, I'd like to write some things. There are a lot of myths in jazz. Like the use of the bass drum. I mean the myth of the evolution of bebop drumming. They attributed bebop drumming to putting the time up on the cymbal."

"Yeah, you read it day after day."

"See, that wasn't true. It really wasn't true. I argued that back when I was in high school and I heard Max Roach and Art Blakey and different people on those early records. I used to argue with my fellow students that it wasn't true. And then when I got to New York, I found out the truth, and then when I moved in with my Dad again, I found out more. They explained to me how they feathered the bass drum. They played four beats to the bar, they kept the pulse down there, but they learned to play with a touch, so that when people like Jimmy Blanton and Milt Hinton came along, who were classically trained—Milt was trained as a violinist, and picked up the bass because he couldn't make any money playing the violin—they had harmonic and tonal awareness and the bass was carrying the foundation of the harmony. So the bass drum couldn't be louder than the bass. It had to be there, to give that extra punch, but it couldn't be louder. I do a thing in my classes, man, where I show that you can't carry no band with a ride cymbal. Can't do it. It's impossible."

"Well, you know, I heard Dizzy complaining years ago that so many of the young drummers couldn't use the bass drum."

"Well, they haven't been taught that. Nobody told them otherwise. When Dizzy stays with them, some of them eventually learn. I did an interview with Kenny Clarke, published in *Modern Drummer*, which clarified what happened. He said that in those early days, he got tired of what he called digging coal. Digging coal refers to what you do on the snare drum, that doom-derry-doom-derry-doom-aderry-doom. And that's the way they kept the time. From the drum, they moved it up to the cymbal, that ting-tingtating tangta-tang. And that's what it was, 'cause he said he had to stop digging coal. I remember seeing his bass drum at Minton's, when I first saw him play. I didn't even know how important he was. I saw a lot of great people and didn't know how important they were. I just knew that I liked them. Anyway, I was looking at his bass drum at Minton's. And he used this big sheepskin, I think it was, beater ball. It was very very thick, to keep a soft tone, because they didn't have any mufflers in the drums. He still had a big tone but it was soft, he'd get a muffled sound out of it, but you still could hear it. That's an important thing, that's the foundation. So important.

"I've had guys . . . Lennie Tristano once said, 'Don't use the bass drum.' I used it anyway. It didn't bother him a bit. It's the way you play it. Jazz encompasses all of the classical disciplines of the instruments, all the disciplines period. Anything of worth I have ever listened to got into my work on my instrument. It's not a matter of labels. The thing in jazz is the interpretation. Guys say, 'Today, what's wrong with the music?' I say, 'It's the repertoire.' Jazz has a history. We have great jazz compositions. We have a jazz repertoire, and people who play the music should be versed in it. The old show tunes, the Ellington tunes, whatever. This music has a tradition, and it's very important. When you have to record, and everything has to be original, so-called? Quote? You go on a date, and you say, 'What tunes are you playing?' And you hear, 'Well, they're all originals.' And I think, 'Oh boy, here we go.' Now sometimes it's hip, but I'll be darned if some of these people have enough background. What of all that went down before? Do you just throw it away?"

"Well, there's another thing," I said. "When you're dealing with an improvisatory music, that repertoire gives the listener a point of departure, whether it's a Broadway show tune or an Ellington or a Benny Golson tune."

"Yes. If you're playing 'A' Train, improvising on 'A' Train, at some point in there you should feel 'A' Train. People who play on the changes, it could be anything. But it's very interesting when a guy thinks melodically. Those cats took earlier tunes and made other tunes out of them. It's interesting to hear front-line people who improvise melodically, whether they're doing it on the changes or on a combination of the changes and the melody. If you're improvising on just the changes, with no reference to either the mood or the melody of the original . . . "

"When you get a tune like *Groovin' High* built on *Whispering*, and then Dizzy starts to play something on top of that, you've got layers of tradition and music."

"And you can have layers rhythmically, too," he said. "That's the epitome."

We paid our dinner checks. The steaks had not been as good as those at London House. Or was this another illusion of memory?

The Silver Screen Room, adjacent to the restaurant in the Sunset Hyatt, where Ed was to play with pianist Harold Danko and bassist John Heard, was almost empty. Ed looked around and said, "This is a reality. It's sad, but it's a reality. Look. The bottom line is that the man pays you two hundred bucks a night to come in, and you haven't got twenty dollars worth of people. I want to make as many friends as I can, because we've got to get these people back in these clubs, man."

"The problem," I said, "is that the constituency for small-group jazz came from the teen-agers who used to stand around near the bandstands in the ballrooms, listening to the big bands, and knowing all the soloists. When the era ended and the small groups went into the nightclubs, those kids, now grown up, followed them. But these were places where liquor is served, and so a potential new audience of kids couldn't get in to hear the groups. So the audience has aged, and not enough kids have replaced them."

"And there's another important thing, man," Ed said.

"Yeah, radio. It has done nothing to build a new audience. Only the jazz stations are doing a job, and they're doing it for people who already love the music."

"That's right," Ed said, and we found a table. "Jazz represents freedom," he said. "It demands freedom, it demands love. It demands individuality, but most of all love and freedom. Because otherwise it doesn't work. Freedom with discipline. A very high form of discipline. You can't patch the solos in. It's a certain thing that happens one on one, a certain magic that happens with the instrumentalist or the vocalist. No matter how much you study, it's a very spiritual experience. This magic that happens, that becomes the gift. Forget all your talent, I don't care who you are, Buddy Rich, Art Blakey, whoever it is, no matter how much talent you have, when it's really at its highest point, it's like a gift. You say, 'How'd I come up with this?' This whole thing is a gift.''

We greeted John Heard, the fine bassist and prodigiously talented artists. John began tuning his bass, Ed sat down at his drum kit, set up his cymbals, pulled a new set of brushes out of a plastic wrapping.

"You and your brushes," I said.

"Buddy too," Ed said, with a grin.

"Yeah, Buddy can play brushes," I said.

John Heard jumped in, "I saw Buddy Rich kick the whole Basie band with brushes."

"That's right," Thigpen said.

"He'd been talking to Butch Miles about it," John said, still tuning his bass. "He did it as a demonstration, to show him how you do it."

Ed ran a pattern across his drums and cymbals, shook his head dubiously, grimaced. "Boy," he said.

"What's the matter?" I asked.

"Doesn't feel right."

"What doesn't?"

"The whole thing. Man, I have to get home and practice. It just doesn't feel right."

Ed tuned the drums, then sat down again at our table. Suddenly his face lit up, he stood up, and he said, "Here you are," and to me, "This is my family. This goes 'way back, to my childhood." He introduced me to Beverly Watkins, principal of a San Fernando Valley school, and her husband Harry. Beverly, Ed explained, is his sister—not really, but really. She and her husband sat down at the next table.

Ed's mother and father separated when he was five. His mother moved with Ed to Los Angeles. She died when Ed was twelve. Ed was boarded out with a family who could not abide his interest in drums. "There were four children in our family," Beverly told me between sets. "My father liked people, he liked people around him. But he didn't go out much. He couldn't even drive. We didn't own a car."

"In Los Angeles?" Of course, in those days the street railway system had not yet been dismantled.

"In Los Angeles." There were certain rhythms and inflections in her speech that were identical to Ed's. Whether they were particular to certain parts of Los Angeles, to that neighborhood, or that family, I do not know.

The neighborhood was not a ghetto. Blacks had begun to move into it, but the Anglos had not begun to move out. "Nobody moved," Beverly said firmly. There were Italian families and Mexican families as well. It was a good solid middle-class working neighborhood. "Families were very tightly knit," Beverly said. She is a beautiful woman, quite distinguished in bearing and appearance. She is of Creole descent, very light-skinned, her name at birth Guero, pronounced gay-ro, probably a variant of a French or Spanish spelling. Her mother had remarried and the stepfather of whom she spoke with such affection was named Collins, Tony Collins. "When there are four kids in a home," she said, "one more doesn't make much difference. I remember Ed brought his little drum set over to our place, and he used to practice there.

"I think he saw in our household what he felt he was missing. My mother never worked outside the home, and she was always there when we came home from school. And you know, a young boy with a drum set, that would drive most people crazy, but it didn't bother her.

"He was pretty much like he is now—very positive, very active, very much in love with life itself. He was the kind who would say that the glass was half full, not that it was half empty, even then. He's always been a giving person. He always sees where he can share."

By the end of the trio's first set, there was a goodly audience for the music. Ed, rejoining us, said, "Oh, that feels better. To see some people. The fans, they're wonderful. They are so interested—in you and in the music."

"Yeah, like the guy in Chicago with the hamburger heart," I said. And Ed chuckled at the memory. I told the story to Beverly, who laughed. "And Ed was so nice with the guy," I said.

"Of course," Ed said. "It was what he had to offer. It was very touching."

I stayed for two sets. I heard the groove that Ed and John Heard attained almost immediately. Ed played some solos. I am one of those who are not partial to drum solos. But I have always liked Ed's. I remember discussing them with him in Chicago. He said you build a small crest, then back off, then build a larger crest, and back off again but not so far, and then a still larger crest, until by this process you achieve a great crest, after which you descend from it quickly and go back to the group. It's not a bad rule of thumb for any of the temporal arts, including the drama and fiction.

And yes, he was as good as I had remembered him. You could watch Ed through a studio window with the sound turned off and see the swing in the motion of his hands, splendidly graceful hands whose movements are not, interestingly, unlike those of Buddy Rich.

The great dancer Carmen Delavallade has a distinctive way of using a rallentando at the end of an arm motion that is unforgettably beautiful. The arm will come back or down or forward in a fluid movement that somehow slows at the end with a subtle graceful break of the wrist. Arnold Ross, with the Harry James band in the 1940s, had a comparable way of slowing a fast run as it reached the bottom, like a skier coming out of a steep slope onto level ground, that I never heard in another pianist. Ed's hands move like that. They pause, float, in the air, then snap. Buddy Rich's did that.

And Ed's solos are endlessly inventive. He is so aware of pitch in his equipment. "A good cymbal," he said, "has at least five tonalities." The solos go to unexpected places, you hear unex-

pected rhythms, but the continuity and form are flawless. In Thigpen's playing, rhythm itself is an entire music. He begins softly and
builds to tremendous power, without ever sacrificing sensitivity or
tone. Yes indeed, he was all that I remembered and more.
Edmund Thigpen is a poet of percussion.

   I told him before the last set that I would probably leave in the
course of it. Harold Danko announced the next tune, *Hey There*.
It stirred memories for Ed and me. He was cooking away on the
snare drum with brushes during the first chorus as I stood up to
go. He grinned and called out to me, "London House!"

Spike's Life

With *The Secret Life of Walter Mitty*, James Thurber gave a name
forever to men who live boring lives sustained by fantasies of high
adventure. The mass of men (not to mention women) indeed pursue lives of quiet desperation, as Thoreau observed. And Thoreau
escaped to Walden Pond only with the help of a mother who
brought him lunch. Heaven only knows how many people in
America and the world pursue numbing careers to meet material
needs and the obligations of family while nursing private passions,
like the adherents of arcane religions—all the secret poets, lyri-
cists, painters, sculptors, composers, violinists, actors, who live out
the week locked in work they loathe, consoled by the anticipation
of escape into some beloved art, amateurs in the true and original
sense of the French word, those who do it for pure love of the
work. The classic example was Charles Ives, who spent his life as
an insurance executive while composing complex and uncompro-
mising music that anticipated much of what was to come in twen-
tieth-century music.

Occasionally the siren song of the muse grows too strong and
someone throws caution and convention to the winds to follow it.
The classic case is that of the French-Peruvian Paul Gauguin, who
at seventeen became a seaman and for six years sailed around the

world, and for the next fourteen years was a Paris stockbroker, painting on weekends with Camille Pisarro and Paul Cézanne. Finally, in 1883, he quit his job, which cost him his marriage and earned him the enmity of his son, and became one of history's great painters. Nine years his junior, the Polish-born Joseph Conrad also became a seaman in the French merchant service, sailing out of Marseilles. He cherished dreams of being a novelist, and finally, with the publication of *Almayer's Folly* in 1895, when he was thirty-seven, became one of the greatest in the English language. And a few years before Conrad wrote his first novel in his cabin on a ship, a Russian naval officer was writing his first symphony in the cabin of his. Nikolai Rimski-Korsakov resigned his commission with the first performance of his opera *The Maid of Pskov*. Albert Roussel was an officer in the French navy before he resigned to study composition.

Those who find in themselves whatever it requires to take the plunge—desperation, perhaps—are rare; and those who do usually do it early. Roussel did it at twenty-five. Somerset Maugham, an obstetrician, saw his first novel published when he was twenty-three.

One can only wonder how many men spend their lives, say, at the drafting tables of engineering offices, dreaming dreams of one day chucking it all and getting the old tenor saxophone out of its case and heading off into a wild blue uncertainty to groove with a good rhythm section and blow some jazz. People like Henry Bertholf Robinson of Boulder, Colorado.

Who? Well you may ask.

Like Spike Robinson.

Who? Well you may still ask.

The late Zoot Sims had never heard of him either. Zoot had just played a set at one of the jazz parties that have sprung up all over the United States in recent years. He was leaving the room when Spike Robinson began a solo on an old silver tenor. Zoot stopped and listened, and listened, and stayed to listen some more, occasionally shaking his head. Everyone hearing Spike Robinson for the first time does that. And it would be all right if he were fresh out of North Texas State University or the Eastman School or one of those many well-oiled machines that turn out innumerable skilled jazz musicians the economy is never going to be able to absorb. But Spike Robinson turned sixty in 1990, and startled jazz fans all over the place were just making his acquaintance. He is better known in Europe than in America, but that is changing rapidly, due to a series of albums made in the last few years, both before and after he took his retirement from the Honeywell Corporation, ending a thirty-year career in engineering.

That a tenor player of Robinson's stature could have languished unknown in Detroit, Minneapolis, Cape Canaveral, Denver, and Boulder, all the cities to which his main career took him, is amazing. To be sure, there were murmurs, rumors, almost a legend, disseminated by those who passed through these places and heard him on his weekend gigs or sit-in sessions, as there were about the pianist Peck Kelly of Texas and John Park of Missouri.

Robinson is of the Lester Young school from which came Zoot Sims, Stan Getz, Al Cohn, and Brew Moore—all players to whom he has been compared. And there are elements of their work in Spike, a highly lyrical player of the mainstream bebop persuasion. Perhaps he is closest to Zoot because of certain figures and turns of phrase he likes and the sunny and throw-away melodicism of his lines. Like so many jazz musicians, he plays much as he talks, and his speech is full of humorous contours and inflections. (Of a bass-player friend who fell down a flight of stairs: "We put him in the hospital. I put his bass in my glove compartment.") His almost indolent eloquence is characterized by surprising asides and codettas. People around him are always laughing, and one suspects, as one does of all continuously funny people, that Spike's endless jesting is a sublimation of pain. His humor tends to the whimsical, and is devoid of malice. The tone of his voice, like that of his playing, is at once airy and woody, and he is prone to a soft articulation in ballads, the notes beginning with an f-f-f- sound, like those of Ben Webster. Leonard Feather said, "He is beyond question one of a handful of giants of the tenor saxophone."

He stands six feet tall, weighs a hundred and sixty pounds, and has wavy gray hair and an indecisive gray mustache. He resembles the bebopper of legend in his casual, round-shouldered, S-shaped posture, but other than that, he looks more like, well, an engineer than a jazz musician. He dresses conventionally and well, even a little elegantly.

His little studio apartment, however, is a mess. Both were described by Colorado journalist Matthew Soergel in a Sunday supplement article:

"Spike Robinson welcomes a visitor . . . and offers a can of cold Budweiser.

"'Do you want a glass?' he asks, then looks absently toward his combined stove, sink, and refrigerator. 'I'm not sure I have one.'

"Robinson does not stand on formality, though for this visit he has taken the TV off the open oven door (it's placed there so he can watch it in bed) and removed his electric piano from over the sink . . .

"Receipts from recent trips to Europe are scattered over the brown wall-to-wall carpeting. ('There's my spring trip there,' he says, pointing to a heap of papers, 'and this one is my fall trip.'), as are letters and memos to himself. More memos, postcards and newspaper clippings are taped to each wall. His only furniture is a waterbed, a chair, two stools, and a couch.

"Robinson wants to be able to move in an hour, to chuck everything in the trash if one day he decides to move to San Diego or somewhere in Europe.

"His needs are simple. You can see that in the car he drives. It's a 1976 Datsun 280Z, rusted out and beaten up, mostly green in color. It has 440,000 miles on it and has rarely been touched by a wrench, except maybe to change the sparkplugs every 150,000 miles or so.

"'It's a marvelous car,' Spike says, though he makes sure he never parks it too close to a dumpster. Then he laughs one of his smoky laughs. It's infectious.

"Friends have told him to write a testimonial to Nissan about the 280Z. Maybe the company will give him a new car. He doesn't need a new car."

It might be added that you can always tell when Spike is about to arrive: you can hear the Datsun's brakes. And the trunk lid isn't green, it's black, obviously a replacement. You have never seen such a car. It's like the wonderful one-horse shay. One day it is going to collapse, leaving Spike sitting on the pavement with a steering wheel in his hands in a puddle of junk in the middle of a street.

His silver tenor was manufactured in 1900. He bought it when he was an impecunious engineering student. He kept bandaids, rubber bands, and sealing wax in its case for emergency repairs, but in recent years he has dispensed with the sealing wax, having, he says, noticed that most nightclubs have candles on the tables. This is wry hyperbole. He's long since had the horn put into good working order.

Spike Robinson is the divorced father of two and the grandfather of three. He has in recent years maintained a close relationship with the delicately attractive white-haired Texas-born Boulderite Betty Weems, a descendant of Parson Weems. She takes care of much of his business. They will no doubt never marry. He wants his freedom. So does she. At fifty-four, she followed her own Walter Mitty dream: she enrolled at Rice University in Houston, took a master's degree, and is now an architect.

Robinson was born January 15, 1930, in Kenosha, Wisconsin. His father, a fight fan, wrote a note saying, "Jack Dempsey the second was born tonight." Hence the tough nickname. But his father was also a jazz fan who took him to hear Count Basie when Spike was eight. Instead of boxing gloves, Spike acquired a clarinet, practiced six hours a day, played along with Benny Goodman records and, later, on alto, with those of Charlie Parker. In high school he organized a big band, mostly of musicians ten years his senior, and, exhausted by playing, almost flunked out of school. On graduating he went to Chicago and played in various bands, always scuffling for money:

"Trying," he said, "to get enough money to buy a candy bar and go to the all-night movie theater. The usher would wake you up with a tap on the head with his flashlight. I saw *The Song of Bernadette* eighty-two times, and I didn't like it the first time."

Spike joined the navy on learning there was a posting for musicians in London. British writer Brian Davis takes up the story: "It is London in 1948. Almost opposite the Windmill Theater behind Piccadilly Circus is a narrow entrance and passage to the Copacabana Club, but just to the left of the club's door, down a steep flight of wooden stairs, is a basement, bare-floored with light bulbs to match and a small stand with a just-about-upright piano. On certain nights an up-turned box at the top (or was it the bottom?) of the stairs acts as a cash desk; you pay your 3/6d and enter the gloom. Along the front are a few rows of hard chairs and those two ancient and incongruous horse-hair sofas along the left of the stand. Down here, if you are fairly uncritical, don't expect too much subtlety or concessions to the squeamish, you are in for a session of never-to-be-forgotten excitement! Bebop in the raw, as 'it is spoke' by Britain's young bloods—this is Club Eleven, London's first modern jazz club; ten musicians and a manager/cashier/compere. Of course, if they were 'with it' there were sitters-in and one such who became a regular was a thin, cropped-haired guy who seemed to come from nowhere, said little, but played the most fantastic Bird-like music on an old silver alto. We now know he was a U.S. seaman based in London but required by the navy to play anywhere in Europe. Union rules extant necessitated his low profile while jamming with the London beboppers and, in fact, things ended rather suddenly when posters proclaimed that guest soloist Spike Robinson would appear at a Ted Heath Sunday Palladium concert! He shortly returned to the U.S.A., leaving a legacy of six Esquire 78s of his music. This was the last anyone knew of the legendary Spike Robinson—that is, until thirty years on!"

The pianist on those 78s was a seventeen-year-old Victor Feldman.

When Spike Robinson got back to the United States, he made a career decision. As much as he loved it, he turned away from music. He wanted to marry and couldn't see himself pursuing an unstable profession. He chose to become, of all things, an engineer.

"I didn't want to go scratching around in New York or some-place," Spike said. "I saw the same thing I'd seen before I left, and even worse. Very meager money. And around that time, a lot of the good players were on hard stuff. Guys I had worked with in Chicago. I thought, 'Naw, I really don't want to get into this bag. That isn't the way I want to spend my life, trying to make enough in the kitty in some juke joint in Chicago to stay in the all-night theater. So that is why I got out of it as a main profession.

"I chose engineering because my father told me that during the Depression, there were two kinds of people who always seemed able to work, piano players in bars, who got free lunch and free booze and picked up enough cash to get by, and engineers. He said that even in the darkest days of the Depression, there were signs out in front of most manufacturing firms saying, Wanted: engineers. When he first started telling me that, I thought an engineer was the guy who ran the train. By the time I came back in 1952, I knew pretty well what engineers did and what they made. Engineering was one of the most desirable things to get into.

"I'd gotten high on racing while I was in England—cars, motor-cycles. I'd sold my alto to buy a road-racing motorcycle, and used navy horns. I had this marvelous Conn alto, an old silver beast that was lovely, and I tried to get the navy to surplus it. Somehow it couldn't be done.

"Some of the records I'd done in England in '51 got picked up by MGM and released here, and they were getting some play in New York. I got a letter from Leonard Feather, who then had a column with *Down Beat*, and each month highlighted somebody you had never heard of before. He wanted to know what I was doing. He wanted an action photo. I thought, 'All the years I've spent in music, waiting for The Break, and now it comes, and here I am in my second year of engineering school.' I wrote him back, saying, 'Gee, I certainly appreciate your interest, but I am no longer in music as a full-time activity.' So often it doesn't come at the right time.

"I began to get calls for jobs, but I didn't own a horn. I thought it would be nice to make that extra loot. I borrowed a guy's horn a couple of times, but I thought I'd been going to the well too often. I thought I'd better buy a horn. Playing again sure beat the hell out of hot-roofing. So I went down to the music store here, but they didn't have an alto. They only had one horn, an old silver tenor, made in 1900, hanging on the wall. So I bought it. I paid eighty bucks for it. I went to the bank and got a loan. I paid for it in ten months, eight bucks a month. It was a good investment. It's paid for itself a couple of times over. I'm still using it."

One of Spike's friends at the University of Colorado (invariably referred to by Spike and its students and alumni as CU) was a music student four years his junior named Dave Grusin, native of Denver. Grusin is one of the few people who is unsurprised by the acclaim being accorded Spike now. "He was just the same then as he is now," Dave said, "and he played the same way—beautifully—although of course he's better now. We used to play weekend gigs together, and we had some wonderful times. One of Spike's jobs was collecting garbage. He found an old baritone under a building in the veterans' housing, and gave it to me. I don't know what ever happened to it. I left it somewhere in New Jersey."

"I gave it to him," Spike said, "because Dave played clarinet in those days. But piano was his main instrument." With a chuckle: "If he'd gone on playing the clarinet, he wouldn't have the Academy Award." Grusin had just won the Oscar for his score to *The Milagro Beanfield War*.

Spike continued his *curriculum vitae*:

"Because of my interest in racing, I thought maybe I ought to point my studies as specifically as I could to the automotive industry, and maybe I could hook up with Ferrari or Alfa Romeo or somebody, and really have some fun. That didn't work out, but after I left CU in '56 with a bachelor's degree, I was offered a job with the Chrysler Corporation, which included continuing for a master's degree at the Chrysler Institute of Engineering in Detroit. I worked half time at a good salary—unheard of at that time, to me; I could now afford a six-pack—and studied half time. I don't know why they chose me, because everyone else there had been a straight A student, and I'd been about a C student. When I was interviewed, I told them I'd been doing hot-roofing during the day, pumping gas at a gas station all night, selling insurance door-to-door on weekends, and playing gigs, which was probably why my grades were considerably lower than they should have been. I guess they bought that, because they took me on.

"I really didn't like Detroit that much. Coming from Wisconsin, I loved the lake area. I loved to be around water. And when I came out here to CU, there was nothing in terms of water. No river, no lakes near-by. Boulder was considerably different then—about 11,000 permanent residents and about 7500 students. Now the town is maybe 14,000 and the student body is about 22,000. There were always articles in the paper describing Boulder as gravel roads and barking dogs. And that's about what it was. After I graduated, I was anxious to get back to water, and that was another reason we moved to Detroit.

"One day we drove out to Cass Lake, which was supposed to be very pretty. It was probably about twenty miles away, and I think it took us something like three hours to get there in the traffic. When we got there they'd closed it because they had too many people, and it took us about three hours to get home. I never went near water again in Detroit in the three years we were there.

"I got my master's at Chrysler and came back out here on vacation in '58. The outlook for engineers in this county was not good. Because of the desirability of living here, they kept wages considerably below national average—except for aerospace. They had to pay because they had to hire certain talents. I hooked up with Martin Marietta. I went back to Detroit, and thirty days later we came back here. I was a principal engineer in ground support equipment. I did a lot of co-ordination with their sub-contractors, one company for silo design, another for propellant system design. I traveled a lot, going back and forth to Los Angeles for meetings, meetings, meetings. I'd try to co-ordinate what the customer, the Air Force, wanted, with what our designers wanted to do, so you wouldn't be putting the toilet where there was already a sink.

"In the early phases of Apollo, they were launching Polaris mis-

siles off barges at Cape Canaveral, simulating submarine launch-
ings. The missiles then weren't very reliable. They would go up in
the air and write Phillips 66 or Eat at Hank's or something, and
then go out of control, and the destruct officer would blow 'em
up and they'd come down in pieces. They'd tumble down in bits
that would land in the trailer courts and on the block houses and
everywhere else.

    "Between all these missile launch block houses, there were great
spaces, each one about the size of a football field, filled with heavy,
heavy, heavy typically Florida underbrush, surrounded by chain-
link fences, so you couldn't get in there, and you'd have been crazy
to try. Everybody knew what was in there. One of the missiles came
down in flames in the space right next to the block house where
we were working. It scared the hell out of the inhabitants, and they
came pouring out, crawling through the fence. I never saw so
many snakes in so many sizes, assortments, and colors. Some of
them couldn't even get through the fence, they were so big. We
were standing on the tops of cars on the asphalt driveway, and the
security people were shooting the snakes with forty-fives.

    "Another morning as we were all arriving for work, there was a
big alligator, about fourteen feet long, lying by the door to the
block house, sunning himself, sound asleep. There was no other
entrance, so one of the guys went and got a big long two-by-four.
He jabbed the alligator in the ribs to wake him up and tell him it
was time to get the hell out of here. Without even opening his
eyes, the alligator moved his tail. You never saw anything so fast.
It came around, and you could have picked your teeth with what
was left of that two-by-four. We all said, 'Hey, let's go to the bar
and get something to drink. Leave that mother alone.'

    "I was offered a permanent job at Canaveral, but I told them,
'First we have to discuss my salary. Then we have to discuss my
alimony, because my wife just isn't going to live here.'

    "The ballistic missile research and development phase was
almost over for Martin Marietta by 1963 and my job became
mostly a matter of paper-pushing, and that bored me to death.
And I kept going by this restaurant and bar south of Boulder that

I visited now and then for years. It had a beautiful view. And I thought, Oh boy, wouldn't it be wonderful to have your own place and not have a manager telling you what to play and when to play. Wouldn't it be lovely to do that full-time. During the day you could practice and just have a ball and make all kinds of money. And so with a couple of other guys I leased this place three or four months before I left Martin. We were very undercapitalized. I thought, My God, $10,000, that's enough to get a restaurant going forever and a day. I didn't know what I was doing.

"And I never worked so hard in my life. I was there twenty-two hours a day. I had to call and see if my wife could send me pictures of the kids. I didn't have the money to hire someone to manage it during those times I didn't want to be there. And I swore that Boulder was ready for seven nights a week of jazz. So five nights I had an excellent pianist out of Denver named Billy Sloan, who's no longer playing, and Paul Warburton on bass. I usually played drums, once I had everything under control. I'd played drums a bit in the navy. I was the only one in the group who'd ever got near a set of drums, so I played drums. It started out like wildfire. On weekends we had Johnny Smith on guitar. Sometimes he'd fly his plane up from Colorado Springs.

"Bullets Smith. Johnny was in those days a great hanger-outer. We'd sit at the bar and have brandies and swap music stories, and later we'd wander down to an all-night restaurant where we could get steaks.

"I had a really good bartender, a great guy, an Italian with a short temper. One of the customers started bugging him. He was also bugging the other customers, so I told the bartender to cut him off. The guy got mouthy and Frank, the bartender, helped him out the front door. The guy took a swing at him, and Frank plowed him one, right in the nose. I didn't know this had all gone down. Johnny and I were sitting there at the bar having brandy and coffee. We closed the place. There was a knock at the front door. I walked down and Johnny walked with me. There was this drunk, and he had a few friends with him. He said, 'I want to talk to Spike.' I said, 'I'm Spike.' He said, 'Why don't you come on out here? I want to talk to you.' I said, 'I'm not coming out there.' The guy said, 'Your bartender hit me in the nose.' I said, 'No, I'm not coming out there. Come back tomorrow and I'll talk to you.' And I shut the door. Johnny said, 'Let's put the cash away and get the hell out of here, because I noticed one of those guys had a tire iron.' We were 'way out of town, with not very much sheriff's patrol. I said, 'Okay, you wait in your car while I put the cash away.' Johnny went out to his car and just sat, waiting for me.

"These guys were sitting in another car. They came over to Johnny and told him to get out, they had some dealings with me. A couple of them had coat hangers, and another had a tire iron. They were bloody well going to do me in. They were drunker than ten skunks. Johnny had a good friend, a guitar player in Philadelphia, who'd pulled up to a stoplight one night after a gig, and two guys jumped into his car and beat him to a pulp, and the guy died. Ever since then, Johnny had carried a gun in his guitar case.

"One of these guys came up to the window and said to Johnny, 'You get your ass out here.' Johnny put the revolver right on the guy's nose. They all took off. I came out and Johnny told me what had happened. By then I was so mad. We went to a restaurant in Boulder, and I was hoping those guys would come in. I was going to take a chair and break it over one of their heads.

"That story has gotten so much embellishment now that it's really out of control. Everybody calls Johnny 'Bullets'. I've heard that story all over Colorado, and it gets better with every telling.

"We packed the place on weekends. But Boulder was not ready. Boulder wasn't anything but a two-night town.

"I found out about my dreams of having your own place. I'd get to the bridge of a tune and somebody would be pulling my coat sleeve to tell me the women's john was overflowing. Next night I'd be at the bridge again and somebody would be telling me, You've got a hell of a fire going in the kitchen.

"This wasn't quite what I thought it was going to be. Because I was a small operation, I had to go into Denver to do all my own buying. I'd go to the meat packers and pick up stuff, then go for something for the bar, you'd have to go to eighteen different distributors, because I wasn't big enough for them to deliver to, or to hire someone to do it for me.

"You'd just be in fat city and you'd go down and buy forty lobster tails for the weekend, and you'd put them in the freezer, and come in the next morning and the freezer had quit at, like, ten o'clock the previous night, and you'd throw all the lobster out.

"We were on a well. There was a swimming club next door. People would go in there and leave the showers going and walk out. Come dinner time, you'd go to serve a customer a glass of water, and no water. You couldn't flush the john. We'd go down the road to get water in a tank from a friend, so we could get through until the water table filled up. It was a rough business, a real headache. I think everybody ought to do it. Everybody ought to run a restaurant for a year at least.

"At the end of a year, I let the lease go. I just wanted out. I had a hell of a lot of bills. If I'd had any brains, I'd have declared bankruptcy and told the bakery and everybody else to go to hell, but I didn't. It took me three years to pay off the debts. I went back into engineering, and told everybody, I owe you so much, and if you'll just cool it, you'll get it.

"I was in dire shape. I saw an ad for a project engineer in Denver. An outfit in Detroit had just bought a screw machine and punch press outfit in after-market products in the automotive field, replacement parts. They wanted someone with some automotive background, which I had from Chrysler.

"I was never a good engineer. I was a common-sense engineer. I probably used only five-tenths of a percent of everything I learned in my university training, but I was a pretty good common-sense engineer. That's probably why I ended up more in production. I was happy as hell to get that job. I was there about a year and a half. And then they were having some trouble with their radiator and auto cooler business, which was a prime contractor to Chrysler. The worst plant was in Ohio. They were losing all kinds of money, and the customer was threatening to take their business elsewhere. Another guy and I went in there and cleaned it up in about two and a half years. Then I got bored. I found out

that the owners were going to sell the company. They offered me
a plant in Allentown, Pennsylvania, and another in Washington,
Indiana, neither of which inspired me too much. They're probably
lovely places.

"I had résumés out, and I heard from IBM and Honeywell.
Honeywell interested me. The vice president of operations hired
me and I moved to Minneapolis and became superintendent of
production of one of their four groups. I stayed there about three
and a half years, and I got bored there, too, I must admit. My
sister, who was living in Colorado, died in 1970, and she had two
kids about a year older each than my two kids. We thought we
could be of some assistance, if we came back to Colorado. I started
putting out résumés again, and talked to Honeywell about a transfer to the test instruments division, in South Littleton, which is
about fifty miles from Boulder. Then my driving career started, a
hundred miles a day, for sixteen years. Honeywell was very good
to me.

"About 1980 or '81, I started to think it's damn near time to
get out of this business, which doesn't interest me."

"You told me that about five percent of it was enjoyable," I
interjected.

"That's not saying much for thirty years, is it?" Spike replied.
"That may be a high number. Did I say five percent? More like
point five. I may have inflated it. But it's somewhere between the
two. I was just never cut out to be an engineer, I hated it from the
time I got into it. I didn't like the field. I liked the money. Engineers are dull. I know a few interesting ones, and I guess there are
dull doctors, dull plumbers, dull electricians. The worst time I ever
had was evenings at Cape Canaveral. All there were there down at
Cocoa Beach were engineers. All those motels were filled with
engineers. You'd go into a bar and *everybody* was talking engineering. Missile men. Oh God! If there's a horrible way to spend an
evening, it's listening to engineers talking about engineering. They
didn't talk about anything else. It was as if nothing existed in the
world except: When did the Vanguard go off, and how did that
compare to the whatchamacallit?

"I used to sit in at a motel where they had Sunday jam sessions. And of course I'd take out the horn now and then to scare away the snakes. But I didn't do much playing, other than to try to keep the chops up a little bit. And I was too busy down there, working my buns off. Anyway, I found most engineers boring because I don't like to talk engineering. And I found it boring from the first day I walked into an engineering class. Maybe challenging, but still boring. As far as: Can I figure this out? type of thing. But not really interesting. I knew from the first day that I would never really be interested in engineering. But nothing else interested me, either. I didn't want to go into medicine, I didn't want to become a brain surgeon. It was the lesser of evils that still paid well. That's how I approached it."

"What happened to your marriage?" I asked.

"It ended," Spike said, chuckling at his own evasion.

"Why?" I said, knowing that no one ever really knows the answer to that question.

"Well," Spike said, "just because I'm an asshole." Then, pensively, "It ended in 1980." After a while he said, "Both my kids were stop-and-start about their education. I told my daughter in 1980, 'In 1985, when I reach fifty-five, the money's going to stop.' I knew I was going to take my retirement from Honeywell. She went back to school and got her business degree with straight A's. My son, who'd been working in a bank, went back to school, Colorado College, and aced through in economics, then came back here and got a master's in business at CU. So they were both fixed up.

"And now here comes '85, and I have no more financial responsibility that way. By 1980, I could see the direction I wanted to go. I got the idea to put out a record. I talked to Rich Matteson, the tuba player, and George Masso, the trombonist, both good friends of mine. George had done what I was thinking of doing. He was teaching at the University of Connecticut. His kids had grown up, and he said, 'Hey, I'd really like to get back to playing.' He got an apartment in New York, and started picking up some jingle activity and getting some gigs. Now he's traveling all the time. I worked with him a few months ago. George recommended that if I wanted to test the waters, I'd better get a record out. Rich Matteson said the same thing. And Rich said, 'Pick three people who are well known and will comprise a hell of a rhythm section. Your name's not going to sell. If you're going to get that album played on the air, it will be because of the other names on it.' So I called Victor Feldman, who was the last guy I'd recorded with. I'd kept in some contact with him.

"Victor said, 'Hey, you were going to call me after that other date. It's been thirty years.'

"I told Victor what I wanted to do, and he said, 'Let me get Ray Brown and Shelly Manne.'

"Then I began to have doubts. I was a little scared, really.

"Victor got hold of Ray, who was traveling with the L.A. Four. Then he tried Shelly. Every time Ray could be there, Shelly couldn't, and vice versa. Victor said, 'Why don't I get John Guerin?' whom I'd heard years before in a concert with Dave Grusin and Chuck Domanico. So we put that album together in a hurry to test the waters. It was released in '82, and it did what it was supposed to do. It got a lot of airplay, particularly on Voice of America. I started to hear from people all over, particularly in Europe, who never knew what happened to me after I left in '51.

"The first record in '82 got me a feel for what could happen. A young woman in Denver knew a fellow in Britain, a critic for *Jazz Journal International*, Brian Davis. I was sitting one night in Denver listening to Art Pepper, right before he died. This young lady said she had written to this fellow in England who was going to send her some tapes of some things I had recorded over there. She gave me his name. He had written an article about the Club Eleven, where I had played. I sent Brian a copy of the record I had made with Victor Feldman and Ray Brown and John Guerin. We corresponded, and he said, 'How about coming over for a tour?' I said, I'd love to. I was sure I could get a leave of absence from Honeywell, two weeks and add my two weeks vacation time. Brian set up an '84 tour, and it was a smash. It was beautiful. I saw so many friends I hadn't seen in thirty-five years, musicians and otherwise.

"I took the proceeds of the tour, which I didn't really need because I was making a good salary, and put it into another record. Martin Taylor, the guitarist, and I had worked a trio thing with Tony Lee, the pianist, a couple of nights at Pizza on the Park. I was very impressed by Martin's playing. I'd also worked with Dave Green and Spike Wells. We went into the studio and did an album, just before I was to leave. I said, 'If we don't like it, we throw it away.'

"In '85, I had another tour lined up, and I told Honeywell that I needed two months leave of absence this year. And they said, 'Okay, we'll do it again. But the only way you're going to get it again is if you become pregnant.' And I tried. God, I tried. But I knew I was done. I'd already booked a tour for later that year, in fact. When I came back from that tour in the summertime, my daughter was just finishing school, and I said, 'Well, this is it, I'm going to retire and go back to playing, I can survive somehow.' I made an album in London with Roy Williams on trombone, and Ted Beament on piano, Paul Bridge on bass, and Allan Ganley on drums. That got a lot of play. I was getting one album out a year, which I still think is essential.

"I came back and was told at Honeywell to cool it. Other people were saying, 'How come he can get all this time off?' And I could understand. Honeywell was putting out a little bait to get some people to retire early. I was the first guy in line. I disappeared, and haven't regretted a minute of it since.

"The pension was sufficient for anything I wanted. My material desires are very, very limited. You can tell from the looks of my car that I'm not trying to accumulate enough to go get a Mercedes next month. The oil's been changed ten or twelve times, the oil filter about twice." Laughter. "I get emotionally involved in things like that. I talk to that car a lot, as I do to the saxophone. They look kinda similar.

"There isn't really anything I want. Well yes there is. There are a few places I'd like to work some time. For historical reasons I'd like to play the Village Vanguard. I'd like to play in Chicago again, maybe Joe Segal's place, because that's where I come from, that area. I'd like to get back to Chicago, I've got some good friends back there. I'd like to play more in the United States. I've been going to Europe two or three times a year, because I made a name there between '48 and '52. The British consider me a Brit. In fact there was an album that came out listing me as British. Except that I don't know how to speak well—they say. They say, 'Gee, you speak funny.'

"About every three years I go down to the plant and walk in the front door and go around and see a lot of friends, and they're scurrying off to their meetings, and I walk out a half hour later and think, 'Oh God, why didn't I do it earlier?'

"I consider myself very fortunate.

"I never wanted to play studios. Playing in the studios or with a big band was like sitting down and reading the same novel you read last night. It became work to me, very quickly. That's why I had a lot of apprehension about going back into it. I thought, 'Are you going to become saturated again? Are you going to have to play things you don't like?' A lot of the people I'm playing with have been in the business full time, one way or another. They've paid horrible dues, traveling on buses in big bands and playing in studios. I couldn't do that. I wouldn't want to recommend that anyone go the way I did either. That's a different type of dues.

"But the thing that really got to me in a hurry, once I got back into it again, from 1984 on, is that there was no reason why all the players were so helpful, and warm, and accepted me. I'll never quite understand. But that's what happened. You think they'd say, 'Let's keep it to ourselves.' Instead they've been 180 degrees to the opposite. I couldn't ask to meet a warmer, more supportive group of people in my life."

From time to time one reads that there are 30,000 stage bands in the high schools, colleges, and universities of the United States. If this is so, there are 450,000 kids playing tenors, altos, baritones, trumpets, trombones, pianos, drums. The instrument manufacturers of South Bend, Indiana, know perfectly well that they are a far larger market than the professional musicians. Most of them will give up music for other professions. Most of them will practice medicine or law, become engineers or businessmen. All of them will always appreciate music. Some of them will go on playing weekends.

And, no doubt, thirty years or so from now, a Spike Robinson or two will emerge from the mass.

Spike said, "I can be in the worst position—I just missed a train, my bag's heavy, I'm frustrated. I think, 'Oh shit, why did I do this?' And then I think, 'Oooooh, well, but yeah, you could be in a three-hour quality control meeting.' And then I feel wonderful again."

Waiting for Dizzy

It felt strange, going out there. And we got lost. "This isn't it," Benny Golson said, as the driver of the van pulled into a parking lot by an office building in Englewood Cliffs, New Jersey. Art Farmer concurred. It looked unfamiliar to me, but then I hadn't been to Rudy van Gelder's recording studio in twenty-five years and was disoriented by the new buildings along what once was a country highway. I had last come out here for the *Bill Evans with Symphony Orchestra* session that Creed Taylor produced for Verve. That was in 1965.

We left the parking lot and traveled a little farther. Benny said, "I think this is it," and the driver pulled into a lane among trees, running in an S-shape in a mini-woodland and strewn with puddles from last night's rain, and suddenly there was the cement block building with a high-peaked roof that Rudy van Gelder had built a good thirty years ago to capture some of the acoustic qualities of a church. A sign affixed by the door advised all ye who entered here that there was to be no smoking or drinking within these walls. Rudy said cigarette smoke penetrated and damaged recording equipment. Everyone who had ever recorded here knew Rudy's quirks, and one of them was that you never touched his equipment.

"You know," Art Farmer said, in his low slow voice and with a somewhat grave and almost frowning expression he takes on when he is about to lay something funny on you, "Jim Hall and Red Mitchell have the classic story about Rudy. Red went to high school with Rudy. Red and Jim were here doing a duo record. They talked about the sound they wanted, and Red was in the control room with Rudy, and Red said, 'You know, Rudy, maybe if we just put a little more of this in there.' And he touched one of those faders, and Rudy said, 'That's it. You don't owe me anything. Just pack up and get out.'"

Benny laughed. "He pushed friendship a little too far."

"That was it," Art said. "If you touched anything in his control room . . . "

We went into the building. The studio was immediately familiar: the peaked wooden ceiling, the cement-block walls, the recording booth. Rudy still wore cotton gloves when he left the booth to adjust a microphone in the studio. I asked him why he did it. He said, "I'll tell you why I do it. Because it doesn't leave fingerprints on the microphones."

Rudy looked much the same. So did Creed Taylor, youthful—almost boyish—at sixty. A Southerner with family roots in New Orleans, he is actually Creed Taylor V, a fact I uncovered after reading that another Creed Taylor had participated in the first battle of the Alamo, when the American forces took the church from the Mexicans. That earlier Creed Taylor—who complained of the way the American forces treated the Mexicans—was a direct ancestor of the present Creed Taylor.

Creed's sandy hair had thinned a little at the back, and he wore slightly tinted glasses after retinal surgery. But he showed no sign of the strain of his eleven-year legal battle with Warner Bros. Records, a battle he had won in Santa Monica after the longest civil suit in the history of the California Superior Court.

One thing was different, though: the studio was filled with television equipment, high floodlights shining down from suspended tubes of black cloth and making pools of light on the floor around music stands and microphones, and cameras, including a monstrous instrument mounted on a boom. The crew was getting set up.

Creed won eleven million dollars in that suit; his lawyers had advised him that he could get much more if he wanted to fight further, but he'd said, No, he'd had enough; he wanted to get on with his work, get back to his career, get back to making records. This first session for his CTI label was to be something extraordinary: the first high definition (or hi-def, as it is already being called) jazz video in America and, probably, the world. High-definition television is already on the air an hour a day in Tokyo, and some form of it will probably be in use in America sooner than anyone thinks. With double the number of lines to the screen, it looks like color photos in motion. The vividness is startling. Outside, crews were getting ready for the sessions in a huge video truck next to a generator truck. These cameras were prototypes, and one of them alone was costing Creed $27,000 a day. The mere thought of the cost of this recording made me uneasy, and only the more so when I mused that this was Creed's own money.

It was a typical Creed Taylor move: daring and original. Like the *Bill Evans with Symphony Orchestra*, which must have been an expensive album; or Bill's three-piano *Conversations with Myself*, which got Bill his first Grammy; or the Freddy Hubbard *Red Clay* album; or *The Individualism of Gil Evans*, made when nobody in the world thought Gil was "commercial" and which Creed made only because he loved Gil's writing. Or the great Jimmy Smith albums. Or the George Benson recordings. Warner Bros had swiped Benson from Creed, who had a contract with him. That's what he sued them for. And now he was suing CBS records to get back the masters of his CTI records.

Creed had called me in California and asked me to come east and work on this hi-def video project. He wanted me to interview some of the musicians, capture if possible some of their personalities and histories on film in segments to be spaced among the musical numbers. It sounded a little nuts to me, but I have great faith in Creed's imagination. He will take chances, go into things with only a faint idea of how they will come out, putting his faith in the people he's working with. And he had ordered up a varied, to say the least, crew of musicians: among them Art Farmer, Phil Woods, Bob Berg, Anthony Jackson, Charlie Haden, Tito Puente, Airto Moreira and his wife Flora Purim, and Dizzy Gillespie. Creed idolized Dizzy, still remembering in awe the first time he saw him, fronting his big band back when Creed was an undergraduate in psychology at Duke University. He was looking forward to Dizzy's arrival. And he was treating everyone like royalty.

In the past few days, we had discussed the project at length. Creed said, "How do we keep it out of the record-store bins marked 'various artists'? What's the unifying principle?"

"Dizzy," I said. Because of the breadth of his influence, which goes far beyond bebop. Creed agreed that it certainly was one of the principles. Dizzy was to come in on the last day and record two pieces of material.

Benny Golson and I had been talking about Dizzy in the van on our way out here from Manhattan. We were to pick Art Farmer up on the way. Art lives in Vienna now, and he was staying in the apartment of a friend; Benny had recently moved back to New York after many years of writing film scores in Los Angeles.

"Dizzy was talking about Art last night," Benny said. "Dizzy said, 'Did you hear Art's recording of *U.M.M.G.*?'" I assumed he meant *Upper Manhattan Medical Group*. "The first recording of it I heard was Dizzy's, that he did with Duke. He just happened to come by the studio that day, when they were recording, and he just happened to have his horn. Duke said, 'Take your horn out.' He didn't quite understand the tune, and so Swee'pea, Billy Strayhorn, said, 'Well look, this is the way it goes.' And he played and it was fantastic.

"Dizzy and I talked about an hour on the phone last night. I called him in Atlanta. I told him that many people can follow those who are already taking the lead. But when he came along, he was stepping out into dark places, at some personal risk, I guess—risk of being ridiculed. Louis Armstrong said something like, 'They play like they're playing with a mouthful of hot rice.' Where's the melody? The bass drum is dropping too many bombs. There were all kinds of derogatory things said about them. And now today, it's the standard.

"When John Coltrane and I—we were together every day during that time—went to the Academy of Music to hear Dizzy in 1945, and they started to play, we almost fell off the balcony. Because we had been playing with local bands. And we all were used to playing . . . " He sang an example of swing era riffing. "And all of a sudden, Dizzy was playing other things, things we had never heard, and you can't imagine the impact it had on me. I told Dizzy last night that that moment changed my whole life, and I've spent the rest of my life trying to comprehend what it's all about. It's so limitless. It's perpetual. Of course, Dizzy is so modest, I could hear the embarrassment coming through the phone."

Benny said, "He was always didactic. Really. He was a teacher without even intending to be. And Art Blakey, too! All of us who came through Art's band, we would do anything for him. Freddy Hubbard and I were talking about that the other day. When I left that band, I was in trouble. I could not play with another drummer. I was irritated, I was annoyed, I would get angry, because I wasn't hearing what I was used to hearing. When I joined his band, I was playing soft, and mellow, and smooth, and syrupy. By the time I left I was playing another way, because I had to. He would do one of those famous four-bar drum rolls going into the next chorus, and I would completely disappear. He would holler over at me, 'Get up out of that hole!'" Benny laughed. "He taught us a lot."

We pulled up in front of a building on the West Side. Art Farmer emerged and we shook hands and embraced. Benny said to him, "Did you bring your box of chops?" Art laughed. Benny explained, "That's Curtis Fuller's line."

"They're on their way. They'll be here by tomorrow," Art said.

We got into the van and the talk turned back to Dizzy. "He makes no claims whatsoever for himself," I said.

"He gets embarrassed," Benny said. "Like a little boy. I was telling Gene about that *U.M.M.G.* thing that he recorded with Duke, and then you recorded. You know, I was talking to Dizzy last night about the time when he and Charlie Parker were together. He said, 'Do you know what Charlie Parker brought? Charlie Parker brought the rhythm. The *way* he played those notes.'"

"The accents," Art said.

"It's the *way* he played it," Benny said. "It was really a combination of the two. I said to him, 'You were so far ahead that when you first recorded, you had Clyde Hart, who was a stride piano player, and Slam Stewart. It took a while for the rest of the instrumentalists to catch up with what you were doing, and the trombone was the last.'"

I said, "Bobby Scott said, 'The rhythm sections were ten years behind Bird and Dizzy.'"

"That's true," Benny said. "They were playing boom-chank boom-chank." Art chuckled. "Art," Benny said, "you know more than I do, because I never really got to know Charlie Parker and you played with him."

"You've seen the movie, I presume," I said.

"I didn't see it," Benny said.

"Yeah," Art said. "I saw it. It didn't get him, but it's not a crime. Because somebody that big, they should either have more input from somebody who knew him, or else do it fifty or a hundred years later. There are too many people around who knew Bird who are disgusted with the movie. If you didn't know him, well then it wouldn't make any difference. And the guy in the picture is nothing like Dizzy. Dizzy is a guy—and Bird was too—when these people walked into the room, you knew there was a presence there. The guy who played the part of Dizzy was very quiet, almost meek, a mousy kind of guy. And Dizzy is nothing like that at all." He and Benny laughed at the discrepancy. "And everyone who knew Bird recognizes that he was very strong intellectually, and had a very strong personality. This guy in the movie came across as somebody who was a little boy, child-like, and never knew what he was doing. Not to take anything away from the actor—he was a good actor. But he didn't know what he was dealing with. The guy in the movie came across as too much of a victim, a sad guy. Bird had a sense of humor. He wasn't going around crying all the time.

"I remember that when we were living in Los Angeles, there was a little black weekly newspaper called the Los Angeles *Sentinel* that came out with a review of Bird. I read it and I was so surprised that I took it over to where he was staying, and woke him up, and said, 'Hey, man! Read this!' The lady who wrote it said, 'This saxophone player carries himself with the air of a prophet. And he's got a little wispy black boy who plays the trumpet and a bass player with an indefatigable arm.' She said, 'He carries himself with the air of a prophet, but there's really not that much going on.' Bird was sitting up in the bed, reading it, and he said, 'Yeah, well, she's probably okay, but the wrong people got to her first.' She was the girlfriend of a trumpet player out there who wasn't into anything."

Benny said, "One of the most ridiculous things I have heard recently was by a female critic who said Kenny G is very much like Charlie Parker. I couldn't believe it. I'm not taking anything away from Kenny G but he's nothing like Charlie Parker.'" And Benny and Art laughed.

For me, too, it was the rhythm in the playing of Charlie Parker and Dizzy Gillespie. Having grown up with Wagner and Debussy and Ravel in my ears, the harmony was not startling. There is little in bebop harmony that wasn't in use in European concert music by the end of the nineteenth century. It was the rhythmic shifting to which Bird and Dizzy were prone that startled me. I had grown up loving Edmond Hall and Trummy Young and George Wettling and Big Sid Catlett and the Goodman small groups, and in them the solos tended to fall into comparatively neat bar divisions, two or compounds of two. Even Coleman Hawkins and Charlie Christian had not prepared me for this swift evolution in jazz. Charlie Parker said once in an interview that he and Dizzy and Don Byas and Kenny Clarke and their friends were not rebelling against anything: they simply thought this was the logical way for the music to go.

I never was able to accept the story that they "invented" bebop at Minton's as a thing the "white boys" couldn't steal. It is at odds with Dizzy's character, his spirituality and unfailing kindness. And anyone who credited that story simply doesn't know how skilled musicians hear. Once I was sitting in Jim and Andy's with Marion Evans, the arranger, when a Les Brown record came on the juke-box. There was a particular smoky sound in the brass that the band occasionally used. I mused vaguely that I wondered what it was. Marion said, "Trumpets voiced in thirds, with trombones doubling it an octave down," and he told me what mutes they were using. He'd never heard the record before. Another time I was at the rehearsal of a large orchestra in Los Angeles, as they prepared to perform Alfred Newman's score for *Captain from Castille* at a concert. There is a particular chord in that music that has always caught my ear, and I expressed my curiosity about it to Dave Raksin, who was standing near me. Dave told what the chord was, its inversion, and spelled it all the way up, including what instruments were on the parts. During World War II, Robert Farnon used to listen to short-wave radio from the U.S., to get the latest pop tunes. He'd write them down as fast they went by, line and changes. I don't hear that well, but I know any number of people who do. The ears of Billy Byers are legendary. So there was no way that, in those early days of bebop, people like Mel Powell or Eddie Sauter or Ray Conniff—any number of people—could be baffled about what was going down on the bandstand at Minton's. In any case, art is never created out of such petty motivations. And if Bird and Dizzy actually didn't want the "white boys" to know what they were doing, why did they so generously show it to people like Stan Levey, Red Rodney, Teddy Kotick, and Al Haig, and hire them to play with them? I hardly ever remember a time when Dizzy didn't have someone white in his group, whether it was Phil Woods in the mid-1950s or, later on, Lalo Schifrin or Mike Longo on piano.

By all reports, Johnny Carisi was always welcome on that Minton's bandstand, because he knew the tunes. If anything—and this was always true in jazz—the idea was to blow anybody off the bandstand who couldn't keep up. One of the men they consistently stomped on was a black tenor player. Dizzy called him the original freedom player—free of melody, free of harmony, and free of time.

Those rhythmic displacements on the first bop records—those starts and stops in funny places in the bar structure, so exciting and surprising finally, weren't what I was used to, and when what Bird and Dizzy were doing began to make sense to me, it was a revelation. My God, such fresh and inventive musical minds.

I first knew Dizzy in 1959, or maybe 1960. I was putting together an article for *Down Beat* that in time took the title *The Years with Yard*. Charlie Parker's nickname was, of course, Yardbird, ultimately shortened by most people to Bird. But I have always heard Dizzy refer to him as Charlie Parker, the name in full, or, sometimes, Yard. Dizzy was playing Minneapolis at the time, and I went up there from Chicago with my photographer friend Ted Williams to take the notes and the pictures for the article that would appear over Dizzy's byline. For some reason now forgotten, we were to meet him in a little park somewhere. As Ted and I approached, we paused to watch him for a minute. Lost in some musical thought, Dizzy was softly dancing, all alone there in the sunlight. I never forgot it; it was one of the most poetic things I have ever seen.

I asked Dizzy about his humor on the bandstand, the jokes, the gestures. He said that if he could do anything to set a sympathetic mood in an audience, for his music, he would do it, and if humor would accomplish that end, he had no intention of giving it up. Even then he was announcing that he would like to introduce the members of his group after which he introduced them all to each other. He still does it. It still gets laughs. But sometimes the humor is quite spontaneous.

Once in the 1970s, he appeared in Los Angeles on a bill with Carmen McRae at a hotel that had decided to "try" a jazz policy. Everything went wrong. The sound system was poor, the piano was out of tune. Part way through Carmen's opening half of the concert, the pedals fell of the piano, and her accompanist was thereafter unable to move well through the chords in her ballads. Dizzy grabbed his horn and rushed on-stage to help her, filling the spaces in her phrases. Intermission came. A crew set up the band-stand for Dizzy's half of the performance.

His microphone stand was high, to pick up the sound of his uptilted horn. But whoever had put it there had left the cord spiralled around the stand. Dizzy came out and looked at it. He shares with the late Jack Benny a curious ability to walk onto a stage and stand there doing absolutely nothing and somehow making the audience laugh. He pretended, as is his wont, that he was unaware that they were there as he examined the problem of the microphone stand. He set his horn on the stage, standing on its bell, its body tilted at a forty-five degree angle. And he studied that mike stand and the cord coiled around it from several angles. The audience had begun to giggle softly. Suddenly he picked it up, held the weighted foot of the stand high in the air, and spun it, so that the cord uncoiled itself. The audience exploded in laughter, and at that point Dizzy affected surprise, as if taken aback by the discovery that he was not alone in the room. He took the mike off the stand, and looked back and forth in mock shock, and then said, "It is twenty years since Charlie Parker and I played Los Angeles." Pause. "It still ain't shit."

The laughter became a roar.

A few years ago, Dizzy changed his embouchure, and now he gets a bigger, fatter tone than he used to. It has acquired a rather velvety quality. I think he paces himself. I doubt that, at seventy-two, he could sustain entire evenings of blazing solos as he did in the late 1940s in front of his big band. But he knows how to handle it.

Someone pointed out to me a while ago that many, perhaps most, of the earlier generation of jazz trumpeters and some of the trombone players sang. Louis Armstrong, Red Allen, Hot Lips Page, Ray Nance, Jack Teagarden, and others would do occasional vocal choruses. Clark Terry still does. Partly it was because they were of a generation that considered they were in show business, they were there to entertain. But I suspect they did it as well as a way to rest their chops. I heard Dizzy in a university concert in

Chicago a year or two ago. He played superbly. And then he did
two numbers in which he didn't play at all. He clowned a little,
and sang—one of the numbers being, inevitably, *Swing Low, Sweet
Cadillac*. And then he went into the closing number, a long burning solo at a fast tempo. He was at the absolute peak of his form,
full of surprises, simple melodic phrases alternating with those cas-
cades of notes. And I concluded he had sung those two tunes to
give his lip time to rest up for this finale.

He is, aside from being one of the major figures in modern
musical history, a very shrewd showman.

The first day of the session was devoted to setting up the sound
and the cameras. The musicians ran the material down. Phil
Woods had been engaged for the session, but he was on his way
back from Europe and Jerry Dodgion subbed for him. The material Benny had written was tough, and Creed realized it was going
to be hard on Art Farmer's lip. He wanted Art more for his solo
value than as a lead player, and set Amy Landon, his assistant, to
checking on several potential players to ease Art's burden. There
is a softness about Creed that causes him to be very reserved, as if
to protect himself from the importuning world; I once took it for
coldness. I was wrong.

The summer of 1989 was viciously hot in the northern east coast
United States. It rained every second day, at most every third day,
and the humidity between rains was almost unendurable, particularly in Manhattan. Those powerful television lights completely
overcame the air conditioning in Rudy's studio and turned it into
a sauna.

We were all drained at the end of the day, when I rode back to
the Omni Park hotel—where Creed had put most of us up—with
Airto Moreira and his wife, Flora Purim. Flora reminded me of
something: that when she and Airto arrived in New York from
Brazil in the mid-1960s, they stayed in my apartment for a week
or so until they found a place of their own. I had completely forgotten about it.

The van crossed the George Washington Bridge. The buildings of Manhattan receded to the south in layers of aerial perspective, at last to disappear in the pale humidity.

Airto said, "We were in Europe for two weeks at Ronnie Scott's club with our band, every night, two sets, very late—we would start at 10:45 p.m., first set, second set one o'clock to two something. We did that for two weeks, then we went all over Europe for almost three weeks with Dizzy Gillespie and an all-star United Nations band. So it was pretty heavy: flying every day, waking up at 6:30 in the morning, going to the airport, the plane leaves at nine, baggage outside the room at six o'clock. Got my luggage stolen, two big bags."

Flora said, "It was great working with Dizzy. Dizzy is one of the greatest teachers, without teaching you. He shows you ways of handling life. When he goes onstage, and the music changes, it's so easy, so humorous. Everything is a laugh, it's fun, and if it's not fun, he doesn't want to do it. He's been a big inspiration to us lately. The last year, we've been working on and off with him.

"We're losing a lot of players who are the center, and Dizzy Gillespie is one of the last of them. If Dizzy hadn't come up with his bebop, we wouldn't be here."

Airto said, "He made the fusion of Latin music and jazz. He was the first one who understood it and tried to play with those guys, and did it."

"He's still doing it," Flora said. "Dizzy is still behind the fusion of Latin and jazz music."

Airto said, "He just blew our minds on the road for three weeks in Europe. Flying every day, as I said. We were so tired, we couldn't even rehearse the sound any more. Dizzy would just come in and play, and then everybody felt good, and thinking if this man is playing like this, at least we should play *something*. And very strong. I don't know how he does that, at seventy-two."

Flora said, "His energy level is very high, and what he stands behind is very strong, even though he's very shy to say it. We've done some interviews together, and sometimes people would ask him why he was still doing it, and he would come off with things like, 'For the money.' Which is not true. He doesn't need the money at all. He's a rich man.''

"He's made some good money," Airto said.

"He's there," Flora said, "because this is life. This is life to him, and to us. There are different kinds of musicians. There are musicians who make their livelihood emotionally, not just financially. I believe Dizzy is one of them. Art Blakey is another one of them. We look up to them as examples.''

The next morning, I rode out to Rudy's with Phil Woods, who'd just got in, and was weary. In Paris, he and Dizzy and a number of other American jazz musicians had been honored by the government of France. Phil's wife, Jill Goodwin—she's the sister of Bill Goodwin, Phil's drummer; and they are the children of announcer Bill Goodwin, whom older readers will remember from the network radio days—said to me once, "Phil's angry at all the right things." It's a remarkably apt description.

Phil said: "Just come back from Paris where François Mitterand presented Milt Jackson, myself, Stan Getz, Jackie McLean, Percy Heath with medals, made us *Officiers* of the Order of Arts and Letters, which is one step above the *Chevalier*, and Dizzy had already been named Chevalier and Officier, so he was named Commandant. It was neat, man. Danielle, the president's wife, a lovely lady, came to two concerts. Some cats were saying that she understood the changes, she was singing along. She loves *A Night in Tunisia* and all that stuff.

"I was trying to relate that to my country, Bush coming up with a polka band or something.

"But how wild. You go to France and they recognize American jazz. It was kind of neat. I'll show you the medal." He pulled it out, displaying it in its velvet-lined case. "I wore it all the way home on the plane. It didn't impress customs at all. Isn't that something? I got a lot of salutes from the police in France. It helps with your parking tickets. This and two dollars will get you a beer at Jim and Andy's. It's amazing, isn't it, how other cultures accept our music so readily, and here, it's hard to get arrested?"

"Where did you first meet Dizzy?" I asked.

"I met Dizzy in 1956, when we did a State Department tour, first stop Abadan, Iran; next stop Aleppo, Syria; Damascus, Bayreuth. All the trouble spots, all the places that are now on fire, the State Department sent Dizzy. I think if they'd sent him one more time, he could have cooled it all out. But obviously the State Department knew something. That's what always bugs me. When there's trouble in the world, our government recognizes jazz. But the rest of the time, we have troubles with the subsidies and all that. We get the roach, what's left over. The National Endowment for the Arts disseminates huge amounts of money. A category called Folk, Ethnic, and Jazz, splits about ten or twenty million— a pittance. Most of the money goes for blue-haired ladies listening to Mahler, conducted by some cat from Israel or somewhere else. You go to France and they give you medals, and wine, and dine you, and treat you like an artist.

"I was with Dizzy for the Mideast tour, and then South America. I had known Dizzy before, but only peripherally. When you work with him, you get to know him. But going to Iran first, that was a killer. And they loved the music. They didn't understand the jazz part, but Dizzy has such an important thing. The rhythm, that grabs people immediately. If you don't know anything about bebop. Dizzy is such a master of rhythm, the Afro, the South American. He was the first cat to fuse the jazz and the Cuban and the South American. Dizzy is the cat who discovered that, the first cat who used conga drums and all that, with Chano Pozo. That's a real big contribution of Diz, which is sometimes overlooked— not by musicians, of course. A lot of people know about the bebop part, but not the rhythm. He loves to play drums.

"When we were in the Mideast, he was out there playing with snake charmers. He'll sit in anywhere—Carnival in Rio, any drummer, any rhythm. He has an uncanny ability to memorize it or feel exactly what they're doing, and then fitting it into the jazz mode, without prostituting either one of them. He's a rhythmic genius.

"That stick he carries—did you ever see that, that thing he made out of a stick and Coca-Cola bottle-caps?"

"Yes, I have. In fact, I suggested to Creed that he use it as a visual motif. He called Dizzy, and Dizzy had lost it, so Creed had one made for him." There's no name for this instrument of Dizzy's invention. It is a pole with a rubber pad on the bottom. He mounted bottle caps on nails on a stick. He can stand in a room and bounce that thing and kick it with his toe and stomp a beat with his foot or shake this thing in the air, setting up the damnedest swing you ever heard, all by himself. I just call it Dizzy's rhythm stick.

Phil said, "I once flew back with him on the Concorde. When you travel with Dizzy, it's incredible. He was carrying that stick, right through the metal detector at the airport. The detector flips out with a hundred Coca-Cola caps rattling. And all the control people cheer and applaud: here comes Dizzy with that silly thing! The big stick. He plays it all the way through the airport; you can hear him come a mile away. He gets away with it."

"There was a time," I said, "when we all thought nobody in other countries could play jazz, but not any more."

"No no," Phil said. "That's no longer true at all."

I reminded him of the group he once led, during his long residence in France, called The European Rhythm Machine.

He said, "We used to call it The European Washing Machine. The cleanest band in the West. Look at the people you've got today. Niels-Henning Ørsted Pedersen. All the way back to Django Reinhardt, Grappelli, René Thomas, Daniel Humair. The list is long. They used to say that the horn players were okay, but the line went that the drummers didn't swing, the rhythm sections were inferior to ours. That's no longer the case. It's all over now. There are some Japanese bands that sound great. There's a cat in Japan who copies Miles so closely that when Miles fired his piano player, he fired *his* piano player in Japan. And the jazz clubs of Russia are flourishing."

A few days before this, the crackdown on the Tiananmen Square protesters had begun, and the executions were under way. Phil said, "We were supposed to go to China, but I told my agent to cancel the tour—and I'd love to go to China. My band is a natural, since we don't use microphones. We're not a fusion band. We play Porter, Gershwin, and what have you. But for the moment I think we'll hold back on that. That's about the only country I've missed."

We reached Rudy's. Phil and Art Farmer embraced. Art told us a story. Some years ago, late at night, Grady Tate had left Baron's in Harlem. As he was getting into his car, a man pointed a gun at him and demanded his money. Grady emptied his wallet and handed the money over. The man said, "Hey, ain't you Grady Tate?"

Grady admitted that he was.

The holdup man said, "Hey, I've got all your classics."

Grady said, "I've got a new album. I've got some in the back. I'll give you some."

The man said, "No, that's cool, man. I'll buy my own."

Phil and Art and Benny and the others went into the studio and began to rehearse. The tenor player was Bob Berg, from Brooklyn. His playing was hot, hard, and beautiful. Flora and the band rehearsed a complex piece by Gilberto Gil called *Quilombo*, which called for her to spit out the words at incredible speed and make them swing. She did it, too, and I was astonished by her. Astonished, too, by how much she had grown since Creed and I first heard her in the 1960s. Airto was cooking all over his complex of rhythm instruments, some of which he invented, working closely with Tito Puente. Airto's beard is now flecked with grey; Tito's full head of curly hair is now white. I talked to him during the lunch break, as most of the musicians and the crew gathered at trestle tables in the shadows of trees to consume the catered food Creed had laid on for them. Though Tito speaks fluent Spanish, his English is without accent—or rather, it is that of New York City.

"When I went to Juilliard," Tito said, as leaf-shadows made by a hazy sun played on his handsome face, "I came from the navy. I was in the navy during the war. They paid for the lessons. I went to study arranging and composition and conducting—not percussion. Nothing to do with Latin music. I went to the old school, the one that was on Manhattan Avenue at 124th Street.

"I studied trap drumming when I was seven years old. In the neighborhood in which I lived, in Spanish Harlem, there was a band that I used to sit in with, and a man named Montecino, who is still alive, showed me how to play the timbales. I already had the execution of the drumming, and that helped me to get into the timbales, which I'm very happy I did now.

"Dizzy was probably the first one to bring the Latin rhythms into jazz—with Chano Pozo. That was '46 or '47. His was the first big jazz orchestra to really utilize these Latin rhythms. Then after that we had Stan Kenton and Duke Ellington, and Woody Herman. I wrote some charts for Woody Herman and we did an album together. I've known Dizzy forty years or more—not longer than Mario Bauza, of course.

"The band that really started what we now call Latin jazz was the great Machito, who passed away about five years ago. He developed the influences of Cuba, Haiti, Santo Domingo, Puerto Rico, and Brazil.

"I grew up with a lot of drummers around me in Spanish Harlem. That's where I learned a lot about the rhythms, thanks to Machito—he was my mentor—and Mario Bauza, who is still around today and is one of the greatest maestros of our music and knows everything about the Cuban music. He's responsible for a lot of our music being played today."

Mario Bauza plays a significant role in the life of Dizzy Gillespie. Born in Havana in 1911, he is one of the many refutations of the idea that jazz and classical music have always been separate and unrelated streams. He played bass clarinet in the Havana Symphony Orchestra, and then, after moving to the United States, played trumpet with Chick Webb, Don Redman, and Cab Calloway. It was Bauza who brought Dizzy into the Cab Calloway band, where his national reputation began to catch hold. That was in 1939, a year before Dizzy met Charlie Parker in Kansas City, and we may assume that Dizzy, then twenty-two, was introduced to the rhythms of Caribbean music at least that far back.

Later that afternoon, during a break, I heard Romero Lubambo, an excellent young guitarist from Brazil, talking to one of the camera crew. He is tall, with a full face and sandy hair. He said, "The whole time I was in Brazil, I liked to listen to American musicians to learn how to improvise, how to play jazz. Now I am playing with the greatest musicians in the world, I think. For me it is fantastic. We used a lot of the American know-how of doing jazz improvising. What I did in Brazil, and what I am doing here, is playing Brazilian music together with the American. For me it is very close, American and Brazilian. Jazz is very influential in Brazilian music and vice versa.

"Until thirty years ago, we didn't have many improvising in Brazilian music. I'm not so old, but it was singing. But not with many improvisation, and then we borrowed the jazz know-how. This is from what I understand.

"Dizzy through his seventy-something years made everybody be happy when they heard his name. Everybody here is happy already, to see him tomorrow. Everybody is looking forward to seeing him laughing and playing, always great. It's nice."

At Newark Airport the next morning, I waited. Dizzy was playing an engagement in Washington, and flying in for one afternoon of this three-day recording. I was thinking about Dizzy's essential character, about the title of one of his finest tunes, *Con Alma*, which is Spanish, meaning with feeling or with soul. It is a wonderfully appropriate title for a tune by Dizzy.

How did this boy, with that curiously elegant natal name John Birks Gillespie, son of a father who abused and beat him in his childhood, who grew up in a society that committed unspeakable acts of racism all around him, and many of them upon him and on his friend Charlie Parker, grow up to be so loving? It has always seemed to me a triumph of the human spirit that anyone born black in America can even bear the company of white people, and for Dizzy, who years ago took up the B'hai religion, to have such love for his fellow man amounts to a miracle. It is not that he is unmindful of the abuses of his people. But he has found laughter even in that. Lalo Schifrin, who was his pianist in the early 1960s, told me of walking up a street with Dizzy in Glasgow or Edinburgh. Occasionally, affecting that very proper English he can turn on or off at will, he would stop someone on the street and say, "Pardon me, my name is Gillespie, and I'm looking for my relatives." He would leave some baffled Scot looking after him as Lalo fell apart with laughter.

His antic humor has been part of his life apparently since he was very young. It dates at least as far back as his early twenties, when he was working in a band in Philadelphia, because someone there named him Dizzy. He no longer remembers who put the name on him, "but," he says, "I'm glad he did." I first heard of him when he got fired from the Cab Calloway band, purportedly for firing spitballs at Cab. But that not only illuminates his life off-stage: it is used very shrewdly on-stage. One of my most vivid memories is of an incident in which his laughter, his clowning, his shrewd showmanship, and above all his kindness, came together on a stage in Canada.

It happened this way.

I was asked to do an evening of my songs at one of a series of concerts sponsored by the Canadian Broadcasting Corporation at a place called Camp Fortune in the Gatineau Hills, outside Ottawa. I was told I could use a large orchestra, which meant arrangements had to be written. I chose Chico O'Farrill to write them, because I love his work, and we were neighbors and friends. When Chico agreed to do the concert, the producer, Peter Shaw, asked him to perform his *Aztec Suite*. It had been written for and recorded by Art Farmer. Peter asked us to track Art down and ask if he would join us in the concert, but Art had moved to Europe and we had trouble finding him. Chico said, "How about Dizzy?"

And I said, "Why not? We can always ask him."

We called Dizzy and he agreed to do it—which meant that he had to read and learn a by no means simple piece of music in one or two rehearsals. But this presented me with a problem. I am essentially a writer, not a performer. Performance takes certain highly honed skills that I lack. And there is no more brilliant *per-former*, questions of music aside, than Dizzy. I told Peter, "There is absolutely no way I'm going to follow Dizzy Gillespie on a stage. I'll open; he can close." But, Peter suggested, this would set up in imbalance. So Chico and I wrote a new song, in long form, that we could do with Dizzy as a closer.

Dizzy, as it happened, got delayed by weather in St. Louis and missed the first rehearsal. Chico rehearsed the orchestra, with Mike Renzi playing the trumpet part in transposition on the piano, no mean feat in itself. Dizzy got there in time for the final rehearsal, and seemed to be memorizing the *Aztec Suite* as fast as he was reading. That was the afternoon I came to appreciate his consummate musicianship, questions of jazz quite apart.

Well, the evening came, and terrified or not, I sang my half of the concert, apparently not disastrously. The audience was warm, and at the end I said something to the effect that I had never before sung my lyrics in the country in which I was born, and I was very glad to be there. Then I said something like, "Now, ladies and gentleman, it is my privilege to introduce one of the great musicians of our time, Mr. Dizzy Gillespie."

Birks came out on the stage, looking (as is his wont) as if he was startled to find people there—and there were five or ten thousand of them, I would guess, blanketing the hillside of a natural amphitheater in front of the stage. He took the mike from the stand, gave a long Jack Benny pause, and said, "Damn! I'm glad I'm a Canadian!" The audience roared, and as usual he had them in his hand before he'd played a note. And then he and Chico and the orchestra sailed into the *Aztec Suite*.

He played brilliantly—this piece he had never played before. There is a gesture he has, a motion, that always reminds me of a great batter leaning into a hit. He has a way of throwing one foot forward, putting his head town a bit as he silently runs the valves, and then the cheeks bloom out in the way that has mystified his dentist for years, and he hits into the solo. When that foot goes forward like that, you know that John Birks Gillespie is no longer clowning. Stand back.

And that foot went forward a lot that night. At the end of the suite, the audience went crazy. They were screaming. Backstage I said to Peter Shaw, "I'm not going out into that. I'm not that nuts."

But Chico and the orchestra and Dizzy were setting up for the number I was to do with them. Now Dizzy's part was a long one, written out on accordion-folded music paper. He started to put it on his music stand—and dropped it. It spilled at his feet, and the audience tittered a little. Setting his horn down on his bell, he got down on his knees and started to fold it, like a man trying to put a road-map back the way he found it. When he had it neatly together, he stood up; and dropped it a second time. He did this three times, until Chico and the orchestra and the audience and I were helpless with laughter and the mood at the end of the *Aztec Suite* had faded into the past. He let the laughter die down. And then he introduced me. He handed that audience to me. I couldn't believe the generosity of this; or the cleverness, the canny sense of show.

And we finished the concert and went to a party. It was probably that night that he told me he had never in his life walked onto a stage without feeling at least a little nervous, and that humor helped to break the feeling.

I got thinking about the last time I'd seen Birks. We'd been guests on one of Steve Allen's TV shows in Los Angeles. Three of these shows were shot that day. We were on the first of them, and one guest on the second show was to be Doc Severinsen. Dizzy said he wanted to stick around after we'd finished and hear Doc play. One of the girls in makeup heard him say it, and passed it along to Doc. I heard Doc reply, "Oh boy! That's all I *need*—Dizzy Gillespie listening to me." A little later he came to our dressing room, and Dizzy greeted him warmly, and they fell immediately into the camaraderie of men in the same profession. They didn't talk about music. They talked about lip salves and medications. Birks said, "I've got something great! Freddy Hubbard turned me onto it."

He opened his trumpet case and gave a small package to Doc. "Try it," he said.

It came time for Doc to do his show. Dizzy stood in the shadows, listening. Doc played with a small group. There were none of the high notes, none of the flourishes, you hear during his usual television appearances. He played a ballad, mostly in middle register, the notes sparse and thoughtfully selected. He sounded a lot like, of all people, Bix Beiderbecke. "He's beautiful," Dizzy said, and if Doc in the spotlight had been able to see the smile of John Birks Gillespie in the shadows, he would have felt compensated for all the dismissals of his jazz playing by critics.

I have a very deep love for Dizzy Gillespie. He has contributed immeasurable joy to our troubled era. And to me, he has contributed insight.

These thoughts were in my mind as he got off the plane, carrying the big, square, black case that accommodates his idiosyncratic trumpet, and wearing sandals and a short-sleeved safari jacket.

He grinned, greeted the driver of the van, and our cameraman and sound technician, and got into the back seat. I was in the front seat, leaning over its back, and I suddenly had a wave of emotion. "Hey, Birks," I said, "I'm awful glad to see you."

He went serious. He tapped the middle of his chest, indicating his heart. His goatee is grey now, and so is his head. He said, "Me . . . too!"

I told him Creed had ordered a new version of his rhythm stick made for him; Dizzy had misplaced the last one, made with pop-bottle caps. This one was de luxe: made not with bottle caps but the tiny cymbals you find in tambourines. I said it was at the studio, waiting for him. "Where'd you find that thing originally?" I said.

"I made the first one," he said, and I remembered the first time I'd seen it. He demonstrated it to Jerome Richardson and me, and we were astonished at the polyrhythms he could set up with it. "I made two or three after that." He chuckled. His voice is low and little thick in its texture, with a touch of the south in its accent. He is one jazz musicians whose speech is not like his playing; in fact they are radically different. "That stick was something. I could be at one end of the airport and be walking with that stick, and all the guys knew where I was, from the rattle. Every now and then I would do it, and they'd know where to find me."

I said, "Everybody I've talked to, Phil Woods, Benny Golson, Art Farmer, said you have always been the great teacher. I remember Nat Adderley said once, 'Dizzy's the greatest teacher in the world if you don't let him know he's doing it.'"

"Is that true? I don't know about that," he said, and I saw that embarrassment Benny Golson had described. This was no affectation of modesty; this was genuine humility. "But what little I do know, I'll give it, any time. So I guess it's not actually someone with a whole lot of knowledge giving it out to people. But anything I learned, I'll tell somebody else. So that's what they mean by that. I will tell anything that I've learned."

"Miles said to me once, 'I got it all from Dizzy.' Art Farmer said that you came in to hear him one night and he realized that everything he was playing, he'd learned from you."

"That's a good question, about those guys. One example is Art Farmer," he said, trying to steer the conversation away from himself. "I made a record with Duke, a Duke Ellington party. I wasn't called to make the record, but I just went by the record date to see all the guys in the band I hadn't seen in some time. And when I walked in, Duke pulled out this *U.M.M.G.*, and said, 'I want you to try this.' So he gave me the part and they played it. And then Strayhorn was there. Strayhorn had to show me a couple of things. There were some very big surprises in that number—the resolutions at certain parts. Out of a clear blue sky, boom! A-flat minor seventh. And how it got there, you don't know. So Strayhorn came over to the piano and showed me and then I didn't have any trouble.

"But Art Farmer!" The sound of South Carolina was in the way he said it: Aht Fahmuh. Driving in South Carolina two or three years ago, I was slightly startled by a sign on the highway that indicated the direction to Cheraw. It looked so matter of fact. I vaguely thought it should say under the name: birthplace of John Birks Gillespie. "Boy!" Dizzy said. "I heard Art Farmer do it. I just happened to have the radio on, and boy! This guy! He must have spent some time on this number, because he knew every in and out of the progressions, he knew all of the resolutions. Boy, he really operated on that. Like a surgeon. Art Farmer is some fantastic musician. He's so pretty. Some guys can play all the changes, and you don't get the significance of the resolutions going from one to the other. But Art Farmer, he's so gentle. Just beautiful. I'm sorry I made the number. But if I hadn't made the number, Art wouldn't have made it, because he liked the record I made with Duke, and he said, 'I want some of that,' and he went and got it.

"Art Farmer. Nat Adderley. There's some good trumpet players around. I think there are more than in the early days. Because we had a hard core of young trumpet players, like Charlie Shavers, Kenny Dorham, Fats Navarro, and of course Miles is in there and, let's see—Dud Bascomb. He was a very tasty trumpet player. We used to talk when I was at the Savoy with Teddy Hill's band and Dud was with Erskine Hawkins. We used to say, 'Man! I wonder what it would be to be with someone like Duke Ellington and Cab Calloway.' And he wound up with Duke Ellington and I went with Cab Calloway. So we got two of the best jobs in New York. But that Dud Bascomb!

"And then there was a trumpet player named Little Willie, who played with Buddy Johnson. He was very talented, too. He didn't get a chance to play too much on records."

"Birks, I want to talk to you about the Caribbean, and the Afro-Cuban, and the Brazilian. It's like Phil Woods and others say, you were the first jazz musician to get into that music, to combine jazz with these various Latin influences."

"And I'll tell you something," Dizzy said, "the Latin guys play jazz better than the jazz guys play Latin." That was something to think about.

He said, "I was always interested in that music. All of my compositions have a Latin tinge. Every one of them. And that means that I am a lover of Latin music. I remember the first time I went to Argentina, I composed a piece that sounded like their music, called *Tango-rene*. I recorded it with the big band. That was a nice trip. I like Argentina very much.

"This year I was in Budapest. In my hotel they had a gypsy band, with a guy who played violin. He was *bad*, boy. I was supposed to come back after our performance in the theater and play a little bit with them. But that's where the tango comes from—that area of the gypsies.

"Which reminds me of a time in Africa. I went to Kenya for the State Department for the tenth anniversary of independence for Kenya. They took me to a dance one night. And I heard these guys playing. And I closed my eyes, and it sounded like calypso, the West Indian guys. So when the musicians asked me how I liked the music, I said, 'To tell you the truth, it sounded very similar to West Indian music.' And one of the guys, he say, 'You know, *we* were here first!' I said, 'Thank you very much.'" And he laughed at the memory.

I asked him what caused that immediate affinity between them when he first heard Charlie Parker in Kansas City, during his time with Cab Calloway.

"The method and music impressed me, the more I heard him play. Because it was so much the way that I thought music should go. His style! The style! Was perfect for our music. I was playing like Roy Eldridge at the time. In about a month's time, I was playing like Charlie Parker. From then on—maybe adding a little here and there. But Charlie Parker was the most fantastic . . . I don't know. You know, he used to do tunes inside of tunes. He'd be playing something and all of a sudden you'd hear *I'm in the Mood for Love* for four bars. Or two bars. Lorraine told me one time, 'Why don't you play like Charlie Parker?' I said, 'Well that's Charlie Parker's style. And I'm not a copyist of someone else's music.' But he was the most fantastic musician."

When we got to Rudy van Gelder's, the camera crew asked Dizzy to wait a few minutes so they could get shots of his arrival. He waited a little, then began to get impatient. He said he wanted to get out and warm up his lip. He waited some more, finally got out, and went directly into the studio, where Benny Golson was rehearsing one of the numbers Dizzy was to record. Everything stopped, and the mood in the place became reverent. Various of the musicians shook his hand, or hugged him, and he wore that great embracing grin. Art Farmer beamed; his hair too is gray now. Phil Woods, in a red polo shirt and a small leather cap, grinned, and shook hands: "Sky King," he said. It's his nickname for Dizzy, because he is always in an airplane, going from one gig to another. In fact, though he lived only a short walk from this studio, he wouldn't even have time to go home to see his wife Lorraine before flying back to Washington later today.

"Hey!" Dizzy said, when he saw the rhythm stick Creed had had made for him. "Beautiful!" And he gave it a few experimental shakes.

He left the studio, went out to one of the trailers that were standing by, took out his horn, and began to practice. After a while he came back, and the recording began. Dizzy played on two tunes, both Latin, and both rhythmically powerful. In each case he mastered the material quickly, and soared off into solos, the notes cascading down from his horn. The takes were interrupted repeatedly. What began to be apparent is that the compound rhythms weren't bothering Dizzy, but the polyrhythms he was piling on top of them were bothering the band. One tune, *Wamba*, kept breaking down at the same point, and Benny Golson, in a red shirt, would start it again. Dizzy's every solo was totally fresh, unrelated in any way to his solos in the previous takes. The studio grew hotter. Dizzy opened the safari jacket and played barechested, always with that uncanny concentration he brings to bear. The rhythm . . . . the rhythm!

I was in the booth with Creed and Rudy; I couldn't bear the heat of the studio, and didn't know how the musicians were doing so. Dizzy kept playing. "That man is a miracle of neurological organization," I said to Creed.

"That's a good way to put it," Creed said.

The tune kept breaking down; I kept looking at the clock. This was the last day of shooting, with that one camera alone at $27,000 a day . . . . And Dizzy had to return late in the afternoon to Washington. There could be no extensions of the date. The suspense was getting to me. Creed showed nothing; not a flicker of anxiety. He is always like that. I don't know how he does it. Maybe the training in psychology . . .

And at last it was over. Dizzy did his two brilliant takes. The musicians applauded. Creed went into the studio to thank him. Dizzy packed up his horn. A limousine took him back to the airport.

I said to Creed, who is never ever demonstrative, "Well, are you happy?"

"No," he said with a trace of a smile. "I'm ecstatic."

All the musicians were packing up. Soon the studio was empty. Across a chair lay Dizzy's rhythm stick, the new one Creed had had made, and that Dizzy loved. Creed planned to send it over to his house, a minor gift. The light from above flooded the stick, Dizzy's music stand, and the microphone, set high for his uptilted horn. It was is if the ghost of this colossus were still there.

Throughout those days, I was forcefully struck by the diversity of America that is represented in jazz. When I was a teen-ager, listening to bands and dazzled by the solos of Ray Nance, Cootie Williams, and so many others, some of them—Zoot Sims, for example—not much older than I, I wondered if this music was just a job to them, one that got boring from doing it night after night, or if it was a genuine passion.

I learned very early that it is the latter.

Charlie Haden said it as well as I have ever heard it expressed after the last session.

He said: "It's very rare in the recording industry for a producer to place such importance on creative values. Jazz, for so many years, has been treated as a tax write-off for most big record companies. And now, more and more, conglomerate corporations that are in the record business are just looking to sell many many records and make a lot of hits and a lot of money. Which is okay, but it's kind of sad that the art forms and the deeper values are forgotten about.

"That's sad for the jazz musician, and other artists dedicated to their art forms, film-making, poetry, dance, painting.

"I feel it is the responsibility of every one of us to improve the quality of life; to make this planet a better place; to bring deeper values back to the society, which are taken away from the people by the conditioning of mass media, of society's profit-oriented racist-sexist values. People are taught by the mass media what they should like, what they should wear, what they should listen to. And then they are sold these things.

"It's very sad that this music is put on the side, and not many people know about the importance of this art form we call jazz. And the other sad thing is that whenever someone has an opportunity to educate people in film about this art form, they always miss the mark. They never show the brilliance of improvisation and what it really is. They show a romantic story, or a story about drugs, or a story about alcohol, or the perennial image of the jazz musician as a child who hasn't grown up; who cares only about sex and alcohol and drugs and music, and really doesn't have any feelings or opinions or ideas or interests about any other things in life. Which is very sad, because it's not true.

"I think that Creed has done a great thing here, by making this record and also making it a video, so that people can see what we're all about, and what we love, and why we're doing what we're doing: we're actually fulfilling a calling to a responsibility to the universe. And that is to make beautiful music, and bring beauty and deeper values to people's lives, so that they can touch the deeper parts inside themselves. And there will be more of us.

"If the leaders of all the countries of the world were able to sit down and think about these things and to bring this music and these values to the people of the world, there would be a different mentality. The governments of different countries would be concerned about life. They would have reverence for life, instead of placing importance on weapons.

"It's all included in this music, the beauty of all those things. Because improvisation teaches you the magic of being in the moment you're living in. You get a different perspective about life. And you see yourself in relation to the universe in a completely different way. There's no such thing as yesterday, there's no such thing as tomorrow. They're only right now, when you're improvising. The spontaneity is there. When you're touching music, you see your extreme unimportance.

"The reason it hasn't been given more to the public, there's no vested interest, there's no profit being made. Since the beginning of this country, if there's no profit being made, they won't give it to the people.

"That's why government subsidy is really difficult. In Europe, you have a lot of countries that subsidize jazz concerts and musicians. It doesn't happen in the United States and it's very sad. The only thing that is similar to subsidization is the National Endowment for the Arts, which isn't nearly enough.

"People should be able to turn on television and see beautiful music. If I were an alien from another planet, and I landed in Queens one night, and I walked to the nearest house and looked in the windows and I saw the kids sitting on the floor, looking at MTV, I would say to myself, 'My God, is this the best that this country's popular artists have? Are these the best values they have to give to their young people?'

"Values of sequins, limousines, wealth, perpetuated every day with the whole superstar structure of the music industry. And every time that you bring music with deep values to people, it touches somebody.

"It's the people who have corrupted the music that we have to worry about, that we have to try and change, and one of the ways of doing this is to just keep playing, and to present the music to as many people as possible, because the more people hear this music, the more people are going to be attracted to it.

"And, hopefully, more endeavors will happen like we just did, because it brings great musicians together who usually don't have a chance to play music with each other, and it allows them to feel comfortable and relaxed in improvisation. And, when music is presented on the same level that the music is played, that's the thing that's really meaningful. When it's presented on a level of reverence and respect.

"People have lost their appreciation for beauty. The great thing about this art form is that musicians care about beautiful sound. They want to make their instruments sound really really beautiful. It's so important, beautiful sound—to be able to hear the beauty of the musician's soul. Every musician . . . they learn their favorite notes, they discover their favorite notes, their favorite sound, and they make their music sound as beautiful as they can for the listener, and that's what makes it so great. It's a dedication and an honesty that you don't find very many places. Improvisation and spontaneity are about honesty. It's completely pure honesty. The musician is baring his soul to the people, and hoping he can touch their lives, in a humble way. Every great musician learns that before they can become a great musician, they have to become a good human being. That's the most important thing, to strive to be a good human being, and to have humility.

"It's like the guy in Washington a few years ago. In the middle of winter, an airliner crashed in the middle of the Potomac River. People were on their way home from work. A guy got out of his car. He saw a woman who got out of the aircraft and couldn't reach the lifeline that was being thrown to her. And he didn't think twice, he jumped into the river and rescued her, and disappeared. Finally someone found him, and said, 'What's your name?' And he said, 'It doesn't matter what my name is, I just did what I had to do.'

"And that's greatness to me."

I got up early the next morning in the hotel and called Phil Woods. Phil and his wife had found me a house for the summer near their own. They live in Delaware Water Gap, Pennsylvania. We got into the car. Phil told me the best way was to go out through the Lincoln Tunnel. I hate the New York tunnels. They give me what Woody Herman used to call the clausters. I'm always afraid the roof is going to fall in and, New York being what it has become, probably some day it will. I wanted to go out over the George Washington Bridge.

Phil said the other route was faster. "Only take us an hour and twenty minutes or so."

"You sure?"

"Promise," he said.

But the whole West Side was tied up with traffic because President George Bush was coming to New York for some event or another. And when we got down in the tunnel, the traffic stopped completely.

"Hey, Phil, you promised me," I said.

"It'll be cool," he said.

At last it crawled forward. But hardly had we come out of the tunnel than it stopped cold again on the highway. People shut off their engines and got out and stood around on the cement. I asked a truck driver who had climbed to the roof of his cab to look ahead what was happening. "Ah the president's coming in or something," he said.

Of course. From Newark airport, where I'd picked up Dizzy the day before. The air was as hot and humid as ever. Phil and I stood around on the highway and told music business stories. We were there a half hour or so. The truck driver said, "Next time, I'm voting Democrat!"

And then, on a parallel highway, we saw it, the cavalcade of black limousines with dark glass, the one with the pennant identifying the president's car. How silly. To tie up this traffic like this. Why didn't they fly him in a helicopter to the Pan Am building? What was all this gasoline costing? I wondered if the man in that dark car would ever recognize the contribution of Dizzy Gillespie to the American culture; it seemed unlikely. And if he ever did, it would be for political reasons.

The traffic started moving again; we'd been on our way for an hour and a half. "Phil, you said an hour and twenty minutes!"

Inevitably, we talked more about Dizzy. "The Sky King," Phil said again.

I said, "I think his sense of humor lets him get away with things the rest of us wouldn't have the nerve to try."

"You know," Phil said, "he didn't do any clowning at all on this European trip. Occasionally he likes to do jokes and sing and scat. But when we did the All Star thing, which was Hank Jones, Max Roach, Stan Getz, Jackie McLean, Milt Jackson, boy was he playing. Because he knew he was with the musicians who grew up with him, and there was no funny business. He was alllll serious, man. Some European critics have said, Ah, Dizzy's chops are gone. I hope they were there that night." Phil whistled. "He was hitting high r's.

"Dizzy changed the way of the world. That music means so much to so many people everywhere."

Phil searched the radio dial until he found a jazz station. We heard a superb pianist whom we could not identify. It turned out to be Kenny Barron. The sky darkened. We were in a cloudburst. I slowed to about thirty miles an hour the sheets of rain swept across the highway and all the crawling cars turned their headlights on. We'd been traveling now more than two and a half hours.

"Phil, you promised me!"

And the sun came out.